When the Boys Came Back

WHEN THE BOYS CAME BACK

Baseball and 1946

FREDERICK TURNER

Henry Holt and Company ★ *New York*

Henry Holt and Company, Inc.   /   *Publishers since 1866*
115 West 18th Street   /   New York, New York 10011

Henry Holt is a registered
trademark of Henry Holt and Company, Inc.

Library of Congress Cataloging-in-Publication Data
Turner, Frederick. 1937–
When the boys came back: baseball and 1946 / Frederick Turner. — 1st ed.
p.   cm.
Includes bibliographical references and index.
1. Baseball—United States—History—20th century.   2. Spring
training (Baseball)—History.   3. World Series (Baseball)
—History.   I. Title.
GV863.A1T87   1996   95-37707
796.357′0973′09045—dc20   CIP
ISBN 0-8050-2645-2

Henry Holt books are available for special promotions and
premiums. For details contact: Director, Special Markets.

First Edition—1996

Designed by Victoria Hartman

Printed in the United States of America
All first editions are printed on acid-free paper. ∞
10 9 8 7 6 5 4 3 2 1

FOR
CHARLES H. TURNER

Contents

PROLOGUE   xi

★ *Part 1*

SPRING TRAINING   1

★ *Part 2*

THE RACE   89

★ *Part 3*

WORLD SERIES   223

EPILOGUE   257

ACKNOWLEDGMENTS   263

BIBLIOGRAPHY   265

PROGRAM: THE PLAYERS
AND THEIR TEAMS, 1946   269

INDEX   277

Prologue

*I*t was March 1946, and two young men stood beside the westbound lane of the Pennsylvania Turnpike near Harrisburg, their thumbs out in the early spring sunshine. Inside their service duffel bags were their just-issued navy discharge papers, and now, like thousands of other young men, they waited as patiently as they could for that next lift. They'd been discharged down at Bainbridge, Maryland, and had been lucky enough to catch a train to Philadelphia, but there they found they couldn't get a bus to the Pittsburgh area for days. In the spring of 1946, the nation's public transportation system was impossibly overburdened with returning service personnel and with civilians who after almost four years of wartime restrictions no longer had to explain to anyone why this trip was necessary.

And it wasn't just the transportation system. To many Americans, especially service personnel, it seemed as if the whole country was in some giant *snafu,* a soldiers' term meaning something like "snarl" or "knot." The war had been over since the previous August, and still tens of thousands of men and women, both here and abroad, awaited demobilization. Overseas, in fact, there had been some increasingly ugly incidents in which GIs registered their anger at the maddeningly slow process. In Europe restless soldiers with too much time on their hands were beginning to commit violent crimes. After early January demonstrations in Paris, Frankfurt, Manila, Guam, and Calcutta, General Dwight D. Eisenhower ordered overseas commanders to expedite the return of all personnel not absolutely essential to the orderly transition to postwar routines. But when the personnel finally got back to the States and were run through the demobilization mill, they found out about the transportation crisis, and so they stood along the nation's roads and highways with their thumbs out,

Stan Musial drawing his navy discharge papers at Bainbridge, Maryland, March 1, 1946. (*The Sporting News,* March 17, 1946)

just like these two ex-sailors near Harrisburg. Some elected to hop freights, huddling in boxcars where sympathetic railroad bulls chose to look the other way; if they were more fortunate they might find space in the aisle of a passenger car where their uniform, perhaps grimy from travel, no longer was worth even a brief indulgence. Some chose to wait in crowded bus depots for the next available seat. And some had to be billeted in temporary camps because even if they could get a bus, a train, or that greater rarity, a plane, there might be no place for them to stay in their chosen destination: America was also beset with an acute housing shortage. If the most common sight these spring days was that of recently discharged servicemen hitchhiking, the second most common was of them sleeping on the benches of public parks.

The two ex-sailors outside Harrisburg were lucky: they had homes to go to, and the lithe, lean-jawed one from Donora even had a job waiting for him. "We finally got a ride from two old guys who were going to Pittsburgh," the man from Donora recalled many years later. "They were in the state legislature, but they were driving so slow I whispered to my buddy, 'Oh, no. We'll *never* get there at this rate.' Well, they started asking us questions, you know, like 'Where're you from?' and so forth, and when they found out I was Stan Musial, why geez, they got it in high gear and drove me right to my doorstep!"

Musial had won the National League batting championship in 1944, then had been drafted and missed the 1945 season. When it became clear Musial would be inducted, Pete Reiser, the Brooklyn Dodgers star outfielder, encouraged him to beat Selective Service to it and sign up with the army. That way, Reiser said, Musial could go to Fort Riley, Kansas, and play with the rest of the boys on what was going to be a great service team. There was a colonel on the base, Reiser told Musial, who was going to take good care of all the ballplayers.

But Musial had other ideas. "I told Pete, 'Naw, I'm going into the navy.' I just liked the navy for some reason—the water and all. You know where a lot of those guys wound up who were at Fort Riley? At the Battle of the Bulge! They sent the whole unit over there. Everybody. Harry Walker, Murry Dickson, all those guys. They were in some battles, I'll tell you! And I think Harry killed twenty-two guys or something like that. Al Brazle captured a division that was surrendering. I often think of that—that I could have gone with those guys. But they sent us to Hawaii. We had a lot of ballplayers down there in a very tough league."

In Hawaii Musial was attached to a ship repair unit at Pearl Harbor where he ran a launch from shore out to the battle-damaged ships that came in, ferrying personnel from them back to port. Three or four afternoons a week he played baseball before stands packed with sailors, "Ten thousand every game." "You know," he recalled, "there were so many men around Hawaii, goddamn *thousands* and thousands of guys, so this was good diversion for them."

Seeing the condition of those ships and hearing the stories their crews told, Musial knew how lucky he'd been. Still, running the launch all morning, then trying to play afternoon baseball effectively before those big crowds took its toll on him. "Finally," he said, "I told our officer that after bouncing around in that launch for three hours in the morning, when I got out there on the field in the afternoon, God, my legs were like rubber. So, I tell him, 'Sir, I'm either going to play baseball on a regular basis or run the launch, because I can't be doing what I'm doing and do a good job playing baseball.' " Probably the sight of all those sailors with comparatively little to do convinced the officer that Stan Musial could be put to better use on the ballfield than on a launch, and he transferred Musial to a special athletic unit where he became the equivalent of a phys ed instructor.

With a substantial number of big leaguers and minor leaguers in Hawaii, the competition was good enough to keep Musial's skills sharp. But in the fall of 1945 his father fell dangerously ill in Donora and wasn't expected to live. The navy cut Musial emergency leave orders, and after an agonizingly slow trip he arrived home to find his father alive and recovering. Thereafter Musial was assigned stateside duty in Philadelphia and Bainbridge until his March discharge. Back home again in Donora, he stayed only about a week before he packed his baseball gear, said goodbye to his wife and child and his parents, and caught a train to Florida. He had a job waiting for him as the left fielder of the St. Louis Cardinals, and he was late: the exhibition season was three weeks old, and many of the players had been in the training camps since the first week in February. The boys were coming back.

PART 1

Spring Training

1

*S*tan Musial echoed the recollections of many of the players returning from the service when he said that the dominant feeling in the camps was one of joyful relief that the war was at last over and old teammates were together again under the sun. There wasn't much talk of the war at first or of what individual players had gone through: those stories would emerge gradually as the season progressed, spun out on the long train trips between cities; told in hotel lobbies before and after games or around a table of card players; or between two roommates, restless and unable to sleep in a hot hotel room on the road. For now, the boys laughed and cavorted and limbered up. Musial, who had a penchant for tricks and parlor magic, brought a false rubber thumb to camp and left it in the hands of unsuspecting teammates and writers who shook hands with him.

The condition of the Cardinals park at St. Petersburg wasn't a laughing matter, however. Waterfront Park had always had too much sand in its soil, making footing tricky, and the playing surface was now in even worse condition after having been used for the past three years as a military drill ground. Playing pepper one day soon after his arrival, Musial slipped and stretched ligaments in his left knee, setting him even further behind the others in his conditioning. Racing for a ball in the lumpy outfield, Terry Moore made a misstep and pulled a calf muscle, an injury that would nag him the rest of the season. And there were off-field problems, too, like the scarcity of rooms for wives and children, higher prices for everything from a shave to a steak, and blowouts on the team bus when recapped tires gave way. But for now, few were complaining. This certainly beat the service. From the perspective of the fans and the writers, it also beat what had almost laughably passed for spring training and big league baseball during the past three years.

In the immediate aftermath of Pearl Harbor, baseball's commissioner, Kenesaw Mountain Landis, had written President Franklin Delano Roosevelt asking for instructions: should baseball be played at all in such an emergency, and if so, under what conditions? As a deep conservative, Landis deplored almost all of Roosevelt's policies and perhaps most especially his racial attitudes and is said to have despised FDR personally, but now baseball's dictator was obliged to ask for guidance from a higher authority. And although Landis subsequently took credit for getting the "green light" from Roosevelt to continue the game through the war years, it may well have been Roosevelt's friendship with Washington Senators owner Clark Griffith that proved more important in the decision. Whatever the case, Roosevelt wrote Landis back in mid-January 1942, saying he thought it would be good for the nation's morale if baseball were played. Roosevelt was a baseball fan and also a superbly canny politician who knew full well what a remarkable position the "national pastime" held in American culture and how much its continuance would contribute to the belief that there were certain aspects of American life that could be counted on, even in the most terrible of emergencies.*

In his letter to Landis, Roosevelt said that, although baseball ought to continue, able-bodied players should not be exempted from service, and before Japan surrendered more than 500 major leaguers and more than 4,000 minor leaguers wore service uniforms.† Some, like Musial, served only briefly and far from the front lines. Some, like Musial's teammate, Enos Slaughter, followed closely behind the advance of the front lines and entertained the troops with exhibition games played on the newly won ground. Some saw heavy action and came back with scars and citations to prove it. And some, like the Cleveland Indians

---

* Before the war's end Roosevelt's sense of the game's cultural and emotional importance was demonstrated many times, both on the home front and on the fields of battle where the game was discussed and even played when the smoke of an engagement had barely cleared. During the first days of the Battle of the Bulge in December 1944, German officers disguised as Americans were sent ahead of the Panzers to infiltrate Allied lines and spread confusion. To counter this, roadblocks were hastily thrown up by American forces and anyone going either way was interrogated. General Robert Hasbrouck, commander of the American Seventh Armoured Division, said that a favorite question at a roadblock was, "Who pitched for the Yankees in such-and-such a year?" "If you couldn't answer," he said, "you were detained."

† Interestingly, as Bill Gilbert points out in his book on wartime baseball, *They Also Served,* Selective Service's Lewis Hershey granted deferments to virtually everyone in the film industry. The reason for this difference in treatment must have been the industry's greater potential for creating and disseminating wartime propaganda.

The outstanding prewar Cardinals outfield, reunited in 1946: Enos Slaughter, Terry Moore, and Stan Musial. They had varied and representative service experiences. (*The Sporting News,* March 28, 1946)

great pitcher Bob Feller and Cardinals outfielder Harry Walker, fought with the troops, played for them, and supervised their recreation and workouts.

Musial's outfield mates on the Cardinals had representative experiences. Center fielder and team captain Terry Moore had been thirty-one when he'd entered the army and had missed the seasons of 1943, '44, and '45. But during those years he'd had the opportunity to play a fair amount of service baseball, some of it in South and Central America where the weather was generally good but the playing conditions were often subpar. When he was discharged in January 1946, Moore stayed on a few weeks in Panama, playing on a civilian team in a league he was leading in batting average when he left for the States and early camp in Florida. Moore saw no action, played in over a hundred exhibition games, and reported to the Cardinals in what he said was reasonably good shape. Yet the war had cost him prime years, and he knew very well it had been a long time since he'd faced top-flight competition.

Enos Slaughter had enlisted in the Army Air Corps in August 1942, with his team in a tremendous pennant race with their archrivals, the Dodgers. He finished the season (the Cardinals won 43 of their final 51 games to finish first), then went to San Antonio for what he hoped would be flight school. "I wanted to be a pilot," Slaughter said, "but they said I was color blind. They wanted me to be bombardier, but I said if I couldn't be the one flying the plane, I'd just as soon not be flying. So, I became a physical education instructor in charge of about two hundred troops." Afternoons and weekends Slaughter played baseball against other base teams in Texas, many of them like his own, stocked with professional players. A half century later he would recall that during the 1943 season there he'd made 116 hits in 233 at bats.

Then Slaughter was told that if he would go with other players to the South Pacific, he would be guaranteed a quick discharge when the war ended. He accepted the deal and followed the American forces as they island-hopped toward Japan. On Tinian the Seabees bulldozed out a ball-field on top of a coral reef, then fashioned bleacher seats out of bomb crates. On Saipan, Guam, and Iwo Jima huge crowds of troops sat at the edges of the rough-hewn fields in the blazing sun, drinking beer and Cokes, and cheering the ballplayers. And on some islands there were still holdout Japanese soldiers in the hills; when the games were in progress, they would come out of their caves to watch. Seeing these "fans" up there on the hillsides, gave the players a funny feeling, Slaughter said.

Slaughter got his discharge March 1, 1946. "When I come back," he said, "I was getting the same contract as before: eleven thousand dollars. They said I was an old man. I was thirty." Later that month, the "old man" came back to St. Louis, "had a hemorrhoid operation, got me a pillow, and drove to Florida."

Harry Walker was inducted immediately after the 1943 World Series and sent to Fort Riley where Pete Reiser met him at the bus stop and assured him things would be great there, that the colonel was a big fan, and that the base team would be a powerhouse. As it turned out, Walker played almost no baseball at Fort Riley because he contracted spinal meningitis there and almost died. When he eventually recovered he was sent to the European theater and wound up on the German-Austrian border in the last desperate days before the collapse of the Third Reich. There

The game goes on. Here American GIs play ball with the smoke of battle plainly visible in the distance. (National Baseball Library and Archive, Cooperstown, N.Y.)

Walker's reconnaissance unit was ordered to hold a bridge against a horde of routed German troops seeking to cross it. Whether or not he killed twenty-two men, as Stan Musial remembered, Walker was forced to kill a good many. He was on point in a Jeep with two machine guns mounted on it when, as he recalled it, "here they come, and I'm trying to stop them, and they *wouldn't* stop. So that's when I had to start shooting, and I just cut through the whole mess, and they were scattered everywhere, firing back and forth at you, and you're just out there on point like a sitting duck."

Days later, when the firing stopped and that part of the war ended, Walker began a new assignment when his commanding office approached him with what Walker thought was a suggestion: that he organize some ballclubs to play for the troops. When Walker said he'd kind of like to go home now that the shooting was over and play ball for money, the c.o. got to the point. "He said to me, 'Walker, I didn't *ask* you if you wanted to do it. I said I *wanted* you to do it. I have about fifteen thousand GIs here, and I've got to entertain them, or they're going to give me a fit. We're not supposed to have anything to do with the Germans, so I want you to get those teams together and play two or three times a week.' "

Walker found earthmoving equipment in Czechoslovakia, requisitioned it, and built a ballfield in Linz. Later he starred on a team that played for the European theater championship in the Nuremberg stadium where Albert Speer once staged the monster rallies for Hitler. Down at one end of the now-ghostly complex was the baseball field, its infield made of finely crushed brick salvaged from shell-damaged buildings, and beyond the outfield fence stretched the concrete expanse of the runway along which the Nazis had once paraded military equipment more sophisticated than any in the world. The stadium that once shook with the thunderous chants of an intoxicated people now heard the cheers of 60,000 American GIs watching a version of their national pastime.

★ ★ ★

With Walker and the others away in the service for varying lengths of time, their places were taken by players of lesser skills, and as the teams' rosters changed with service call-ups, the leagues' standings gyrated wildly. The season of 1942 was not that much affected, though already the great players Feller, Hank Greenberg, and Cecil Travis had left. But beginning in '43, with the departures of Ted Williams of the Boston Red

Cardinals outfielder Harry (the Hat) Walker (*left*) was a much decorated veteran of the European theater and in the immediate post-war weeks organized a team of GIs that played their games in the Nazis' huge stadium in Nuremberg. His teammate, Howard Krist, a highly valuable pitcher before the war, was unable to bounce back from his service injury and never won another big league game. (Bob Broeg, *Redbirds*)

Sox, Yankee Joe DiMaggio, Reiser of the Dodgers, Johnny Mize of the New York Giants, and Slaughter, Moore, and Johnny Beazley of the Cardinals, the level of play definitely dipped, and it was to sink even lower during the next two seasons. Graybeards who under normal circumstances would have long since grabbed a lunch bucket and joined the workaday world, now hung on, often with pathetic results. These were players such as the great slugger Jimmie Foxx and two-time American League batting champion Al Simmons who tried to play in 1943 at age forty-one and hit .203; or Ben Chapman, a star outfielder for several American League teams, who turned pitcher in 1944 and '45. Fat Freddie Fitzsimmons, a big winner in the 1920s and '30s, pitched for the depleted

Dodgers at age forty-two in 1943 and was awful. Manager Joe Cronin of the Red Sox had gotten too old and fat to bend over at shortstop, but his squad was so thin he shifted over to play first base and hit only .241.

At the same time other old-timers who had put their mitts away and gone to work now returned to the diamond. Hod Lisenbee pitched against the Yankees of Ruth and Gehrig in 1927 but hadn't pitched in the big leagues since 1936. In 1944 at age forty-six he made a comeback with the Cincinnati Reds. Pepper Martin, the hell-bent-for-leather star of the Cardinals in the 1930s, returned to his old club in 1944 after four years of retirement. Babe Herman had been a feared slugger with the Dodgers in the 1930s but hadn't been in a major league game since 1937. In 1945, though, the Dodgers suited up the forty-two-year-old Herman and used him as a pinch-hitter.

Then there were the kids who should have been learning their profession in Class D baseball but who were now forced to learn it before the fans in big league ballparks. Joe Nuxhall was fifteen in 1944 when he toed the pitching slab for Cincinnati and got his ears pinned back by the Cardinals. In that same season seventeen-year-old Eddie Yost played briefly for the Senators. And there was Tommy Brown of Brooklyn's Bensonhurst section. In childhood Brown learned a baseball's tricky hops playing on the cobbled streets down near the navy yard. At twelve his childhood ended when he went to work on the New York docks, and by fourteen he was playing on weekends with those four and five years his senior on the diamonds at Brooklyn's Parade Grounds. In 1943 when he was fifteen a Dodgers scout invited him to an Ebbets Field tryout along with about 2,000 other aspirants.

"After the first day," Brown said, "if they called your name, you came back the next day. Next day, same process. They finally got it down to about thirty kids. So the following day I played in an intersquad game in Ebbets Field, and they told me they'd be in touch with me." In early December with parental consent Brown signed with the Dodgers, the team whose every doing he'd followed for years. That spring they sent him to Newport News in the Piedmont League. "I was hitting .297," Brown said, "and the manager got a telegram and said to me, 'You're going to Brooklyn. [Leo] Durocher wants you to play shortstop.' You could make a movie out of it, I guess, but I didn't really want to go. But I rode the train all night and got to Ebbets Field in the morning. We're playing the Cubs a doubleheader, and I didn't expect to play. Durocher says,

'You're playing shortstop. Both games.' I coulda hit the floor. I was sixteen, and I used to keep a scorecard on these guys!"

Between the old-timers and the raw kids was an odd collection of men who had no past to speak of in the game and no future in it either, but who in 1943, '44, and '45 passed for big league players. Eddie Boland, an outfielder who'd had what the players termed a "cup of coffee" with the Phillies back in the mid-'30s, played for the Senators in 1944—on his vacation from the New York Sanitation Department. Sig Jakucki was a boozing, brawling journeyman pitcher who had never won a big league game and had been bouncing around in the minors for eight seasons until the St. Louis Browns found they could use him in 1944 when he was thirty-six. As it turned out, Jakucki was more than the equal of the league's hitters of that season and the next one, too, but he was completely uncontrollable and a menace to club morale. The Browns also had Pete Gray in the outfield. Gray had lost his right arm in a boyhood accident, yet he'd been able to excel in the minor leagues. With the Browns in 1945 Gray was simply overmatched, even by the pitching staffs of that season.

These years also saw the birth and rise to popularity of the All-American Girls Baseball League, begun by Cubs owner P. K. Wrigley in 1944 as a novel way of satisfying the homefront's hunger for baseball. The AAGBL game was a hybrid of baseball and softball and was short on slugging and long on strike-out pitchers and stolen bases. Still, it was a recognizable version of the national pastime and took fans' minds off the war and the loss of the star players to it. When the boys came back from the service and big league baseball returned to its prewar level, the popularity of the AAGBL sagged appreciably, and despite various measures designed to revive its popularity, the league eventually folded after the 1954 season.

During these years the level of major league play did not have to suffer quite as much as it did, for skilled and able-bodied players were available who might have made up for at least some of the losses to the service, but organized baseball had a firm if unwritten color barrier that forbid any owner, no matter how talent-starved his team, from dipping into the ranks of the Negro leagues. To be sure, the Negro league teams had themselves been hit by call-ups. Still, during the seasons of 1944 and '45 talented players such as Satchel Paige, Artie Wilson, Roy Campanella, Sam Jethroe, Willard Brown, Gene Benson, Roy Partlow, and

Hilton Smith were available to any white owner who wanted to sign them. So too was the almost mythical slugger Josh Gibson, though by this point heavy drinking had apparently already eroded his great skills. Bill Veeck, the Young Turk who wanted to buy the hapless Phillies in 1943, recognized the nature and extent of this untapped pool of talent. His plan, which he unwisely revealed, was to buy the Phillies and stock the team with black players. Had he been able to do so, the Phillies with Paige, Partlow, Wilson, and the others, would have walked to the pennant. As it was, once the other owners heard of Veeck's plan, they arranged for the Phillies to go to another, more orthodox buyer, and Veeck and the blacks were frozen out.

2

*T*hrough these years and until his death in 1944 Commissioner Landis did his best to assure the public that organized baseball was solidly behind the war effort. Roosevelt had given the game the green light, but Landis wasn't about to let the President seem a greater patriot. Those foolish pregame drills players had been forced to perform during World War I (using bats in place of rifles) were not to be repeated, but the parks could be used as collection centers for vital materials, for bond drives, and as parade grounds for military units. Players could be encouraged to buy war bonds through voluntary salary deductions, decorated veterans could be honored before games and toss out ceremonial first pitches, and Landis could tinker with the schedules, reducing the number of road trips a team made during the season and even during the World Series. Landis also thought the sight of players stretching under the palms and sun of Florida and southern California during spring training wasn't the image the game ought to be projecting when servicemen overseas were shivering in foxholes or slogging through the savage heat of South Pacific jungles. So he drew a Landis line above the Mason-Dixon and east of the Mississippi and decreed that no teams could train south or west of it except the Browns and the Cardinals who had the latitude to train in Missouri.

The decree added its bit to the bizarre quality of wartime baseball with the sight of Giants players at their Lakewood, New Jersey, camp, warming up in earmuffs and scarves while a campfire crackled on the sidelines. The Red Sox went into camp in suburban Medford to limber up in New England's grudging spring. The Braves went as far south as Wallingford, Connecticut. The Cubs and White Sox went to French Lick, Indiana, while the Dodgers worked out at West Point—not an entirely unhappy compromise for their manager, Leo Durocher, since it kept him within range of the lights of Broadway. Transformed into spring training camps, these heretofore prosaic locations were rendered oddly exotic, but as the *Sporting News,* "Baseball's Bible," candidly observed in the spring of '46, "Now that it is all over, nobody pretends that those northern seasons were anything but synthetic representations of the real thing."

The "real thing" began earlier than ever with precamp workouts held by some clubs for players who had been in the service. The Cubs, defending National League champions, were returning to owner P. K. Wrigley's private island of Santa Catalina, but in mid-January they got the jump on the other clubs by opening a "rehabilitation" camp in Lake Worth, Florida, for their ex-servicemen. The Yankees, Cardinals, Senators, and others soon followed suit. Braves manager Billy Southworth sent his returning servicemen south to Hot Springs, Arkansas, on February 1, for medicinal baths he hoped would restore a prewar suppleness to their muscles. Within the first ten days of February almost a thousand players, the largest group ever, began to head south and to southern California, and more were to follow as their discharges came through.

The bloated rosters revealed the fact that general managers and managers really had little idea what the final look of their teams would be like. Which replacement players could continue to play now that the boys were back? Among those returning, what was the current level of their skills, and, if they were really rusty, how long might it take them to get sharp? White Sox manager Jimmy Dykes, who'd come back to baseball after World War I, said it would take many of them a full season to round into prewar form; he himself had had to return to the minors and play his way back up to the A's. Which younger players, who hadn't been ready before the war, might have matured playing service ball? And then there was that most intriguing of spring's possibilities: what youngster might blaze up out of nowhere to become what the writers called a "phee-nom"?

So, in addition to the early starts and the outsized rosters, the clubs scheduled a record number of exhibition games; some clubs were set to play as many as 50. The Dodgers were down for 44, some of which were split-squad affairs with players divided into two teams, which gave everybody more work. The world champion Tigers were scheduled for 43 games, while the Pittsburgh Pirates were to play 39 games in 21 towns, beginning at their San Bernardino base, then barnstorming eastward.

Even as the first players reported in Florida and California the owners sounded a warning note: discipline in the camps of the war years had been pretty lax, and even during the regular season some players had taken advantage of the emergency situation to play fast and loose with the rules and to talk back to management. Now, the owners said, those days were over, and rules would be strictly enforced. Sig Jakucki was home, waiting for a call that would never come.

Some personnel decisions seemed easy enough, such as the Browns refusal to offer Jakucki a contract. Similarly, they didn't offer one to Pete Gray who was at home in Nanticoke, Pennsylvania, waiting for some other club to contact him. The Reds, who had lost 93 games in 1945, let three-quarters of their infield go, keeping only defensive whiz Eddie Miller at shortstop. But even the better clubs were also cleaning house. The Dodgers, a respectable third in 1945 with 87 wins, knew they couldn't hope to compete with the same personnel and so made wholesale deletions, including that of Eddie Basinski, a concert violinist but a mediocre infielder. Gone also were pitchers Cy Buker (7 wins against 2 losses) and Tom Seats who'd won 10 games. Though he felt he could still play and later was bitter about being dropped, infielder-outfielder Frenchy Bordagaray was induced to hang up his spikes and accept a manager's job in the Dodgers' farm system. Even the champion Tigers were at it. Almost as soon as they'd defeated the Cubs in the Series they began dismantling their squad, and in spring training a front office source said that of the thirty players who had appeared in the Series no more than thirteen would be with the team this summer. The Red Sox announced that veteran outfielders Pete Fox and Indian Bob Johnson would not be back.

Johnson's situation was representative of baseball's version of the nationwide phenomenon called "reconversion." He'd been a star for Connie Mack's Philadelphia A's through the 1930s and into the '40s, averaging 99 runs scored per season, 104 driven in, and 25 home runs—impressive numbers by any standard. "People don't realize what an outstanding player he was," Red Sox Hall of Fame second baseman Bobby Doerr said. "I know I didn't until I got to see him play every day with us. He could hit, he was an outstanding defensive outfielder, and he had a fine arm." In 1945 Johnson had driven home 74 runs and had hit a respectable .280 on a poor Sox team. But he would turn thirty-eight this season, and the Red Sox outfield was suddenly crowded with the return of Williams and Dominic DiMaggio to join youngsters Tom McBride, Leon Culberson, and Catfish

Metkovich. It was Metkovich who'd predicted what would happen to Bob Johnson and others like him after the last game of the '45 season. In the clubhouse the outspoken Metkovich advised his teammates to take a good look around them, because, he said, many wouldn't be back now that the "real" players would be returning. So it proved for Johnson who drifted down to the American Association this season.

Representative, too, was the situation of Danny Gardella. Unlike Johnson and Pete Fox, Gardella had never been a star. In 1945 he'd been good enough to hit 18 home runs for the New York Giants, but he was an undisciplined batter with big holes in his swing, and he had severe defensive liabilities. He could hit for distance, though, and manager Mel Ott had to go along with him because he had no one better. At bat, Gardella said he could overcome some of his deficiencies because he was very strong despite his small stature (he was 5'7½" and weighed 160 pounds). Gardella was one of the first ballplayers to regularly lift weights and in the Polo Grounds where the Giants played he could muscle the ball down its short foul lines for home runs. He was also a genuine eccentric who sorely tried the patience of the Giants management with his antics.

"I loved music," he said, "particularly operatic music, and I would uninhibitedly burst out in song from time to time. What the hell, why not sing and holler? You're young, you're healthy, and you're playing baseball. You're also nitwit enough not to remember anybody else's misery. So, I sang." For the most part Gardella confined his operatic outbursts to the clubhouse or the train, and manager Ott turned a deaf ear, though it must have galled this graduate of old John McGraw's take-no-prisoners school of baseball.

Other Gardella stunts weren't so easily overlooked. In a game at Cincinnati's Crosley Field Gardella was half asleep on the bench with his shoes comfortably unlaced when Ott called on him to pinch hit. Gardella didn't want the manager to see how really out of the game he'd been, and he went to the plate as he was—and hit a home run. Then Ott had to watch his player flopping around the bases with his shoes coming off. Another time when the team was on the road Gardella spotted infielder Nap Reyes preparing to go up to the room they shared. Gardella raced ahead of Reyes, scribbled an apparent suicide note, then climbed out the window. "I was hanging onto some awning rods outside the window," he laughingly recalled, "about thirty stories up. I heard him come into the room and pick up the note and then make a lunge for the window. I said to him, 'Nap, don't make a grab for me!' I was afraid he'd try to grab me, and those rods could easily have let me down into eternity." On a night trip into Chicago Gardella climbed into the luggage rack above his seat and tied himself to it with his belt, waiting for traveling secretary Eddie Brannick to come through on his nightly check. Then he swung down and dangled there before the startled and enraged executive. "Brannick didn't regard it as a joke," Gardella said, "but took it instead as a reflection on his inability to get us a sleeper into Chicago. He never really cared for me after that."

In the off-season of 1945–46 the Giants sent Gardella a contract calling for a $500 raise to $5,000, and Gardella sent it back unsigned. When the team train left New York for spring training in Miami in February Gardella still hadn't signed—and he missed the train. He subsequently arrived at the club's Venetian Hotel headquarters late, unshaven, and broke. "The war was over," he said, painting the large picture. "Johnny Mize was coming back, Sid Gordon, Willard Marshall—all those good ballplayers. It wasn't that they [the Giants] wouldn't have considered me, because I was on the way to improving. But I got down to Miami late, and when I went into the dining room to get some money from Brannick I wasn't looking too good. They always wanted you to wear ties, whereas I didn't have what you might call the sartorial elegance of a big leaguer." Brannick told Gardella he wouldn't get a penny until he signed his contract, and words were exchanged. "Yeah, I sassed him," Gardella admitted. "He insulted me, and I gave it right back to him. They might have taken it during the war, but not now when they didn't have to, not from this Italian dwarf, Danny Gardella." The Giants released Gardella promptly, and no other big league team made an offer. But neither the Giants nor baseball had heard the last of him.

★   ★   ★

So much for the Jakuckis, Gardellas, and Pete Grays. Harder for management to assess were the potential contributions of those players whose careers had taken a dramatic upturn during the war years. It was easy enough to see that the level of competition had been down, but such players as Johnny Dickshot, Chuck Workman, Nick Etten, Red Barrett, and Ken Burkhart had performed too well to be written off automatically as mere wartime players.

Dickshot of the White Sox had never before 1945 hit as high as .260, but that season he was among the league leaders in average, triples, and stolen bases. Workman of the Braves had never shown more than occasional power and was a poor fielder at third base, but in 1945 he'd also hit 25 home runs. The Yankees first baseman Etten led his league in home runs in 1944 and runs batted in the year following. Pitching being always a scarce commodity, managers were very reluctant to write off hurlers like Barrett and Burkhart of the Cardinals or Senators knuckleball specialists Roger Wolff and Mickey Haefner. Until last season Barrett, a wise-cracking right-hander, never had a winning season in the majors; in 1945 he won 23. Had he suddenly learned how to pitch to spots with his mediocre stuff? His teammate Burkhart was a twenty-nine-year-old rookie in 1945 when he won 19 and led the league in winning percentage. Haefner won 16 and Wolff, all but unhittable, won 20 for Washington.

No team had bigger questions of this sort than the Tigers, whose championship had been built on the pitching of Dizzy Trout and Hal Newhouser, neither of whom had ever posted a winning record in the majors before the war but who during the '44 and '45 seasons had a combined record of 99-47. And the Tigers had barely missed winning another pennant in 1944 with Trout, Newhouser, and young slugger Dick Wakefield who was now coming back from the navy.

Trout was a burly, fun-loving right-hander who'd learned his craft at Terre Haute, Indianapolis, Beaumont, and Toledo before sticking with the Tigers in 1939. Until the players began leaving in droves in 1943 Trout had been mediocre, then he became a star, posting win totals of 20, 27, and 18, and down the stretch run to the pennant he'd been magnificent. But Trout hadn't run up those records facing the likes of Ted Williams, Joe DiMaggio, Cecil Travis, Charlie Keller, or Sam Chapman. There were plenty of rest stops in the enemy lineups of 1943–45, but these were now to be filled by tough hitters, not easy outs. Was Trout up to this challenge? Was his left-handed counterpart, Newhouser, whose wartime turnabout was even more spectacular? Newhouser had gone from an 8-17 pitcher in 1943 to 29-9 the year following, and 25-9 in the championship season.

The pitchers were almost complete opposites. Where Trout was outgoing and well liked, Newhouser was moody and had made plenty of enemies on his own club during his swift rise to the majors. In a period when it was unusual for a player, especially a pitcher, to reach the majors to stay with less than four minor league seasons behind him, Newhouser had come up to the Tigers with only one. Intense and given to outbursts of temper, the young southpaw found himself unequal to all of the challenges of big league life. "Hal took himself real serious," said his longtime pitching rival Bob Feller, a fairly intense man himself. "When we'd get our picture taken together before a ballgame, I used to kid him a lot. He wouldn't respond very much. Hal was just a real serious guy." Ted Williams called him a "fiery guy." You'd "hit one off him," Williams recalled, "and it was like you had taken his blood."

"When he first came up," said teammate Barney McCosky, "he was the kind of guy if you did anything wrong, he'd turn around and look at you like he's saying, 'You're not playing hard behind me.' And if you'd go to the clubhouse after a game where he got knocked out or he lost the game, every stool in that clubhouse was in one corner. He'd pick them up and throw them. . . . We'd have to look for a stool to sit down on." Pitcher Virgil Trucks said he and another Tigers pitcher, Hal White, took to following Newhouser into the clubhouse just to watch those tantrums. At one point in the 1943 season, Trucks recalled, Newhouser had lost something like nine straight games when they followed him down after another shellacking. They pretended to be solicitous of his well-being, babying him and telling him he had to take special care of himself since he had so important a string going. "He had to smile," Trucks said. "He couldn't help it." Trucks wouldn't go as far as to say Newhouser was hated by some of his teammates, "but he was probably disliked more than any other ballplayer on any club I was on."

Then, with many of the stars away—and possibly with some of the pressure removed—Newhouser turned to his veteran catcher, Paul Richards, for advice, and Richards, a genuine student of the game, told Newhouser he'd never be a winner unless he took hold of himself and quit acting like a spoiled kid. In spring training, 1944, Richards began to work on Newhouser, smoothing out his delivery, coaching him to release all his pitches the same way, and forcing him to curb his tendency to look for scapegoats when things went wrong. The results were as immediate as they were dramatic, and that season Newhouser won the first of his two consecutive Most Valuable Player awards. But as Newhouser told his biographer much later, he had plenty to think about during the winter of 1945–46 and on into spring training. Naturally, he said, he was apprehensive about the new season. He'd pitched against the good hitters for four years without much success, and now that they were back he had to wonder how well he'd do. Anybody with any common sense, he said, would have the same question.

If outfielder Dick Wakefield was having similar thoughts, he wasn't letting on. After two separate hitches in the navy the former "bonus baby" from the University of Michigan had breezed into Detroit on the eve of spring training, telling anyone who would listen that while stationed at Pearl Harbor he'd made eight bets with Ted Williams on who would outdo the other in various batting categories. "Either that Ted Williams or your Uncle Dick is going to be a broke cookie at the end of the 1946 season," he told the writers. "But neither Williams nor anybody else is going to outhit your old Uncle Dick." Here, in truth, spoke a young man who in 1943 had broken in by leading the American League in hits and doubles and had batted .316. The following season, though he'd had service duties, he'd done even better before going back into the navy for 1945. Depending on your point of view, Wakefield was either the second coming of Williams or a batter whose one and one-half seasons of excellence had been achieved against the equivalent of Triple-A opposition. In the early days of spring training Wakefield's hands were badly blistered from batting practice, and the *New York Times* reported he wasn't "hitting a lick." Wakefield himself said he wasn't worried.

★ ★ ★

*A*nd what about the established big leaguers, some of whom like Bob Feller had been away for almost four full seasons? How much of their skills had they left behind on battlefields and in frigid foxholes, in boats slamming against ocean swells, on makeshift, adamantine fields where they played irregularly against opposition well below major league standards? Was Jimmy Dykes right when he said it would take all the players a year to return to their former levels, no matter how great they'd been? Cubs pitcher Bill Fleming who'd attended the club's rehabilitation camp thought so. Judging from his own experiences pitching for the Fort Lewis army team, Fleming said most ex-servicemen would prove a disappointment to the fans, "at least for the early part of the season," simply because they hadn't been facing enough top-flight competition to keep their skills sharp. "The competition just wasn't good enough," Fleming said. "You never had to bear down and go all out as you do in the majors."

The evidence from the performance of the few major leaguers who'd come back at the tag end of the '45 season was mixed and too slender in quantity to be a reliable guide. The great slugger, Hank Greenberg of the Tigers, hounded into the service in 1941 before Pearl Harbor by a thinly

The great Willard Mullin's front-page cartoon for *The Sporting News*, celebrating the return of the players from the war and the end of ersatz, wartime baseball. (Courtesy of Shirley Mullin Rhodes and *The Sporting News,* April 18, 1946)

veiled anti-Semitic press, came back from the Burma-India theater with four battle stars to play 78 games and help his team to the pennant. To some, he seemed slower of bat and heavier of foot, but Greenberg was thirty-four, and he had driven in 60 runs—a pace that over a full season would have given him about 120. This spring Greenberg wasn't hitting in the early going, but he reminded writers he'd never been much of a spring hitter. His manager, Steve O'Neill, said Greenberg would be returning from the outfield to his natural position at first base since the Tigers had traded their first baseman, Rudy York, to the Red Sox. The move was bound to save wear and tear on Greenberg's legs, O'Neill said, and he was counting on him to provide his old-time power in the middle of the Tigers order.

Greenberg's teammate, Virgil Trucks, had missed the 1944 season and most of '45. He'd been set for his navy discharge as early as July, but his papers languished on an officer's desk in Oklahoma until the end of September as the pitcher helplessly watched his team fight down the stretch with Washington. Meanwhile, Trucks found a catcher able enough to handle his fastball, and he began throwing and running on the base field in his dungarees and spikes. When his papers were finally processed Trucks was in fairly good shape, though not in the prime condition he would have been leaving spring training. When he reported to the Tigers, O'Neill sent him right out against the Browns in a game the Tigers had to have to clinch the pennant. By the time Greenberg hit a game-winning grand slam home run in the ninth, Trucks was on the bench, but he'd pitched creditably and O'Neill started him twice in the World Series. Before the war Trucks had been a rising star, yet this brief showing wasn't enough to judge what he might do after so long a layoff and with the league back at full strength.

Cecil Travis also put in a brief 1945 appearance, and it hadn't been reassuring. In 1941 Travis was baseball's best all-around shortstop and batted .359 with 55 extra-base hits, but that was before almost four years in the army, including service in the Battle of the Bulge. When he'd been drafted, Travis said, he thought he might be in for a year or so, "but you didn't think you were going to be there so long, like it was. I went in about the ninth of January 1942, and I got out September fifth of '45."

In December 1944, Travis was with the 76th division in France when Hitler began his desperate breakout maneuver. "You were moving fast in that action," Travis recalled. "Heck, you was in that snow, and you was out in that weather, and you was lucky you got to stay in an old barn at night. The thing about it, you'd sit there in those boots, and you might not get 'em off for days at a time. And *cold!* You'd just shake at night. Your feet would start to swelling, and that's how you'd find out there was something really wrong—you'd pull your boots off, and your feet is swelling." Travis was lucky because the medical staff caught his condition in time to save his feet, and after hospital convalescence he'd returned to active duty.

After VE Day, Travis took an option the army offered: if he would agree to ship over to the Pacific theater, they'd give him a leave to visit his wife and newborn baby. "I got home around the first of August," he said, "and while I was there they dropped the bomb, and I didn't have to go over there. Otherwise, I'd'a had another tour, I guess." When he received word of his discharge, Travis, with his wife and the baby drove through the night from his north Georgia home to Washington, where manager Ossie Bluege wrote him right into the lineup. It was, he said, "sort of a strange predicament," being asked to play regularly when he was so far out of condition, but he'd made the best of it, trying to help the Senators to the pennant. Travis played far beneath his prewar excellence, both in the field and at bat. His frostbitten feet were tender, his reactions tentative and slow. But, he said, that brief trial wasn't enough to tell him how much he'd permanently lost, and coming south for spring training he felt good.

Pitcher Phil Marchildon had also made a cameo appearance at the end of 1945, and in this spring was trying to overcome both a severe groin injury and a case of nerves. In 1942 Marchildon won 17 games for a dreadful last-place Philadelphia A's team and then had departed for the Royal Canadian Air Force and a new career as a tail gunner in a bomber. Late in the summer of '44, Marchildon's plane was hit by German anti-aircraft fire over the Kieler Bucht area, and the crew bailed out into the bay. When Marchildon and the navigator finally made it to shore they were captured, and Marchildon was sent to a POW camp in Poland where he languished under deteriorating conditions until the camp was moved by forced marches back near his place of capture. When British forces liberated the camp at the beginning of May 1945, a badly malnourished Marchildon was evacuated to an English hospital.

That summer, back in his native Canada, Marchildon wasn't doing much of anything until he got a call from Philadelphia. It was Connie Mack: the A's were dead last again, crowds were thin, and Mr. Mack (as the players respectfully called him) wanted Marchildon to come down to Philadelphia and work out. Marchildon told Mack he was in no shape to pitch in a league game, and when coach Al Simmons got a look at the pitcher he begged Mack to send him to California to recuperate. But Mack was "too tight" for that, Marchildon said. Besides, he had another idea: how about a "night" at Shibe Park honoring the war hero who would then start the game? After two brief appearances, Mack sent Marchildon out on the big night. Twenty thousand fans turned out, and in pregame ceremonies Mack presented him with a $1,000 war bond that Marchildon said was really worth only $750; with the good crowd Marchildon claimed the owner-manager "made his money back and then some." Once the game itself began Marchildon's poor physical condition soon made itself evident, and going after a ball topped down the third base line he tore a groin muscle and left the game. Not only was that the finish of his season, but the injury persisted into spring, and now Marchildon gingerly went through his drills heavily taped.

He was also finding it difficult to focus on baseball. "I'd kind of drift away from concentration," he said. "I'd think about how lucky I was to get out of it all." His mind kept jumping to the fact that five crew members had died in that crash, something he hadn't learned until after the war had ended. His nerves, he found, just weren't the same. "I was more fidgety than before," he said. "I was always pretty serious, but I guess I was more so now." "War nerves," people were calling this, and, of course, many others, both in and out of the game, had the condition. Marchildon's teammate, third baseman George Kell, noticed Marchildon's nervousness and commented on it. A writer sitting in the dugout near Marchildon recorded the pitcher's constant and seemingly involuntary fidgeting during the course of a game. The man simply wasn't able to sit still, he reported.

Over in Orlando at the Senators camp, pitcher Walt Masterson had a similar case of nerves. He'd been at Midway and Guam, then had returned at the end of last season. "It was not a happy time coming out of the service," he told a writer, "which I guess it should have been." The service, he said, "messes up your head. When you get to the position where you don't care whether you live or die, you're kind of strange to be around." When the Senators journeyed to Cuba for some games this spring the players were startled when the evening cannon boomed from the battlements of Morro Castle. "There was a mad scramble for cover among the players who'd been in service," Masterson said with a laugh. But the psychological readjustment was real, and it wasn't funny. It took the Senators pitcher well over a year to realize that he was in control once again of his own destiny.

★ ★ ★

*N*o player's return at the end of the '45 season had been more enthusiastically greeted than that of one of the very first to leave, Bob Feller. When he left for the navy Feller's fame transcended the sport he played and made his name and face one of the most recognized in America. Not only was he baseball's greatest pitcher when he enlisted the day after Pearl Harbor, but his life embodied so many of the nation's cherished values that it read like a story out of the *Saturday Evening Post* with illustrations by Norman Rockwell. Here was a kid from a farm in the American heartland who'd grown strong rising with the roosters to do the morning chores alongside his father. Then he'd pack his baseball gear in a gunnysack with his books and his lunch and catch the bus to a school where he was one of seventeen students. At the other end of the day, if there was light left after evening chores, the father would catch his son's pitches. By the time he'd finished grade school the kid had a grown man's fastball, and then he added a curve. He had a thumb that was long and recurved— an inheritance from his mother—and he used it to get a remarkable break on this pitch.

During the year's shorter days the two played catch in the barn with light provided by what was then called a "Delco electric plant," with its generator, thirty-two batteries, and wind-charger. Later, Bill Feller cleared a field on the farm, and together the man and the boy built a regulation ballfield, complete with bleacher seats, scoreboard, and refreshment stand. They also charged admission to see the kid strike out opposing batters with his blazing fastball and that knee-buckling curve.

Feller spent the summer between eleventh and twelfth grade pitching for the Cleveland Indians, then stepped from the graduation platform to the big league spotlight to achieve a dominance over the league's batters some said would never be seen again. An instructive anecdote from Feller's prewar seasons came from the Red Sox's Bobby Doerr. Doerr said his manager, Joe Cronin (like Doerr, a Hall of Famer), gave him a bit of advice about hitting against Feller that Doerr found useful. Cronin told the young second baseman, "Bob, when you hit against Feller, just divide

Top: Bill Feller (*left*) who built his son a ballfield on his Van Meter, Iowa, farm. *Below:* Feller pitching to service mates somewhere in the South Pacific. (National Baseball Library and Archive, Cooperstown, N.Y.)

the plate in half. Don't worry about the outside half because you won't be able to hit anything of his out there anyway. But anything from the middle of the plate in that you think you can get your bat on, be ready. Don't be thinking of balls and strikes, just what you think you can get your bat on." Doerr said he'd had fair success that way and in fact had broken up two of Feller's many no-hit bids with late-inning hits. "I don't know what I hit against him," he said, ".200 maybe, .150. But against him that was pretty good."

At both the beginning and the end of his navy stint Feller pitched some service ball, but for the most part he'd been at sea in combat situations. He'd wanted to be a pilot but was turned down when he failed the high-frequency hearing test, a consequence of his farm days when the unmuffled roar of the tractor motor sounded in his head until he fell asleep. But Feller wanted no safe recreational job and requested duty where he would see action, so he served as the chief of an anti-aircraft gun crew on the *USS Alabama* in the South Pacific. In what spare time he had he played catch on the ship and a bit of softball on the islands. And he kept in shape by leading the men in calisthenics. When he was rotated back to the States and Great Lakes training center in mid-season, 1945, he went back to work on the weights and doubled his already impressive regimen of calisthenics. When he was discharged in mid-August he felt he was ready to pitch for the Indians. Two days later in Cleveland, 47,000 turned out to see the returned hero and give him a new Jeep for his Iowa farm. The day-long festivities had so worn him out, he recalled, that he was ready to go to bed before game time, but once on the mound again Feller rose magnificently to the occasion. He struck out the first batter to face him, fanned eleven more, and won the game. He went on to win four more games against three defeats and posted a fine 2.50 earned-run-average.

Feller had told the writers then that he felt he was back at full strength, and he said so again this spring in Florida, though his early performances were less than dominating, and there were remarks to the effect that it was too bad that "Rapid Robert" had left that incomparable fastball behind in the navy. "I never cared about getting anybody out in spring training," Feller claimed many years later. "I just wanted to get myself into shape, practice all my pitches, and if we won, fine. I never heard any manager or general manager say, 'He got beat in Alabama by the Giants, and we're gonna cut his salary.' I never heard them say, 'You shut out so-and-so in March, and we're going to give you a couple extra thousand for that.' " What was the point of trying to strike batters out in spring train-ing, he wondered, if you already had a spot on the team? He remembered once when the Indians were barnstorming up through Oklahoma and some raucous fans kept asking why the great Feller wasn't striking all the hitters out. And Feller gave it right back to them, asking them caustically what they wanted for their money, twenty-five strikeouts for twenty-five cents? There would be no exhibitions of his legendary strikeout skills down in Florida. The former farm boy with the All-America smile was in fact a grimly determined professional who designed his own condition-ing program with very specific goals and then went at it with single-minded devotion. To win and to win consistently, he thought, a pitcher must have confidence, and that could only come from "knowing in your mind that you've done just about everything you could possibly do to meet the task at hand." If you were truly prepared, he felt, "then when you walk out there, you're supposed to take charge." Of course, he added, "some days you're going to have it and some you're not."

This year, perhaps more than any other, Feller aimed to "have it" far more often than not. Keenly aware that he'd lost the heart of his career and his earning capacity, he wanted 1946 to be his greatest season yet. One of the things he felt might help make it so was to throw more break-ing pitches, particularly more sliders. Sometimes described as a "nickel curve" because it didn't break as much as a curveball, the slider was intended to upset the batter's timing and give him something more to con-sider beyond the standard pitcher's repertoire of fastball, curve, and change-of-pace. The pitch looked like a fastball as it left the pitcher's hand, then had a late, darting break. Before 1940, though, few pitchers threw it, and even fewer had mastered it enough to rely on it to get batters out. Feller said he'd begun experimenting with it as early in his career as 1940, and in 1941 he said he was "throwing quite a few of them."

Aboard the *Alabama* and later at Great Lakes he continued to work on the pitch. The trick to throwing it consistently well, he thought, was to visualize the ball coming out of your hand like a bullet out of a rifle bar-rel. And the way to have your hand in the barrel-like position at the release point was to keep your elbow stiff as your arm came down through its throwing motion. Feller found that this way he could throw the slider with only five miles per hour less velocity than his fastball—which meant batters were looking at a late-breaking pitch coming in around 90 miles per hour or better. He planned to use it more than ever in the upcoming season, though he knew its effectiveness could be guaranteed only by his ability to intimidate batters with his famed fastball and his curve.

★   ★   ★

*A*mong the "big boys" whose return from the service caused Hal Newhouser to have long thoughts during the off-season, the biggest in his league were Joe DiMaggio and Ted Williams. Newhouser, of course, wouldn't have to worry about Greenberg on his own team or the big boys who were coming back to the National League, but the pitchers over there would now have to face again the likes of Musial, Slaughter, Johnny Mize, and Pistol Pete Reiser. None of these National League sluggers, though, had achieved the stature of DiMaggio with his 56-game hitting streak in 1941 or Williams who'd hit .406 the same season. Both men had been away since 1942, and coverage of their returns was heavy right from the beginning of 1946 when DiMaggio began workouts at the New York Athletic Club.

He'd been in the army since the winter of 1943, but even his 1942 season (.305, 21 homers, 114 rbi's) had been conspicuously below the standard he'd set in his first six seasons. Maybe his mind had been on his top-drawer draft status then, or maybe it was, as he'd claimed, that the ball was different and wound with inferior wool. Or maybe it was his marriage, which wasn't too tightly wound, either, and during the war would completely unravel. In any case, DiMaggio had something to prove to himself this year. He was a tremendously proud man, driven to perform up to his own Olympian notion of excellence, and in September 1945, just out of the army, he'd seen what a few of the service returnees had been doing on the field. They'd looked bad, he told the writers, their legs were obviously out of shape, and the outfielders had looked "terrible" going after fly balls. At bat, their timing looked way off to DiMaggio. Playing service ball, as he'd done, was one thing, DiMaggio said, but playing for the pennant was another. "I said to myself," DiMaggio revealed, "that when I came back to baseball it would only be after long preparation"—one reason he'd resisted playing a few games at the end of last season. So, he was running on the indoor track, working on the stationary machines, and trying at the same time to get his weight back over 200 pounds. He'd long been plagued by a nervous stomach, and in the army had been in sick bay with ulcers, though there were some who meanly suggested he'd faked the condition in an attempt to get an early discharge.

Williams wasn't in DiMaggio's class as a ballplayer. DiMaggio could do everything on a baseballfield with an apparently effortless excellence. He could hit, of course, but he was also a superb fielder, and his manager, Joe McCarthy, said he'd never seen a better base runner. Williams, by contrast, was not that interested in fielding, throwing, or running. His teammate, Dom DiMaggio, Joe's younger brother who played center field next to Williams for many years, joked that the slugger's favorite expression when a ball was hit their way was, "Come on, *Dom!*" One spring before the war, though, Williams had actually approached DiMaggio and asked his advice about fielding. "He came over one day when we were in the field," DiMaggio recalled, "and said, 'Dommie, how do you go in on those ground balls and set yourself to throw?' I looked at him and said, 'Since when did you ever consider fielding part of baseball?' " But Williams insisted he was serious and was going to work at becoming a better fielder, and for a time DiMaggio said he did work at it. "He wasn't a bad fielder," DiMaggio said. "I'll tell you this: nobody ever played that wall [in Fenway Park] any better." Some of the Red Sox pitchers, however, had a different view of Williams's work in left field and were known to resent his often casual approach to defense, especially when balls were hit past him to the wall and he would lope after them and flip the ball to the relay man, allowing an aggressive base runner an extra base.

What Williams could do was hit. He could hit better than anyone playing, and some said he could hit better than any man who'd ever lived— which was precisely what the lanky left-handed slugger had publicly aspired to. A man has to have goals, he said, and that was his: to have people say when he walked down the street, "There goes Ted Williams, the greatest hitter who ever lived." When Williams said things like this at the outset of his major league career people scoffed at the brash busher, but after the season of '41 when he'd outhit even the streaking DiMaggio, few were scoffing. The great Rogers Hornsby, hardly generous in his assessment of the modern ballplayer and whose .424 batting average stood as the best in modern history, said he thought Williams had a chance to better that mark since he so seldom swung at bad pitches. After ringing up that astonishing .406 in 1941, Williams led the league again in 1942 in average, home runs, and runs batted in—baseball's Triple Crown. Then he'd entered Naval Flight School.

But since he was Ted Williams, his entrance into the service couldn't have been made without controversy. With American forces in the South Pacific being pounded by the Japanese and with the German juggernaut driving eastward into the Soviet Union, Americans weren't looking indulgently at any man requesting a deferment for nonmedical reasons. Williams had done so, claiming—rightly—that as the sole support of his mother he was entitled to a III-A classification. Mrs. Williams had recently divorced Williams's father, and her son had entered into some sizeable short-term financial obligations on her behalf. He couldn't possibly fulfill these, he told the draft board, unless he played baseball. So, in characteristically stubborn fashion, he decided he had to play in '43, and to hell with the writers and the fans who booed him lustily and sent him slips of yellow paper in the mail. What did they know of his private situation? Nor did Williams want to share any of it with them. Then in mid-season he'd enlisted and in November entered the flight training program where he soon set a cadet gunnery record on his way to becoming a flight instructor. Now the Kid, as he was called, was back, bigger, stronger, apparently a bit less testy, and more single-minded than ever in pursuit of his lofty, lonely goal.

In the middle of February he'd driven from his San Diego home to Florida with his wife Doris and A's coach Earle Brucker and his wife. Brucker subsequently recounted the trip for J. G. Taylor Spink of the *Sporting News:* how the nervous Williams couldn't sit still at the breakfast table of the cafés they stopped at but was up and down throughout the meal; how he insisted the others join him in contests to see who first could make out the license numbers of approaching vehicles; how incessantly he queried Brucker about the repertoires and habits of pitchers who'd come into the league in the Kid's absence.

In Florida he told the writers he'd been playing a lot of handball in San Diego because he'd put on more weight in the service than he realized. But he was also wondering whether that added poundage might not mean some added distance to his drives. He was an odd mixture of brash confidence and doubt in these early days at camp—in one breath, making claims he could match Ruth and Cobb at their best, in another, admitting that he really hadn't looked too good in what little service ball he'd played in Hawaii. Then he would tell himself aloud that if Hank Greenberg could pick it up at his age, the Kid surely could at twenty-seven. Could he hit .400 again? Williams said he doubted it: he was never fast, he said, and he certainly hadn't picked up any speed in the service, so there wouldn't be many "leg hits" to boost his average. Then, too, he had to wonder whether the pitchers were going to be giving him many good pitches to hit. They might prefer to walk him rather than give him a ball he might hammer into the seats. And Williams would take those walks, too, rather than swing at pitches he knew weren't strikes. As he talked with the writers, Williams's hands clenched and unclenched around the handle of his bat, which he seemed to carry everywhere. He was itching to see these new pitchers and to get a look as well at some of those guys who had come on so strong while he was away—Newhouser, of course, Roger Wolff, and Dave Ferriss on his own club.

★　　★　　★

*O*ver in the training camps of the Giants at Miami and the Dodgers at Daytona Beach the arrivals of Mize and Reiser were eagerly awaited. The writers would be scrutinizing Mize because the "Big Cat" was thirty-three this season and hadn't played much during his last two years in the service. Moreover, in his last season before joining the navy in 1942, the phlegmatic, moon-faced slugger with the rhythmic swing had posted the lowest average of his career—.305—so the question was, what did Mize have left? Early signs weren't encouraging. Mize looked slow around the first base bag and wasn't driving the ball. Mize had never cared that much for the writers. He was a conscientious if colorless workman who went about his job with an unobtrusive determination, and to him the writers with their questions were a distraction. Yet now he sought to remind them that like Greenberg of the Tigers he'd never been much of a spring hitter. The writers watched and waited to see whether the Big Cat would begin to uncoil against some pitches and drive them out of the park. Without the Mize of old the Giants would be headed nowhere except to the league's lower depths.

Age wasn't a factor with Reiser. He was twenty-seven and presumably in his prime. If he was healthy, he might be the best all-around player in the game, and his team would have to be considered very strong contenders for the pennant. Reiser had exploded into the National League in 1941 as a twenty-two-year-old when he'd led the Dodgers to the pennant. He could do everything: hit, hit for power, run, field (at several positions), and throw. In his first full season, he'd led league batters in average, runs scored, doubles, triples, and slugging percentage. Years later his teammate Billy Herman would tell pitcher Vic Lombardi that Reiser in that season was the greatest player he'd ever seen—and Herman had played in Chicago with the likes of Kiki Cuyler, Chuck Klein, and Gabby Harnett, all of them Hall of Famers. Originally scouted and signed by his hometown heroes, the Cardinals, Reiser had been declared a free agent along with hundreds of others by Judge Landis who said the Cardinals' vast farm system amounted to a kind of "chain gang." Then in a complicated procedure Reiser wound up with the Dodgers.

He had an infectious choirboy grin that hid a flaming competitiveness, born, perhaps, out of his situation as one of twelve children growing up in Depression-era St. Louis. Reiser loved to play anything—baseball, soccer, football—and wanted to be the best on any field, anywhere. After his career was over he told writer Donald Honig that when he stood at his center field defensive position he used to say to himself, "Hit it to me, hit it to me." And therein lay his problem, or at least part of it: Reiser was so competitive that he lacked elementary judgment in the field, refusing to admit that there were some balls hit his way that he simply couldn't catch up with. His 100-percent style had already cost him several injuries before his great season of 1941, and in July of the following year it cost him his season and his team another pennant. The Dodgers had come into St. Louis leading the Cardinals by thirteen and one-half games and looking for the kill. Reiser himself had been on a tear. In the field, he caught everything hit anywhere near him and had made 19 hits in his last 21 at-bats. His average stood at .383, and there seemed no limit on what he might accomplish when in the twelfth inning of a scoreless game Enos Slaughter led off for St. Louis with a long drive to right-center field off Dodgers ace Whitlow Wyatt. Reiser's first thought, he told Honig, was that the ball could be caught—which is what he thought about almost any ball hit his way. Reiser also felt certain that if he didn't catch it, Wyatt and the Dodgers would lose. He raced straight for the wall, narrowly missed colliding with the flagpole, intersected with the ball, and gloved it. Then he hit the cement wall in full stride. The impact knocked the ball from his glove, but he somehow retrieved it and threw it to shortstop Pee Wee Reese. It wasn't in time, and Slaughter scored, ending the game. Reiser said the collision felt like a "hand grenade" had gone off inside his head, and he woke up the next morning in the hospital. Dr. Robert F. Hyland, the Cardinals team physician (who was consulted by many other clubs as well), examined Reiser and recommended he not play again that year.

Within days, though, Dodgers president Larry MacPhail and manager Durocher had Reiser back in the lineup, and Reiser himself wanted to be there. Weak and plagued by blurred vision, he hit less than .200 the rest of the season. Meanwhile, the Cardinals kept chipping away at Brooklyn's lead, then in the stretch passed them to win.

Playing service ball at Fort Riley, Reiser brought with him his rage to win, and during a meaningless game he dived through an outfield hedge in pursuit of a ball, fell down a ten-foot ditch that lay behind, and badly jammed his throwing shoulder. Reiser was ambidextrous and had once been a switch-hitter. Now he became a switch-thrower, throwing left-handed of necessity, though it was clear that his throws from that side weren't major league caliber. His best three defensive positions (center field, third base, and shortstop) all demanded a strong arm, and when he reported to camp at Daytona Beach Reiser didn't have one. Dodgers president Branch Rickey expressed alarm, and though the "Mahatma," as the writers had taken to calling him, was often given to purposeful hyperbole, in this instance his concern seemed genuine. In his first exhibition game Reiser played center field and at bat had a double, two singles, and three walks. He said he thought he could lead the league's hitters once again. But no baserunner had forced Pistol Pete to make a throw, and no one knew whether his arm was in condition to do so.*

★   ★   ★

*T*he writers' favorite cliche of spring training was the incomplete quotation, "Hope springs eternal. . . ."† And of the sources of spring hopes none was deeper—because unfathomable—than that provided by the arrival of the rookies in the big league camps. For who, watching some fleet young outfielder, slick-fielding infielder, or hard-throwing pitcher, could say what the kid might accomplish? Add one outstanding rookie and the fortunes of an entire squad might be dramatically improved. Was there in this bunch of unproven youngsters the next great hitter, the next Bob Feller?

---

* Reiser's return captivated the imagination of the sporting public and a novel based on it by John R. Tunis, *The Kid Comes Back,* became one of the best-sellers in 1946.

† The fuller quotation from Pope's "Essay on Man" is if anything even more appropriate to baseball's rites of spring:

> Hope springs eternal in the human breast:
> Man never is, but always to be, blest.

This spring there were more rookies in the camps than ever before as front office personnel, managers, and coaches tried to assess the current and potential talents of players whose development in many instances had been interrupted by years in the service. Some of the rookies had been on the verge of making it to the big leagues when they'd been called to serve; if they'd played service ball, their talents might actually have been sharpened, both through accrued experience and through proximity to established big leaguers. But if they hadn't been able to play, they might well have regressed. Still others, who before the war might have been several seasons away from the majors, might have matured physically and mentally through service experiences (including service ball) and might now be ready for a serious look. Further complicating the picture was the relationship between the talents of the rookies and those of the returning servicemen whose years away from the game might have robbed them of some of their skills: a war-ripened rookie might now be the equal of a veteran player whose abilities time and the war had dulled.

The Yankees, for instance, had their incomparable catcher Bill Dickey returning from two years in the navy. In his last year of play (1943) Dickey had hit .351 in 85 games, but he would turn thirty-nine before the All-Star break, and in the Yankees camp some were beginning to see young Bill Deininger as the "second Bill Dickey." Deininger, too, had been in the service but was so impressive in camp it was said several other clubs had already made the Yankees attractive offers for him. Was the young man now equal to or maybe even better than the great Dickey at thirty-nine and with two years of rust on him?

There was only one Bill Dickey, of course, but virtually every club had situations of this sort, and most had their rookies to tout as the huge squads unlimbered and the exhibition games began. And most, too, had prized rookies still awaiting their discharges, like the Phillies who were waiting on outfielder Del Ennis, the Reds who were eager for pitcher Ewell Blackwell to join them, and the Braves who were counting on left-hander Warren Spahn's imminent release from the army. In addition to catcher Deininger, the Yankees were excited about the play of infielder Bobby Brown to whom they'd paid an unprecedented $35,000 bonus. In the Cardinals camp they were talking about Dick Sisler, son of Hall of Famer George Sisler. Over the winter the big first baseman-outfielder had won raves playing in Cuba under Cardinals coach Mike Gonzalez. Gonzalez sent back reports of young Sisler's distance hitting that had the Cardinals wondering aloud whether the rookie might replace wartime incumbent Ray Sanders. The Cardinals inter-city rivals, the Browns, were talking up infielder Bob Dillinger, called the "Player of the Pacific" for his outstanding service ball performance. Dillinger was one of those who before the war had been on the brink of making a spot for himself with the varsity. Now the speedy, line-drive hitter was a mature twenty-seven, and the Browns had already made a place for him with the release of the veteran Don Gutteridge.

In Clearwater the Indians were excited about a twenty-three-year-old left-handed hitting outfielder from Akron who'd played in three minor leagues before entering the navy in 1943. With Mansfield of the Ohio State League, Gene Woodling had hit .398, easily the league's best mark. In 1941 he moved up to Flint of the Michigan State League and led it with an average of .394. After missing most of the next season with an injury Woodling led the Eastern League with a .344 average. Indians manager Lou Boudreau had the squat slugger installed in center field in the early games and said the job was his to lose. Out west in the quiet opulence of Catalina Island where the Cubs trained, manager Charlie Grimm was threatening to replace his wartime slugging star, right fielder Bill Nicholson, with a twenty-four-year-old service returnee, Marv Rickert. Nicholson had developed a pronounced hitch in his swing in 1945 and despite hours of work in the batting cage was hitting less than .200. Rickert meanwhile was hitting over .400. He had one of those classic baseball backgrounds writers loved and that were so indicative of the hold the game had on the national culture: the Rickert family men had made up eight of the starting nine on a logging town semi-pro team in Long Branch, Washington, before the war, and Rickert said the lone "foreigner" had been converted by marrying into the family. After hauling ammunition in the Aleutians during the war, Rickert said he felt little pressure in his battle with Nicholson for the starting job on a baseball team.

Having backed up the truck and hauled off so many wartime fill-ins, the Dodgers had a camp full of rookies, including pitchers Joe Hatten and Hank Behrman and outfielders Dick Whitman, Carl Furillo, and Gene Hermanski.* Southpaw Hatten was a rookie who'd evidently matured playing service ball. He'd never had a minor league winning percentage

---

* Wartime fill-in Tommy Brown was reversing the normal flow of things. Now that he'd come of age, Brown was going into the service just as everybody else was getting out.

better than .500 before the service, yet in four years of service ball he won more than 80 games, and after watching him break his big curveball over the plate for strikes, Leo Durocher flatly declared Hatten would be one of his starting four. Behrman was a Brooklyn native said to have an even better arm than Hatten's. After three years in the army Behrman was back and raising eyebrows with his mound poise as well as his curve and fastball.

Hermanski was a left-handed hitter from nearby Newark. "When I was a kid growing up in the Depression," he said, "either you played ball or you became a hoodlum, one or the other. Saturdays, Sundays, we'd play all day long and challenge a team maybe four or five blocks away, the Hustlers or the Blue Comets. And one time we got enough money to buy caps and sweatshirts—I'll never forget that day as long as I live—and we went up to DiViga's on Market Street in Newark, the sporting goods store, and got the caps and sweatshirts. I got home that night and wore them to bed!" Despite serving two hitches in the coast guard, Hermanski had managed to play almost every day during his service summers and had improved his offensive game considerably. By signing up for one training course after another he'd been able to stay in the New York area the entire time and play over a hundred games a summer. He played for the coast guard, the navy, and under an assumed name for a crack semi-pro club, the Bushwicks. When it came time to report to the Dodgers early camp for service returnees at Sanford, Florida, Hermanski was not only in top physical shape, he was also much farther along in his development than other rookies who'd shipped overseas.

The turnout at Sanford was huge, but Hermanski got his swings in the batting cage and shagged his share of balls in the outfield (where he was less skilled), and after several days got word that Rickey wanted to see him. The youngster dutifully met with Rickey, and after an exchange of pleasantries Rickey said softly, "By the way, son, do you know you haven't signed your contract yet?" Then Rickey produced a copy of the contract that called for $400 a month. Hermanski said he thought he was worth a little more than that, that he deserved $4,000 for the season. Rickey was aghast—or pretended to be. It was, he said, an outrageous request from such an unproven player. In fact, with his usual shrewdness Rickey had been keeping a close eye on Hermanski all during his service hitches and knew he might well make the Dodgers this year, if not as a starter, then as a valuable reserve. Now, though, he told Hermanski he could either sign the contract at Rickey's figure, or he could immediately leave camp.

Hermanski couldn't sleep that night with worry, but at last he made up his mind to show up at the field the next day, still unsigned, and see what would happen. In an intersquad game he had an outstanding day at the plate, and afterwards Rickey crooked his finger at him. "He put his arm around me," Hermanski recalled, "and said, 'You know, Gene, you still haven't signed that contract,' 'I know I haven't, Mr. Rickey,' I said. He says, 'What was that figure you wanted?' I told him. He says, 'Okay, you got it.' " Hermanski was sent on to Daytona Beach to join the competition there for outfield spots along with Furillo and Whitman.

Whitman also hit left-handed but unlike Hermanski had played only a handful of games in two and one-half years in the army. Like a number of other ballplayers he'd been in the Battle of the Bulge where he'd suffered frostbite to his toes, and had been seriously wounded when a shrapnel fragment angled through his back, came out his shoulder, and grazed his head. He remembered falling into the snow with a sharp pain in the side of his head and thinking, "My God! Half my head must be gone!" He got up, turned around, and went back to ask the man behind him how bad it was. "He was in the machine gun section," Whitman said, "and he was carrying the tripod. But all I could see left of him was his shoes: he was just blown all over."

Despite his considerably different service experience, Whitman found he had more in common with Hermanski than the fact that both were left-handed hitting outfielders, for the wily, parsimonious Rickey was also working on Whitman, trying to deflate his sense of his potential worth to the Dodgers. One day after watching Whitman work out Rickey said to him, "Oh, son, that war was just a shame! Clomping around with those boots, your feet got all fat on you. You can't run as fast as you used to." "Well, I guess not," Whitman had replied and went on with his work. But "fat" feet or no, Rickey and Durocher liked the fact that Whitman made consistent contact at the plate and that he could hit coming off the bench. Durocher's managerial style was to make a good many moves during the course of a game; having a left-handed pinch-hitter in reserve was an appealing prospect to him.

★ ★ ★

Two of the spring's most ballyhooed rookies were Gil Coan, an outfielder of the Senators, and Ralph Kiner of the Pirates. Coan was a graduate of the extensive network of textile mill teams in the South and, to a lesser extent, the Northeast. In the Carolinas, Georgia, Alabama, and Tennessee a textile mill of any size fielded a semi-pro ball team that played against similar outfits. On Saturdays they played night games long before that practice came to the majors, and some teams played Sundays, though, as Virgil Trucks pointed out, Sunday baseball was frowned upon in many parts of America's Bible Belt. Some of the players had had professional careers and a few had even been big leaguers once; rather than accept demotion by their parent club to some alien town, these players had dropped out of Organized Baseball and come back to play for the local mill team.

In 1944 the Ecusta Paper Corporation team in Brevard, North Carolina, was planning on Coan for its upcoming season. He had a service deferment because of a childhood athletic injury that left him with little more than a stump for a left thumb, but his batting was unaffected. Fielding could be a problem since he couldn't squeeze a ball caught one-handed with a mitt he remembered as "about the size of a motorman's glove." But as spring approached Coan thought about an offer to turn professional that he'd refused a few years back because it would have meant leaving Brevard and a girl he'd met there. But after two years on the Ecusta assembly line where they turned out cigarette paper, a shot at professional baseball was looking a good deal more attractive. He'd married the girl and found his work at the mill hazardous and unpleasant, standing ankle-deep in water all day, surrounded by the roar of the huge machines. So, a friend contacted the general manager of the Chattanooga Lookouts who remembered Coan and invited him for a tryout. "This was wartime, remember," Coan said, "and these clubs were looking for ballplayers of any kind." Chattanooga offered Coan a contract calling for $275 a month. He was making eighty-five cents an hour at the mill, and here was an offer that would bring him more money in a summer than he could make in a year at Ecusta. Coan signed and went to spring training with the Lookouts who subsequently shipped him to Kingsport of the Appalachian League to begin the season. With Kingsport and Chattanooga Coan hit a combined .353 and stole 26 bases. At Chattanooga the following year Coan led Southern League batters in games played, hits, doubles, triples, home runs, stolen bases, and batting average. The *Sporting News* named him Minor League Player of the Year, setting the stage for his arrival at Tinker Field in Orlando this spring, billed as the American League's next great star.

"I was just a wide-eyed kid, agog at the whole thing," Coan said. "I could not believe it. In '45 when I had a year like that I was just having a good time. I didn't think much about getting to the major leagues, but I thought it would be great if it ever happened. Then I went to spring training in Florida, and there is the whole Washington ball club, and so many of them were just coming back from service: Buddy Lewis, Stan Spence, Mickey Vernon, Cecil Travis, Jake Early, Early Wynn. . . ." There had been so much publicity about him before he even arrived at camp, Coan recalled, that Clark Griffith almost "couldn't afford *not* to have me in Washington." When he reported, though, Coan was actually considerably out of shape: he'd spent much of the winter working in Texas at a family-run cattle auction business and eating a lot of his sister-in-law's good cooking. At Chattanooga the lithe speedster had finished the season weighing 163 pounds; when he stepped onto Tinker Field he weighed a bulky 206.

Other problems ensued. The subtropical heat bothered Coan, he got blisters from an ill-fitting pair of spikes, and he couldn't pick up the movement of the ball coming out of the newfangled pitching machine the Senators had installed. Then, too, the veteran players weren't nearly as enthusiastic as the writers and Clark Griffith about this much-heralded rookie. "It was different then," Coan said looking back. "This was their bread and butter. I can remember the first time I took batting practice, and I hit a ball back through the box. And the next pitch—I don't remember who the pitcher was—he threw it right at me, and he says, 'Don't you hit that ball back through here in batting practice.' Well, I got up, and I remembered that."

Out on the other coast the talk was of a twenty-three-year-old slugger, Ralph Kiner, who'd been in the Navy Air Corps most of the last three years. During that stretch Kiner hadn't played in more than a dozen games, but when he reported to the Pirates El Centro training camp he was in top shape. He was also a young player seasoned well beyond his years and his games in organized baseball because he'd spent most of his youth in southern California. He was born in the tiny southwestern New Mexico town of Santa Rita. His father had played some semi-pro baseball around there, but when Kiner was a small boy the father died, and the family subsequently moved to Alhambra in the greater Los Angeles area, a development, Kiner said, "that was probably the biggest thing that happened to me as far as being a ballplayer is concerned." By age eight he

Two of the brightest rookie stars of the spring camps: Ralph Kiner of the Pirates and Gil Coan of the Senators. Kiner (*above*) would prove to be the genuine article that year, leading the league in homers. Coan (shown here with his mother as she saw him off for spring training) would need more seasoning but eventually became a solid player. (*The Sporting News* archives)

was shagging flies for a semi-pro team and by twelve was playing with adults—"always right field, because that's where they put the worst player, and I was way over my head, age-wise." The next year Kiner played with the Yankee Juniors, a team whose equipment and uniforms were furnished by the New York club. The team was coached by a former Pacific Coast League star whose job it was to keep an eye out for those youngsters who looked as if they might be potential professionals, and there was a verbal understanding that if you played for the Yankee Juniors, when it came time to turn pro, the Yankees had the first shot at signing you.

From the beginning Kiner always outdrove everybody anywhere near his age with the bat. His swing produced high, soaring fly balls that naturally caught the eye of the Yankee Juniors coach, but when it came time to turn pro, Kiner surprised the Yankees by turning down their substantial offer to sign instead with Pittsburgh. The scout who got him for the Pirates was former major league pitcher Hollis "Sloppy" Thurston. "Hollis Thurston," Kiner said, "told me, 'You've got to be crazy to sign with the Yankees because they'll bury you in their farm system.' Which in those days they did. You could be in the minors seven years before you even got a chance to get to the major league club. You'd go to their D ball club, play there a year. Then there'd be C and maybe B, then maybe A, Double-A, and then Triple A, where they had two great teams, Newark and Kansas City." The Yankees, of course, were loaded with outfielders, from the varsity with DiMaggio, Charlie Keller, Tommy Henrich, and Johnny Lindell all the way down through the system. Kiner's contract with Pittsburgh guaranteed him an easier, quicker route to the majors. He was to start at A-level ball and go to spring training with the big club in 1941. He also got a $3,000 bonus with the promise of an additional $5,000 if he made the majors.

This spring Kiner was ticketed for Hollywood in the Pacific Coast League—was, that is, until the crusty old Pirates manager, Frankie Frisch, got a look at the Kiner who'd come back from the very demanding regimen of naval flight school and who had been hitting and running daily since his discharge. This Kiner was 30 pounds heavier, most of it muscle, and was, in his own words in "great shape, unbelievable shape. I figured I had to have a great spring to make the club."

Like Mel Ott, Frisch had been to the rough school of John McGraw of the Giants and then had been a player and manager with the famed Gas

House Gang in St. Louis. "He was really a tough guy," Kiner recalled, "very sarcastic, very caustic. He never really liked the modern-day ballplayer, but I think he liked me. Hell, he *had* to like me, because I could hit. I had a great spring." Indeed: in his first 44 at-bats, Kiner made 22 hits, and in one game against the White Sox he drove home 10 runs. Frisch told the writers he'd seen some pretty fair players come up in his time, and here was one of them. "He's got it," Frisch said flatly.

3

By far the most talked-about newcomer in the spring camps was a player whose team made it clear from the outset that no matter how well he did in Florida, he would not play in the major leagues this season. His name was Jackie Robinson, and he was the first African-American signed by a major league club in this century.

Throughout his long reign as commissioner, Judge Landis insisted, whenever the subject of Negroes in Organized Baseball came up, that there was no rule and no gentleman's agreement prohibiting their participation. It wasn't up to him as commissioner, he claimed, to facilitate the entrance of Negroes into the game; it was up to the owners to sign some. Yet his actions repeatedly spoke otherwise, and after the judge's death in 1944, his successor, U.S. Senator from Kentucky Albert B. Chandler, claimed he had documentary proof of Landis's opposition to the game's integration. A late 1930s poll of National League players appeared to show that the majority of them had no great objection to playing with Negroes, and there were some observers, particularly among members of the Negro press, who felt Landis was primarily expressing the covert sentiments of the owners. After Branch Rickey had revealed that he'd signed Robinson to play for Montreal, a Brooklyn farm club, in 1946 a secret vote of the owners went 15–1 against integration with only Rickey himself voting for it.[*]

In the aftermath of the signing Rickey's motives were widely debated. Some viewed him as baseball's Lincoln. Others noted that when he was general manager of the Cardinals in the 1920s and '30s he rigorously

---

[*] When reports of the vote subsequently surfaced, the owners denied it had ever taken place. Only Chandler and Rickey maintained it had, and no paperwork related to it has ever been discovered.

Top: Jackie Robinson on his first day at the Dodgers training complex in Florida after a harrowing trip south with his bride. He didn't even have a team uniform yet. (UPI/Bettmann) In the March 28 issue of *The Sporting News*, Dan Parker's column suggested Rickey's signing of Robinson and pitcher John Wright might simply be another of his publicity stunts. *Below*: The caricature of the Pullman porter accompanied Ed Burns's account of the Pirates–White Sox barnstorming trip through thc West.

enforced Jim Crow rules at Sportsman's Park; to these observers he was a magniloquent, money-grubbing humbug. Others, in both the African-American and white communities, were more cynical still, suggesting that Rickey had picked Robinson as the pioneer, knowing Robinson would fail, thus confirming the belief of the bigots who said Negroes simply weren't big leaguers. Even some of the players in the Negro leagues felt Rickey had picked the wrong man, that Robinson was by no means the most talented player they had. Though Rickey had signed him as a shortstop, those who'd played alongside Robinson with the Kansas City Monarchs doubted his arm was strong enough to make it at that position. A better choice, they felt, was outfielder-first baseman Monte Irvin, who was a more accomplished player and a more seasoned one with six years of pro ball under his belt to Robinson's one. Irvin himself later suggested he might have picked catcher Roy Campanella to be the barrier-breaker. Still other Negro leaguers, their hopes so long deferred, felt that whether Robinson made it or didn't, his was a singular situation that had little to do with them. "We never dreamed of it," veteran Negro leagues outfielder Sam Jethroe said of the possible wholesale integration of the game. "Never. When they got Jackie, it never dawned on you that they was going to incorporate that way. You just say, 'Well, Jackie's going, and more power to him.' " Yet by the time Robinson reported at Sanford at the beginning of March, Rickey had also signed pitchers Roy Partlow and John Wright, and within a month he would sign Campanella and pitcher Don Newcombe. All were black.

Racial integration of the game had begun to be an issue at the end of the 1920s and had remained one all through the Depression era. With the coming of the war, however, many other matters seemed more important, such as the very survival of the game itself in so great an emergency. But the war actually precipitated integration. Billed in part in American propaganda as a contest between the racial attitudes of fascism and those of democracy, the war inevitably threw the spotlight on America's failure to live up to its own egalitarian professions. And the longer the war went on, the more glaring those failures looked. Black GIs like Monte Irvin who had been exposed to more tolerant racial attitudes overseas now returned to the United States with a new perspective. Irvin recalled conversations among black troops returning home from Europe in which hopes for racial progress mingled with an emerging determination not to meekly accept the prewar status quo. Even before shipping overseas Irvin had seen the sure signs of a new attitude. At Camp Claiborne in Alexandria, Louisiana, Irvin saw black soldiers riot in furious protest over their relentlessly shabby treatment there.* Within the first four months of 1946 there were other signs that in fact the status quo would not—could not—be maintained in any sector of the national life. In January a Harlem preacher and politician named Adam Clayton Powell Jr. published a program of political action for African-Americans in the postwar era, *Marching Blacks.* In March, Robinson's former teammates at UCLA, Kenny Washington and Woody Strode, signed contracts with professional football's Los Angeles Rams.† And in April the U.S. Supreme Court refused to review a lower court ruling that upheld the right of Negroes to vote in Georgia's primary elections.

Organized Baseball could hardly have remained immune from this trend, but as in other instances the game was slow to recognize this, and when Rickey signed Robinson and the other black players, baseball was unprepared. The reactions of the quasi-official baseball weekly, *The Sporting News,* over the winter and into the spring of '46 were symptomatic—by turns critical of Rickey, skeptical of his motives, and disparaging of Robinson's baseball abilities. In November 1945, the paper editorialized that if Robinson were six years younger and a different color, he might possibly rate a look in Class C ball. By late March with Robinson in camp with the Montreal Royals the paper ran a column by veteran New York sportswriter Dan Parker, ridiculing those who would see Rickey as baseball's Great Emancipator and broadly suggesting instead that this was little more than another "publicity dodge" of the Mahatma's. Robinson and pitcher John Wright, Parker wrote, "are going through the motions at the Royals ballpark in the Negro district of Daytona Beach, while the Dodgers are working out 'across the tracks' with the white folks." Surface indications were, Parker continued, "that both players are being treated the same as their pink-cuticled brethren under the skin." In the adjacent column there appeared a grotesque caricature of a black Pullman porter, this as an illustration for a story by Chicago

---

* The Camp Claiborne incident was not an isolated one. There were serious riots also at Fort Bliss, Texas, Camp Van Dorn in Mississippi, and San Luis Obispo, California.

† After his football career was over the statuesque Strode went on to a career in films. "Early on John Ford said something to me," Strode recalled. "He said, 'Woody, I can't make you a star: you're the wrong color. But I'll tell you what I can do for you: I can make you into a character actor.' And that's what he did."

sportswriter Ed Burns. Baseball, the *Sporting News* made clear, might some day be integrated, but Rickey had gone about it in the wrong way, and the game simply wasn't ready for Robinson.

As for Robinson himself, his eyes were wide open to American racial realities and had been well before he ever thought of playing for the Dodgers. Like Irvin and others, he had had his bruising encounters with prejudice while in the service, none of the branches of which was integrated until well after the war was over. At one point in his army hitch Robinson passed through Fort Riley, and Pete Reiser remembered the day a black lieutenant showed up at the ballfield, hoping to join the team. An officer there told him he'd have to play with the colored team. "That was a joke," Reiser said. "There was no colored team. The black lieutenant didn't speak. He stood there for a while, watched us work out, and then he turned and walked away." It was Robinson. "I can still remember him walking away by himself," Reiser told Donald Honig. Later, at Fort Hood, Texas, Robinson was court-martialed—and acquitted—for refusing to move to the back of a military bus.

After his discharge Robinson found that Organized Baseball's racial attitudes had been changed some by the war—but not much. Responding grudgingly to pressure from the black press, members of the Boston city council, and Boston *Record* sportswriter Dave Egan, the Red Sox agreed to hold a "tryout" at Fenway Park in April 1945 for Robinson, Sam Jethroe, and Marvin Williams of the Negro leagues' Philadelphia Stars. In the nearly deserted park the three players "went through the fundamentals," Jethroe said, with coaches Duffy Lewis and Larry Woodall. Then a call came down from somewhere in the grandstand, "Get those niggers off the field!" Afterward, no one would admit who'd said it, but Boston *Globe* sportswriter Clif Keane who was there said he and everybody else who was present heard it. For years people said it was Tom Yawkey, the Red Sox owner, but Keane said, "it wasn't Yawkey." Keane said he'd subsequently heard who it really was but the secret would never be divulged by him. Whoever it was, the tryout came to nothing for Robinson and the others. "They said we all had possibilities," Jethroe recalled, "but they said it wasn't the right time." But it was, and a month later, operating behind the odd ruse that he intended to form another all-black baseball league, Rickey was actively scouting the Negro leagues for the right man to break the game's color barrier. And now, less than a year after that, here was Robinson in Florida with the Royals.

On his trip to Sanford, Robinson and his wife had been abused, harassed, and bumped from planes in a harrowing, humiliating trip, and on his first day at the park he didn't even have a minor league uniform. With his wife he lived apart from the other rookies in the black section of town. Over the ensuing weeks of spring training, exhibition games would be canceled by city officials in Jacksonville and Deland because of Robinson's presence, and at Sanford a policeman walked onto the field and ordered Robinson and Wright to leave the premises immediately. Some of the Dodgers players from the South also resented his presence in camp, and veteran infielder-outfielder Augie Galan claimed that in an intersquad game Dodgers pitcher Hugh Casey threw at Robinson on four consecutive pitches.* In addition to all this Robinson was plagued that spring by a sore throwing arm, while at the plate his anxiety to prove his abilities and vindicate Rickey caused him to overswing. But despite all this the "great experiment" was proceeding, and there was no going back. Baseball would never be the same.

---

* I have been unable to find corroborating testimony to this effect. Gene Hermanski emphatically denied it ever happened. When asked about it, Dodgers pitcher Vic Lombardi said simply, "I wouldn't even touch that."

4

Baseball wasn't the only thing changing in America. Nothing else would be quite the same, either, despite what appeared to be an almost desperate wish that things would return to the way they were remembered to have been before the war. The entire world had been shaken to its very core, and every mortal and every mortal institution had been affected. Large portions of England, Europe, the U.S.S.R., and Asia lay in ruins. Croplands were devastated, port and transport facilities smashed. Famine, the black horse that follows the red one of war, was now loose upon the European landscape, prompting President Truman to establish a "Famine Emergency Committee" within the Department of Agriculture. America, Truman asserted, could not close its eyes to the suffering that had come in the war's wake, and Americans would just have to keep their belts tightened to aid the starving and the homeless, some of whom were now arriving in the States as "Displaced Persons" even as the ballplayers were rounding into shape in Florida and California.

This spring Europe was still burying its dead while its blasted soil sent up the stony crop of grave markers and memorial monuments. In America, preparations were being made to bring home the remains of 200,000 GIs. In a fledgling organization called the United Nations, which had been founded to prevent future such catastrophes it was becoming clearer daily that this successor to the failed League of Nations was fraught with international tensions that might well cripple and even kill it before the first year of peace was out. East and West had sharply parted company on so many issues—Manchuria, Korea, Yugoslavia, Bulgaria—that the U.N. seemed a good deal less like a forum for peace than a stage for acrimonious posturing behind which the world powers determinedly pursued their own interests. Speaking in early March at Westminster College in

Missouri, Winston Churchill summed up the grim realities of East-West relations by asserting that an iron curtain had been rung down by the Soviets all across Europe. He urged even closer cooperation between his country and the United States. The next day the Russian newspaper *Pravda* denounced the speech as a patent effort to wreck the U.N.

Even the decisive Allied victories and unconditional Axis surrenders that had ended the war now seemed oddly less clean and final. In Nuremberg the Nazi war crimes trials proceeded apace, but in the middle of March when Herman Goering took the stand the trials seemed in danger of being transformed into a platform for the dissemination of Nazi propaganda. Goering, his mind cleared of drugs and alcohol, mounted a sly and occasionally brilliant defense during which the legitimacy of the tribunal itself was called into question. In Asia, Japan had been flattened, but large numbers of Japanese troops remained unrepatriated, well armed, and in a mood said to be something less than humble.

Over all this loomed the shadow of the new and ultimate weapon, the atomic bomb. So unprecedented had its effects been on Hiroshima and Nagasaki that battle-toughened veterans and homefront civilians alike had been awed by newsreel footage of the remains of what had once been cities and the shadows of incinerated human beings branded on the pavements. A weapon so monstrously potent as to alter the balance of world power probably couldn't be kept an American state secret, but the question remained of how to share atomic knowledge; this spring the Manhattan Project's General Leslie Groves was under fire for his efforts to keep the awful genie in an American bottle with a military cap on it.

On the home front the problems of housing and transportation that greeted the returning vets were accompanied by a sharply rising crime rate and the immensely complicated problem of wage and price adjustments. Inflation threatened to explode under the pressure for price hikes and wage demands, and over the year the cost of living would rise 18 percent from 1945. Employers who during the war years had been prevented by government regulations from raising the prices of goods and services beyond set limits sought relief from regulations they claimed were now obsolete. And until such relief was granted, they said, they would continue to resist labor's demands for higher wages. The consequences of what was frankly acknowledged to be a wage and price war were dozens of major strikes and hundreds of disputes laid before the National Labor Relations Board. In the first four months of 1946 there were strikes by electrical workers, metalworkers, meatcutters, steel workers, tugboat operators, and auto workers. And now John L. Lewis was threatening to take his United Mine workers out, a development that would have a dramatically negative effect on the Office of Economic Stabilization's efforts to rationalize what verged on economic chaos.

The baseball world was subject to many of these trends and tensions. The housing shortage, for instance, was a problem for the teams in their spring training camps, and several clubs told players' wives not to plan on coming to Florida or to southern California because there simply weren't available rooms. For players who'd been away for years in the service this didn't sit well, and some brought their wives anyway. In Florida, hotel space was so tight one wag said there was a waiting list for seats in the lobbies, and when the teams went north to their home cities they would find the same problem there. At the end of spring training the Braves were forced to take out an ad in a local paper asking Boston area residents if they had any space for players and their families.

Inflation was an even greater and more intractable problem, one that would get worse as the season went on and the federal government failed to develop a wage and price strategy equal to the massive challenge of reconversion. At first, in the enthusiasm of the return to the sunny training camps these economic bends could be the stuff of jokes: in Florida the players found barbers charging upwards of a dollar for a haircut, and one player said he would cut his own throat rather than pay seventy-five cents for a shave. But very quickly the matter turned serious, especially since players didn't begin drawing their salaries until the opening of the regular season. Despite the glamour attached to being a big leaguer, most players never saw big money and didn't really expect to, but this was a different world now. Back in the 1920s and the Depression years many of them had been rural men or from mill towns, and they'd come up the hard way.* These men considered themselves lucky to have such a job. They might complain about the miserly practices of owners like Connie Mack of the A's, Clark Griffith of the Senators, and the tight-fisted St. Louis

---

* Donald Honig draws the reader's attention to the hard, lined faces of the young men who played baseball in these years in his *Shadows of Summer: Classic Baseball Photographs, 1869–1947.* The players shown in his pages look more like middle-aged cowboys, miners, and mill hands than they do ballplayers, and it is instructive to compare these faces with those smooth and well-fed ones of today's professional athletes.

Dodger Frenchy Bordagaray tries to beat inflation in spring training by having his wife cut his hair. Bordagaray played through the war years for Brooklyn, then was induced to retire to manage in their farm system. (*The Sporting News,* March 28, 1946)

Cardinals tandem of Rickey and owner Sam Breadon. Still, they knew well enough that many others back on the farm, in the factory, or out on the breadline in the 1930s had it far worse. Now, however, they found themselves like employees everywhere, squeezed by postwar prices that were rising much faster than their salaries.

From management's point of view, 1946 was already looking like the costliest one in the game's history, beginning with this very long spring training. True, the owners were looking forward to a banner year at the box office with the return of the players, the end of restrictions on the number of night games that could be scheduled, and the eagerness of the fans to turn their attentions again to peacetime diversions. But, they pointed out, the salary total of the two leagues was inching toward a staggering $5 million, and if baseball was not to become captive to a ruinous wage spiral, salaries would have to be carefully controlled.

★   ★   ★

*A*s they faced the new season with its new challenges to tradition, the owners' first order of business was to settle the contractual status of those players who'd been away in the war. After that they could turn their attentions to the problem of rising salary expectations—a problem they shared with employers all over the nation.

Most owners simply sent their returning servicemen contracts calling for the same amount the players had been drawing before the war, as Sam Breadon had done with Slaughter. Their reasoning was that since these players had been away from the game, some for more than three seasons, they certainly couldn't be worth more now than they had been before entering the service. But some players were angry at what appeared to them to be an arrogant and willful disregard of everything that had happened during the war, and a few of them wondered whether they even still belonged to their old clubs. When the Red Sox automatically renewed his contract at $10,000 Dominic DiMaggio said it made him "sore." After three years, four months, and nineteen days of military service, DiMaggio said, he resented *anyone* telling him what to do and ordering him to report for duty in Florida. Before leaving the service DiMaggio sought the advice of a navy lawyer as to whether he was bound to return to the Boston club or whether he might be a free agent, able to sell his services on the open market. The navy lawyer wasn't very helpful; the situation had no precedent, he said. DiMaggio wrote Red Sox general manager Eddie

Collins that he wasn't so sure he was still Boston property and that in any case he wasn't going to sign with anyone at the same prewar figure, which brought manager Joe Cronin out to see DiMaggio in San Francisco on the double. Subsequently DiMaggio signed with the team for $15,000 and an attendance clause guaranteeing him additional money if the Sox drew more than 500,000 paid customers. Collins was unhappier with the attendance clause than he was with the raise DiMaggio had pried from him. The Red Sox, Collins told DiMaggio, had never granted any player such a clause, and after the season was over, Collins tried to wriggle out of it.

Other players also showed their restiveness with the old, autocratic way in which baseball conducted its business. Like other GIs, they felt especially touchy on the subject of their rights as men who'd answered the call of duty. The GI Bill of Rights was a legislative effort to respond to that general touchiness, rewarding servicemen and servicewomen with various safeguards and special dispensations. Among other things it provided that all returning service personnel be rehired in their prewar jobs for a year, unless they were so physically impaired that they couldn't perform their former duties. This was a provision that made the owners, accustomed to a seigneurial latitude in labor relations, uneasy, and they asked Commissioner Chandler for relief from it. Chandler quickly complied, ruling that a club might dismiss or demote a player after only a thirty-day spring training trial or after fifteen days of the championship season. Here again, the owners relied on baseball's special and unique status within American culture, a status they thought exempted them from regulations applying to everyone else. But Tony Lupien felt owners weren't exempt and challenged them.

Lupien was a Harvard-educated first baseman for the Phillies. When he'd been discharged from the service late in the 1945 season, he'd rejoined his team and performed creditably. During the off-season, however, the Phillies obtained former Most Valuable Player Frank McCormick from Cincinnati to play the position and informed Lupien they'd sold his contract to Hollywood of the Pacific Coast League. Lupien protested, first in private to club officials and to Chandler, then in public when he was summarily rebuffed. The GI Bill, Lupien told reporters, was specifically intended to protect GIs from just this sort of thing. "Now," he said, "that bill either applies to ball players or it doesn't. That's what I'm trying to find out." Boston *Record* sportswriter Dave Egan, who had been active in campaigning for the integration of the game, now took up Lupien's case, writing acerbically that those players who'd served hadn't done so for the "dubious privilege of selling apples on street corners and in common justice are entitled to the same rights as all other citizens." With the case beginning to generate unfavorable publicity for the Phillies, the club decided to handle it speedily and secretly, agreeing with Hollywood that it would make up the difference between Lupien's minor league salary and what he would have made with the big club. When Lupien learned of this, he decided it would be better to play in the Pacific Coast League and hope to make it back to the majors than to sit out the season in protracted litigation. But he still felt he had a strong case, and he freely advised other players who found themselves in similar circumstances. Two of them, Seattle Rainiers infielder Al Niemiec and Washington Senators outfielder Bruce Campbell, would sue their clubs under the GI Bill of Rights, and both would win.

The problem of rising expectations, though, was much bigger and more serious than that of GI rights, which was, after all, short-term. With the return of the players from the war there was a growing feeling within the baseball world that in the emerging postwar economic climate players were being crudely exploited at current salary levels. Even the *Sporting News,* generally conservative in its approach, said as much in a February article on costs and predicted that whether the owners liked it or not, the era of larger salaries was bound to come in the wake of the war. Of the 480 players to be carried by major league clubs this season only fifteen were to get $20,000 in straight salary and only six were to draw more than $25,000: Greenberg, Feller, Joe DiMaggio, Williams, Wakefield, and Indians player-manager Lou Boudreau. At the other end of the spectrum, there were nineteen National Leaguers and thirty-one American Leaguers who were making less than $5,000.

The players had no real way to push for higher wages. They were bound to their clubs by the so-called "reserve clause" in their contracts, which not even a world war and an atom bomb had been able to break. Section 10(a) of the Uniform Player's Contract bound a player to his club until such time as the club either released him, sold him, or traded him away. Thus a player could either play for the club that owned him, or he could find another line of work.

To be sure, a dissatisfied player could always hold out for a higher salary and refuse to report until his club met his demands or a compromise was reached. But the holdout was a weak and ineffective bargaining tool because it was far too costly for the player and, unless he was a star of the greatest magnitude, the club still held the upper hand since there was nowhere else the player could go with his services. In 1946 there were probably fewer than a dozen players generally regarded as absolutely indispensable and who thus could have held out with some hope of success. More typical was the situation of players like Cardinals third baseman Whitey Kurowski and his teammate, pitcher Max Lanier.

Kurowski was a tough, thickly built man from Reading, Pennsylvania, who'd survived a childhood bout with osteomyelitis in his right arm, had put in five seasons in the Cardinals farm system, and then had played an important role in the Cardinals three consecutive pennant winners, 1942–44. Surgery for the osteomyelitis had cost Kurowski four inches of bone in his wrist and forearm. At the plate his shorter arm caused the right-handed hitter to bring his top hand over quickly in his swing, making him a dead pull hitter. In the Cardinals pennant years he'd delivered some big hits, none of them bigger than his home run in the ninth inning of Game Five of the 1942 World Series, clinching the championship for his team. In the field his arm wasn't the strongest, nor was his range more than average, and Kurowski used to joke to shortstop Marty Marion that he ought to give the far-ranging Marion part of his salary since Marion got to so many balls that Kurowski couldn't. But he was a battler at third base, something his pitchers appreciated. As Max Lanier put it, Kurowski "wasn't afraid to get in front of that ball." In 1945 Kurowski had driven home 102 runs and had batted .323. His salary was $12,500—on the high end for the Cardinals—and now he wanted $14,000 from Breadon.

In the old days Rickey had handled St. Louis salary negotiations, and a player talked salary with Breadon only if an impasse had been reached with Rickey. If anything, Rickey was more parsimonious than Breadon, often beating his players down to an even lower figure than Breadon had suggested and pocketing the difference. Bob Broeg, the long-time St. Louis *Post-Dispatch* writer, told a story about Joe Medwick, the Cardinals great slugger of the 1930s, emerging from one of those bruising negotiating sessions with Rickey and asking anyone who'd listen if they could imagine what it was like trying to get a raise out of a man who was back there in his office shaving without lather. "If he'd have bled any more," Broeg had Medwick wailing, "he'd have looked like Count Dracula!"

With Rickey now doing business in his characteristic fashion over in Brooklyn Breadon handled contracts himself, and it wasn't much of a relief to Cardinals players. In Kurowski's case, Breadon made it clear from the outset that he wasn't prepared to go that high for his third baseman. When Kurowski stuck to his position and indicated his willingness to wage a stubborn holdout, Breadon began publicly to explore the possibility of trading Kurowski to Brooklyn, Pittsburgh, or the Phillies. Meanwhile down in Florida, Cardinals manager Eddie Dyer began using Red Schoendienst at Kurowski's old position. Schoendienst was five years younger than Kurowski, was making much less money, and as a rookie in 1945 had led the league in stolen bases while playing in the outfield. But Schoendienst was a natural infielder, capable of playing well at second, short, or third, where he was clearly a better defensive player than Kurowski. On the Cardinals with their traditionally deep farm system, this was a familiar problem for the incumbent player. "If you weren't in there [the lineup]," said Whitey Kurowski, "they always had three or four guys waiting to take your place." While Dyer looked at Schoendienst, Kurowski continued to hold out, and then at the end of spring training he signed for about the figure that Breadon had in mind all along.

Max Lanier had battled Cardinals salary practices almost since the day they'd signed him. Within a week of that signing in 1934 he had quit when the club assigned him to a lower minor league than had been agreed upon. But Lanier was simply too talented for Rickey and the Cardinals to write off as a malcontent, and two years later they re-signed him. Still, as Lanier well knew, the Cardinals had so many talented players under contract they could afford to treat players pretty much as they pleased. "At one time," Lanier recalled, "they had about thirty ball clubs, and they kept us hungry." The competition within the St. Louis system was "murder," he said. "When I was coming up, they had, just in left-handed pitchers, fellows like Howie Pollet, Harry Brecheen, Al Brazle, Ernie White, and Preacher Roe. That was pretty stiff competition." Lanier not only survived it, he became one of the premier left-handers in the league. The broad, beetle-browed North Carolinian threw a good, rising fastball and a curve that veteran Pirates catcher Al Lopez told rookie Ralph Kiner was "the damnedest one you ever saw." Fellow holdout Kurowski said he loved playing behind Lanier because everyone knew that if the opposition got two runs, "that's just about all they were gonna get." And what Kurowski and his teammates particularly admired about Lanier was that he regularly beat their bitter rivals, the Dodgers.

In 1944 Lanier won 17 games and another in the Series. His salary was $10,000 and after missing the next season in the service Lanier found Breadon proposing a new contract at the old figure. He balked. "Breadon?" Lanier said, "You'd like him if you met him—till it came time to sign the contracts. He just wouldn't give an inch." In previous negotiations Breadon had used Lanier's teammate and star right-hander Mort Cooper as a bargaining tool against him. Once, when Lanier made what Breadon considered an exorbitant salary request, Breadon countered by pointing out that Cooper had won more games the previous year than Lanier yet was getting only a little more money than Lanier was now asking for. "I said to him then," Lanier recalled, " 'Well, he should be making twice what he's making, but I don't care what *he* makes. I know what *I'm* worth.' " The way Breadon kept Cooper's salary demands down, Lanier claimed, was that the pitcher would routinely ask Breadon for loans during the off-season, and the owner would grant them on the condition that Cooper sign a new contract at Breadon's figure. But in 1945, following three consecutive 20-win seasons, Breadon tired of Cooper's salary demands and traded him to the Braves for Red Barrett (who'd gone 9–16 the year previous) and $60,000. It was the kind of move Breadon could make because he had so many talented pitchers in the pipeline.

Lanier came to St. Petersburg with the rest of the players but was still unsigned as workouts began. After a few days Dyer, who was in his first year as manager and was understandably anxious to get all his talent on board, offered to intercede on the pitcher's behalf. Speaking with Breadon by long distance phone, Dyer told him that Lanier was worth more than was being offered, and Breadon had quickly responded, "I'll give him $500 more. He can take it or go home." Lanier took it, but he was resentful, and he remained so.

5

*T*here was one recourse this spring that a dissatisfied player might investigate, but it was so odd—bizarre, really—that at first not many gave it serious thought. Beginning in mid-February rumors circulated that five Mexican brothers in the import-export business intended to stock an independent league in that country with players from Organized Baseball. At first the rumors mentioned only minor leaguers, and when one of these, pitcher Jean Pierre Roy who was Brooklyn property, showed up at the Dodgers camp and affirmed his loyalty to that organization, the whole thing seemed more shadow than substance, part of the chaotic phenomenon called reconversion. Jorgé Pasquel, president of the alleged new league—instantly branded an "outlaw" league by Organized Baseball—was talking big, claiming the league was real and that he would be able to announce the signings of some top-level major league stars. The Mexican League was no "outlaw" circuit, Pasquel said, but would be a bona fide major league south of the border, and he said construction was about to begin on a new 50,000-seat stadium in Mexico City. But when all Pasquel could come up with was the signing of free agent Danny Gardella, there were more snickers than murmurs of concern.

Gardella had met Pasquel at a New York City gym where the player worked in the off-season. The Mexican businessman took an instant liking to the cheerful, helpful man who supervised his workouts and who always seemed to have a joke or a song for his customers. "One day in the gym," Gardella said, "he says to me, 'If you ever get in trouble or need something, call me. We need baseball players in Mexico.' So, after the Brannick business I called him and he offered me $15,000, about three times what I was making." Gardella also agreed to recruit major leaguers for Pasquel's league, and within the next few weeks he talked with pitchers Adrian Zabala and Sal Maglie and infielders George Hausmann and Roy Zimmerman, all of the Giants. But none of them committed themselves at the time to the Pasquel brothers, and so the Mexican business still seemed a harmless sideshow.

But then the Pasquels announced they'd come to terms with Luis Olmo of the Dodgers and had made six-figure offers to Bob Feller, Ted Williams, and Hank Greenberg, and suddenly the sideshow looked like a credible threat to Organized Baseball's historic hegemony, unchallenged since the short-lived Federal League of 1914–15. Olmo was a right-handed hitting outfielder from Puerto Rico who'd hit .313 and driven home 110 runs in the war-weakened league of 1945. With the return of Reiser and the rest he might not start for Durocher this season. But at the very least he'd be a valuable man to have in reserve, the kind of player a team had to have if it was going to contend for the pennant all through the long season—especially the Dodgers who had to be concerned about Reiser's history of injuries and Dixie Walker's advanced age. His loss was significant, and Rickey issued an alarm, calling on Commissioner Chandler to issue what Rickey styled a ukase, barring any players who jumped their contracts from returning to Organized Baseball.

Chandler was still very new to his job. He'd already stuck his neck out on the explosive issue of integration, telling members of the black press that as far as he was concerned if black soldiers could make it fighting in the South Pacific, they could make it in Organized Baseball. Here was an opportunity to curry some favor with baseball's power structure by taking a tough stance on the sanctity of contracts and the inviolability of the reserve clause which management had always regarded as baseball's foundation rock.

In selecting Chandler for the job the owners had made it clear to him that they expected him to be their man, and at the same time they took back some of the dictatorial rights they'd been frightened into granting Judge Landis in the wake of the Black Sox scandal. Now they wanted Chandler to stand up for owners' rights as he'd done in the matter of the contractual status of the service returnees. When Feller confirmed he'd been contacted by the Mexicans and Williams said he had as well, Chandler swung into action, issuing the ukase Rickey had called for. All players in Organized Baseball who jumped their contracts, Chandler said, would be barred from playing for five years unless they returned to their rightful owners by Opening Day. Nor was this all, for Chandler added that at the end of that suspension period he would review the players' cases individually; reinstatement, he implied, would by no means be automatic. Considering the brevity of the average player's career, the ruling was tantamount to a lifetime ban, and it was certainly more than enough to give pause to all but the hopelessly disaffected.

But the Pasquels themselves had nothing to lose by continuing to pursue major leaguers, waving bundles of cash under the noses of those who could never expect to earn nearly so much, even if they were to play for a decade or more. The Cardinals Dick Sisler revealed he'd been approached, and it was said that so had the same club's Fred Martin, a pitcher, and infielder Lou Klein. Mexican baseball had long provided off-season play for members of the Negro leagues, and now Jorgé Pasquel even began courting Rickey's pet project, Jackie Robinson. When Rickey accidentally encountered a Mexican League agent at the Brooklyn training complex, the Bible-quoting Dodgers executive offered to fistfight the man. Then he asked for a restraining order.

Robinson said he wouldn't be interested in going south, no matter what kind of money was being offered. And apparently there was plenty available. Jorgé Pasquel said he wasn't afraid of a fight with Organized Baseball and had a war chest of $30 million. What the North Americans were pleased to call "Organized Baseball" was a slave market, he said, with the reserve clause binding players to their clubs for life. It was also an illegal monopoly, he charged, and he intended to break it any way he could.

At the end of March the Pasquels made good on at least some of their threats, signing Dodgers catcher Mickey Owen, Maglie, Hausmann, and Zimmerman of the Giants, and shortstop Vern Stephens of the Browns. The defections of Owen and Stephens were considered the most ominous. Owen was a hustling veteran of the Dodgers pennant races of the early '40s, a man who called a good game and had the respect of his pitchers. When he signed with the Pasquels, Leo Durocher tried to dismiss the loss, claiming he had no big plans for Owen this year anyway. It was a poor bluff, and everybody knew it: Owen would have caught the majority of his team's games. As for Stephens of the Browns, he was precisely the kind of star Pasquel had said he'd sign. He'd led the league in home runs last season, and the Browns, much thinner in talent than Brooklyn, were plainly shocked by his decision. Manager Luke Sewell said he thought Stephens's decision was motivated by the fear that with all the stars returning from the service "he might not stack up so well." But Stephens's teammates openly admitted the team could hardly be expected to contend for the pennant without him.

Giants manager Mel Ott huffily claimed the defections of Maglie and the others were insignificant, but then he and team officials convened a clubhouse meeting to discuss the situation—and to smoke out any others who might also be planning to jump south. When the meeting began, pitcher Bill Voiselle was in the bathroom shaving. Voiselle was hard of hearing and had been exempted from the service because of this. As he stood in front of the mirror, lathering up, he sang aloud the popular number, "South of the Border," happily oblivious to what was going on in the locker room. Suddenly an excited teammate burst in and shouted to Voiselle that he'd better cut out singing that song and get to the meeting. He was already in Ott's doghouse, Voiselle said, and after that he was in it permanently.

There followed a lull in the Mexican business with no more signings, though still plenty of rumors, and Jorgé Pasquel announced that his league's opener would be delayed by several days. American manufacturers, he said, were refusing to sell major league–quality balls and bats to the Mexicans, and since he wanted everything to be first rate, the opener would be delayed until shipments were received. Whether this was the real reason for the delay or whether the Pasquels had hoped to be able to announce more signings wasn't clear. But at the end of March the new league began play with Mexican president Manuel Ávila Camacho sitting in Jorgé Pasquel's box at Mexico City for the game between Mexico City and Vera Cruz. Mickey Owen was player-manager for Vera Cruz, Stephens was his shortstop, and Danny Gardella was in the outfield where he promptly lost two fly balls, leading to his team's defeat. After the game Pasquel ordered him to see an eye doctor.

A few days after the opener the Mexican League story took yet another twist when Stephens showed up on the Texas side of the border and announced he would rejoin the Browns. The Pasquel's money was real enough, the husky shortstop said, but the living and playing conditions weren't at all what he'd been led to expect, and he'd had enough. The parks were rock-hard, all-dirt affairs, Stephens reported, none of the clubhouses had showers, and even in the hotels the shower knobs marked "C" gave you hot water (*caliente*), not cold. He didn't know the language, and after two days he'd started talking to himself. Stephens said he fully intended to repay the Pasquels what he owed them and was just happy to be out of that situation and back in America.

It turned out that Stephens had communicated his instant unhappiness to his father who had then gone to Monterrey to meet him. Then the father and son had driven to Laredo and Vern Jr., disguised in his father's clothes, had walked across the international bridge to the American side. From there the two drove to San Antonio where Stephens caught up with the Browns who welcomed him back with enthusiasm. Though he gave no reason for the cloak-and-dagger nature of his departure, Stephens pointed out that most of what he styled the Mexican "big shots" walked around with pistols on their belts, a practice he said he found unnerving. Danny Gardella, who remained happily behind, later described the Pasquel brothers as "scary" men who slept with pistols under their pillows. Jorgé Pasquel was also a very excitable man, the outfielder said, and after a win in the table tennis games he loved to play against his imported stars, he was liable to fire off his pistol in celebration. Gardella claimed that he once got a glimpse into a room of Jorgé Pasquel's mansion and saw "enough guns in there to fight Sam Houston all over again."

Probably Stephens and Gardella exaggerated the threat posed by the Pasquels, but there is no doubt Jorgé Pasquel was indeed excitable and autocratic. He was also politically well connected, and he had not only put his family prestige on the line with his new league, but his country's as well. He would not take lightly the losses of the American players he'd been at pains to lure south and whose presence in the league had been so well advertised. Thus, when Mickey Owen showed up north of the border hard on the heels of Stephens and announced that he too had seen enough, Pasquel was enraged and said he'd sue the catcher. Down in Florida Rickey was taking a hard line, saying that it was too late for Owen, that he would never play for the Dodgers again, even though Chandler's deadline was still a couple of weeks away. Rickey had been the first to understand that the real issue here was Organized Baseball's reserve clause. He'd built the Cardinals and their farm system on the foundation of the clause and had done the same at Brooklyn, and he felt there was a great deal more at stake than the status of Mickey Owen. To take Owen back under any circumstances, he felt, was to equivocate in a matter fundamental to the survival of the game. It was far better, then, to make do at catcher in 1946, with rookies Ferrell Anderson and Bruce

Edwards. Probably Rickey ordered his manager to back him up in the Owen matter, because as soon as Rickey spoke, Durocher echoed him, saying that it was a matter of no concern where Owen happened to be at the moment: he could go back to Mexico or stay on his farm in Missouri and feed his livestock, Durocher said. He had no plans for Mickey now.

Suddenly friendless and unable to sell his baseball services anywhere in America, Owen lingered on his farm, waiting for Rickey to relent—or for Durocher to convince Rickey that Owen was needed in Brooklyn—and when he didn't, Owen did the only thing he could: he returned to Mexico and resumed his duties as player-manager at Vera Cruz.

6

*T*he distraction of the Mexican League notwithstanding, spring training moved toward its appointed and traditional conclusion with the clubs making their late roster cuts, then getting ready to break camp and barnstorm north toward home. As they did so prewar form began to emerge in ways that were reassuring to fans and sportswriters.

The Yankees under their great manager Joe McCarthy looked very much like the Yankees of old. Their slugging outfield of DiMaggio, King Kong Keller, and Tommy Henrich was reunited and hitting with characteristic power, especially DiMaggio. There was some question about the strength and depth of McCarthy's pitching staff, and star second baseman Joe "Flash" Gordon would miss the beginning of the regular season with a nasty spike wound in his hand. But as so often in the past the Bronx Bombers appeared to be the team to beat, especially with the defending world champion Tigers in some disarray.

Having torn apart their team after the '45 Series, the Tigers hadn't yet been able to reassemble the pieces into a strong squad. Newhouser, Trout, and Trucks had all thrown well in the exhibition games, but the offense had been strangely sluggish. Line-drive hitting outfielder Barney McCosky was having some trouble getting his swing back after three years in the navy, and Dick Wakefield so far looked nothing like the hitter he'd been in 1943 and '44. Outfielder Pat Mullin, a sensation before missing four seasons in the army, looked rusty at the plate, too. Worse yet, the team's big gun, Hank Greenberg, wasn't swinging with his old-time authority. By the time the Tigers were to break camp, rumors were circulating that he would retire at the end of the season—or even before if his performance didn't dramatically improve: he'd worked too hard to be a great star to embarrass himself with a decidedly subpar performance.

The team that looked most likely to give the Yankees trouble wasn't the defending champion Tigers but the perennially disappointing Boston Red Sox. The return of Williams, Dom DiMaggio, Johnny Pesky, and Bobby Doerr had been an enormous boost to the anemic offense of the wartime years, and the Sox had also added a slugger in first baseman Rudy York.

York had been hounded out of Detroit by fans and writers who couldn't forgive him for failing to fill Greenberg's big shoes. He had certain defensive liabilities (former teammate Trucks claimed York would never go to his right on balls hit that way), and because he was what the players called a "guess hitter" he could look awful when he guessed wrong about what the pitcher was going to throw. The hulking Cherokee from Georgia also brought to Boston a reputation as a drinker who often fell asleep in hotel beds holding lighted cigarettes. "Rudy led the league in hotel fires," laughed Barney McCosky, "but he could hit, and he was tremendously strong." McCosky recalled a train trip to Cincinnati on the eve of the 1940 World Series when he'd run into York coming back from the club car. York had been drinking and now engaged the rookie in an animated conversation, all the while squeezing McCosky's hand and assuring him he'd have a great Series, that there was nothing to worry about. Finally McCosky, on his knees from York's crushing grip, managed to gasp, "Rudy, *please!* I'm not gonna have *any* kind of Series if you don't let go!"

York was a streak hitter who in his hot spells could carry a team's offense all by himself, driving in big runs game after game. Once he'd hit 18 home runs in a single month, breaking a record held by Babe Ruth, and that same month had set another record by driving home 49 runs. And despite his reputation as a drinker, he was a sound and very astute baseball man. His new teammates noticed he brought this dimension to a team that had always lacked it: York, the Sox said, was wonderful at stealing an opposing team's signals and at picking up an enemy pitcher's pitching patterns and mound behavior. Red Sox catcher Roy Partee remembered him chain-smoking Camels while he paced the dugout, studying the opposing pitcher and discarding one cigarette after another. Then York would declare, "We're gonna get this guy in about the fifth inning." He was amazingly accurate in his predictions, Partee said. Pitcher Joe Dobson said York was just as astute in diagnosing a problem with Boston pitchers. "He'd see me doing something wrong," Dobson recalled, "and come over from first base to tell me about it. 'You do what I say,' he'd tell me, 'and you'll be all right.' " York also had a habit of spitting into the pocket of his mitt, and Dobson recalled that on occasion the ball would come back from Rudy nicely prepared in the event the pitcher might want to throw a spitball. With York in the field and in the dugout the Red Sox felt they played with a greater sharpness and were, as a team, more in the game than they had been before. His contributions, they felt, couldn't be measured in statistics but in wins.

York wasn't the only thing different about this year's Red Sox: for the first time since the almost mythic days of Babe Ruth, Smoky Joe Wood, and Ernie Shore the Sox had pitching. In Tex Hughson, Dave (Boo) Ferriss, Mickey Harris, and Dobson, manager Cronin had four high-quality starters. The Sox also had a good-looking relief pitcher in Earl Johnson, a much-decorated veteran of the Battle of the Bulge. Johnson, once a hard thrower, had left his fastball in the service and now had to depend on changes of speed and a sinker, but his pitches were producing rally-killing outs in the exhibition games, and in Boston's beguilingly mis-shapen park a manager always knew he needed a reliable man in the bullpen.

Reporters in the Red Sox camp at Sarasota had been eager from the beginning to get the great Williams's opinion of last year's rookie phe-nom, Ferriss, and they'd crowded around the batting cage as the Kid took his first swings against him. After he'd had his cuts Williams came out with a big grin. "I like him," he told the writers, "I like him. That ball's alive. It's always doing something. Don't put him down," he lectured the writers, "like you guys always do. He'll be all right." For the young Ferriss, about to face the restored league for the first time, this endorsement by the game's sharpest student of hitting was a tremendous boost.

Hughson was a big, raw-boned right-hander from Kyle, Texas, with a rising fastball and a hard, late-biting slider, and he could throw both pitches with an accuracy remarkable in a power pitcher. He didn't have much of a curve, but because of his control of his two outstanding pitches he didn't need a very good one. Hughson was also a fierce competitor who believed he could dominate any hitter who ever swung a bat. "When he walked out on that mound," said Dave Ferriss, "he took charge. He was the king. *Tough.*"

Harris was another confirmation of the baseball stereotype of the whacky left-hander: a garrulous, fun-loving Brooklynite who kept his teammates loose and whom they called "Mickey Himself" in affectionate reference to his boisterous self-confidence. Fellow Red Sox pitcher

Top: For the first time almost within living memory the Red Sox had some strong pitching arms to go with their traditional big bats. At top are starters Tex Hughson, Mickey Harris, Joe Dobson, and Dave (Boo) Ferriss. One season later all of them would suffer injuries that blighted their careers and ruined the Red Sox pitching staff. (*The Sporting News,* May 16, 1946) *Below*: Some of the Sox's hitters, including, left to right, Wally Moses, Johnny Pesky, Ted Williams, Bobby Doerr, Rudy York, manager Joe Cronin, Dom DiMaggio, Pinky Higgins, Hal Wagner, and pitchers Mickey Harris and Dave Ferriss. (*Ted Williams, My Turn at Bat*)

Broadway Charlie Wagner summed up Harris's mound character by saying that he had the "guts of a daylight burglar." Harris had what the
players called a "live" arm, though he wasn't the most consistent of per-
formers. He had a good curve and a fastball that tailed away from right-
handed batters, making him as effective against them as he was against
left-handers with whom he enjoyed a southpaw's natural advantage.

Joe Dobson was typical of the kind of man who played professional
baseball in the decades before the war. The youngest of fourteen children
of a Texas farm couple, he'd grown up on the road in the 1920s and the
Depression years as his family migrated slowly westward into Arizona.
Whatever work they found along the way, they did, Dobson included: ten-
ant farming, stoop labor, road construction, carpentry. A solid, unspec-
tacular performer, he was precisely the sort of fourth starter a team had
to have if it wanted to stay in the race all the way to the wire. His fastball
was better than average, but his bread-and-butter pitch was his curve,
which he threw at different speeds depending on the situation. Like
Hughson and Harris, he was coming back to baseball from the army, and
if anything he seemed the better for his seasons away.

Thus for the first (and practically the only) time in his tenure as
Boston's manager, Joe Cronin had pitchers to go with his hitters. And yet
there were many in Boston and around the league who felt that whatever
the quality of his staff, Cronin was a poor handler of pitchers. Baseball in
1946 was still several seasons away from developing the specialty of the
pitching coach, and on the Sox as on other teams the manager served in
that capacity, whatever his talents as a judge of pitchers might be. Jimmie
Foxx, the old A's and Red Sox slugger, was one of the more vocal critics
of Cronin's handling of his staffs through the years. Cronin didn't know
how to handle his pitchers, Foxx claimed; that was the reason Connie
Mack had won pennants and Cronin hadn't. The writers who watched
Cronin spend hours talking hitting with Ted Williams said he was an
offense-minded manager with little feel for pitchers and their special
problems. Shortly, a Boston writer named Harold Kaese would write in a
Saturday Evening Post story "What's the Matter With the Red Sox?" that
Cronin "tortured" his pitching staffs with his inconsistency, sometimes
staying too long with an obviously failing starter while at other times
using a very quick hook. Others added that Cronin had ruined a number
of promising young hurlers and now would find a way to squander the
evident talent of his present staff.

Cronin's defenders blamed Fenway Park's short left-field wall as the real source of the team's chronic pitching woes. His pitchers, then and in later years, were generally among these defenders, though none could mount a defense that was exactly ringing. "When he had the pitching, he won," Dave Ferriss said simply. "I had no complaints about him." The closest any of them would come to criticism was when Joe Dobson said that Cronin was a hunch manager who, once he had a hunch about a pitcher, stubbornly stuck with it, despite any contradictory evidence. In such situations, Dobson said, "he just stuck that big Irish jaw out there, and you couldn't sway him."

As the Sox exhibition season drew to a close, observers looked at all those big bats and this remarkable quartet of starters and wondered if Cronin could manage his team well enough to challenge the Yankees all season long or whether this would be another year in which October's question in Boston would once again be, "What's the Matter With the Red Sox?"

★   ★   ★

/n the National League the team to beat looked like the Cardinals; few thought the reigning Cubs would be able to mount a credible challenge. After narrowly losing out to the Dodgers in 1941, the Cardinals had roared from behind to overtake the Reiser-less Dodgers the year following, then had won again in '43 and '44. But in 1945 the Cubs had slipped past the Cardinals on the season's penultimate day. Chicago had more draft-exempt players than any of the other contenders, but they also now had fewer players returning to them who looked as if they might really help. Only pitchers Hi Bithorn and Johnny Schmitz, outfielder Rickert, and first baseman Eddie Waitkus seemed important additions, and of these only Bithorn was of proven quality. Starting infielders Don Johnson, Billy Jurges, and Stan Hack all had a lot of mileage on them, and pitchers Claude Passeau and Ray Prim were thirty-seven and thirty-nine respectively. 'Oom Paul Derringer, who'd won 16 for the 1945 champions, had retired at thirty-eight. The club had one of the league's weakest farm systems, and little help was expected from it.

By contrast, the Cardinals had a wealth of returning talent to join what had already been a strong squad, and the Rickey-built farm system was still producing more. In fact, Sam Breadon believed he was in a position to safely sell off some of his players. Despite their success through the years, the Cardinals had never drawn particularly well, and Breadon needed cash to finance construction of a new park he was planning. Thus, in the off-season of 1945–46, Breadon shocked Cardinals fans and his own players by peddling star catcher Walker Cooper to the Giants for a whopping $175,000. He sold versatile infielder Jimmy Brown to the Pirates for $30,000. And hard-hitting first baseman-outfielder Johnny Hopp went to the Braves for $40,000 and infielder Eddie Joost. Breadon reasoned that with the return of Musial, Slaughter, and Moore and with young Dick Sisler evidently ready to make a big contribution Hopp was expendable. Lou Klein, Schoendienst, and Emil Verban could easily take up any slack caused by the departure of Brown. The big gamble was clearly the sale of Cooper. Breadon thought that with the well-seasoned Ken O'Dea and young Del Rice on hand to open the season he could afford to let Big Coop go. Moreover, waiting to get out of the service was still another catcher, Joe Garagiola, a youngster from St. Louis's Italian Hill about whom there were glowing reports from the South Pacific. This kid, the reports said, could do just about anything. He was a skilled receiver, could throw with the best at his position, and hit with power. Players returning from overseas talked about a tremendous homer he'd hit out of the stadium in Manila, a drive that rivaled one hit there by Babe Ruth.

Behind all this, Breadon's sale of Cooper was also motivated by personal feelings, for the catcher had become a pain to Breadon just as his brother had been. He'd tangled with both Rickey and Breadon about salary, and once, according to Terry Moore, had had the gall to call Breadon a "cheap so-and-so" to his face. Then, after Breadon had hired Dyer to manage the team, reports got back that Cooper didn't like Dyer and would rather not play for him. Breadon obliged Cooper and fattened his wallet in the process.

Despite the sales of Cooper, Brown, and Hopp and lingering concerns about the physical condition of some of the returning servicemen, the Cardinals were installed as almost prohibitive favorites as the Florida phase of spring training came to a close. Only the Dodgers were regarded as a real threat and this as much because of their manager, Leo Durocher, as because of the talent he had to work with.

Durocher's team had a plethora of question marks on it, foremost of which was Reiser, whose arm continued to plague him. Then there were all the young players Rickey and Durocher were counting on to join the veteran nucleus that included Dixie Walker, Billy Herman, Augie Galan,

Pee Wee Reese, and Kirby Higbe. Could service ball sensation Joe Hatten live up to his advance billing? What could be expected of Hank Behrman, of whom it was already being said that he had a million-dollar arm and a ten-cent head? In outfielders Furillo, Whitman, and Hermanski and power-hitting first baseman Eddie Stevens the team had youngsters of evident talent, but they were all green, and no one could say how they would stand up under the pressures of a hot pennant race.

7

*T*he X-factor in assessing the Dodgers and in handicapping the National League race was Durocher. Even those who hated his guts—and there were many—had to acknowledge that he could get more out of a team than anyone else could. His third-place finish last season with a roster decimated by service call-ups was still fresh in everyone's mind, and now Reiser, Reese, and the rest of his boys were back. But Durocher was enigmatic because of his personality. He was a West Springfield, Massachusetts, gutter-fighter, a pool hall hustler, a card shark who would cheat a friend and expect kindred treatment. He was a compulsive liar and some said a thief as well. A story that he'd once stolen Babe Ruth's watch followed him from his early playing days with the Yankees. For years it was a staple with opposing bench jockeys. One time Walker Cooper had come up with a few old pocket watches that he distributed among his Cardinals teammates. From their dugout they swung the watches back and forth, hollering over at Durocher, "Hey, Leo, we've got Babe Ruth's watch here!"

Off the field Durocher kept company with those like himself: gamblers and tough guys, race track touts, sharp dressers in bold pin-striped suits and two-toned shoes, and flashy women. Balding and big-nosed himself, Durocher enjoyed a sort of success with such women and once described to a young aspirant his personal secret: when you pick up a woman for a seven o'clock date, Durocher told the young man, "You've got to make your first move fast. You make sure you put your hand on their snatch at 7:05. Seven oh five!" Ever the gambler, Durocher had figured the odds. One of two things could happen, he thought: either the woman knocks your hand away, in which case there was still plenty of time to get another date; or she doesn't, in which case it was, "Well, then, hello, dear." This

Durocher and Rickey in a traditional pose. Rickey regarded Durocher as his pet moral reclamation project and stuck with him through one scrape after another. But the Mahatma was nothing if not a shrewd judge of talent, and he would early on have abandoned Durocher as a permanent hard case except for the fact that he recognized that Durocher was a superior manager. (UPI/Bettmann)

spring Durocher showed up in Florida with a showgirl half his age whom he'd met on a USO tour in Italy. They were seen everywhere after his day was done at the park, so evidently it was "hello, dear."

Some of his players tried to keep up with him off the field and almost always came to regret it. Infielder-outfielder Augie Galan who served Durocher manfully both before and during the war, recalled getting involved with him and coach Charlie Dressen in a scheme to make a killing on a race at the Narragansett track. At a party in the club's Cincinnati hotel a tout named Sleep Out Louie told Durocher and Galan about a horse named Anzac. When you see him posted to run at Narragansett, the tout said, "You can bet this hotel on him!" But when Durocher finally got the word some days thereafter that Anzac was to go, he failed to tell

Galan until the very last minute and never told Dressen at all. Galan was only able to get a small bet down while the manager himself cleaned up. That, said Galan, was Durocher: "You could not trust him."

Durocher's gambling habits were no secret, and several times in the past Rickey, who regarded him as his pet moral reclamation project, had to bail Durocher out when he got in too deep with the gamblers. Durocher also took his own players' money in the card games that were so conspicuous a feature of long road trips. Pitcher Kirby Higbe was one of his favorite marks. Higbe, Durocher said gleefully, "couldn't beat your aunt from Duluth" when it came to playing cards. Galan said Higbe often lost a month's salary before the month was well started, and how the pitcher's wife survived was a mystery to everyone on the club. Eventually Rickey ordered Durocher to keep Higbe out of the card games.

There had also long been ugly rumors that Durocher bet on baseball games, too, including, some said, games in which his own club was involved.* This, of course, had been baseball's equivalent of original sin ever since the Black Sox scandal of 1919, and after that event, which came so close to wrecking the game, no major leaguers had been found guilty of it. Nor had Durocher ever been so much as investigated on such charges. But more than anything else said about him, this allegation clung like malodorous smoke to the Dodgers manager, and before this year was out there would once again be whispers in clubhouses, press boxes, and night spots that Durocher had money down on some Dodgers games.

Durocher came into this spring beneath his usual cloud of controversy, and not coincidentally it had to do in part with gambling. In June of the previous season a fan named John Christian had attended a Dodgers game with a friend. Christian was a Brooklyn-born vet now out of the service with a medical discharge. During the Dodgers-Phillies game of June 9, Christian had relentlessly heckled Durocher from his seat behind the dugout, calling him a crook and asking him how much the gamblers were paying him to throw the game. After a while a special ballpark cop named Joe Moore came by Christian's seat and said Durocher would like

---

* Like the story of Babe Ruth's watch, this one followed Durocher to the end of his days. In the winter of 1969–70 then-baseball commissioner Bowie Kuhn authorized an investigation of rumors that Durocher had bet on several late-season games involving his team, the Chicago Cubs. That was the season the Cubs had squandered a huge lead over the New York Mets and had eventually finished a distant second. Kuhn's investigation turned up nothing suspicious, but in Chicago, at least, the rumors persisted.

to meet him after the game. When the game ended Moore escorted Christian beneath the stands to the entrance to the Dodgers clubhouse. What happened next may never be known, but whatever it was Christian emerged from the park with a broken jaw, head injuries, and a black eye. Christian claimed Moore hit him with a sap, and once he was down, Durocher slugged him with Moore's brass knuckles. Christian sued, and now as Durocher evaluated his talent and dealt at the same time with the presence of Robinson and John Wright in the Dodgers camp the case was continued to May. Everyone understood, however, that a conviction would be disastrous for Durocher—and the Dodgers.

Many hoped he would be convicted and suspended from the game. They included National League umpires, who hated him and dreaded working Dodgers games because they knew Durocher would be on them all game long. Jocko Conlon, who umpired in the league for a quarter of a century, said that a group of umpires had once gone over the rosters of the teams to pick out the major troublemakers. "Durocher was the worst," he said, the "king of complainers," a man who could "never, never, never accept a tough decision" that went against his team. Even some of his own players hated him at one time or another, including Dixie Walker, Arky Vaughan, and Billy Herman. Vaughan, a fine hitter and versatile defensive player, wasn't even in camp this spring because he refused to play for Durocher. And Herman had once become so furious with Durocher that he threw a ball at him during infield practice.

The incident occurred in 1943 before Herman left for the service. Herman had long been one of baseball's best place hitters, exceptional at hitting the ball through the hole at second base when the hit-and-run play was called and the baserunner was moving. In 1943, though, with so many players away in service, Durocher was forced to use him as a clean-up hitter. Yet in a game in which the Dodgers had men in scoring position and one out, here was Durocher signaling Herman to take a two-balls-no-strikes pitch—a situation that cried for the clean-up hitter to swing away. "Billy had those big banjo eyes," Augie Galan said, "and when Leo had him taking again at three and one they got even bigger." Eventually Herman lined into a double play, and the inning was over. Enraged that his manager's curious strategy had so compromised his at-bat, Herman took the field for infield practice and deliberately fired a throw into the Dodgers dugout, nailing the unsuspecting Durocher right between the eyes. Down he went as if shot. At the end of the half-inning Galan, a self-described agitator, came in from left field to find Durocher slumped on the bench behind an ice pack. Galan had seen the whole thing, yet now he asked solicitously, "Leo, what happened?" Durocher briefly removed the ice pack, Galan said, "and you could still see the print of the stitches."

Yet Herman, Galan, and Walker all respected Durocher's managerial abilities, how thoroughly he knew the game. So too did Monte Irvin who was to play major roles in two pennants Durocher won in the 1950s with the Giants. "Greatest manager I ever played for," Irvin said unequivocally. "He had everything: instincts, brains, a knowledge of the opposition. Smart as hell. He was always a couple of innings ahead of the other guy in his thinking." But, Irvin added, Durocher had one major flaw: he couldn't always distinguish between the player you needed to goad to get his best, and the player who profited by encouragement. Some guys, Irvin said, simply fell apart under Durocher's needling, and he didn't seem to realize that. On the Giants Irvin had watched as Durocher rode the great Johnny Mize to distraction. "He'd get on him something terrible," Irvin said, "to the point where he couldn't play his game: 'Get off the fuckin' bag, you goddamn donkey!' Johnny got so he couldn't do anything. Then he went over to the Yankees and had another productive five years." In a sense, the flaw carried over to Durocher's treatment of the opposition whom Durocher relentlessly rode from the dugout or the coaching lines. Sometimes his foghorn invective rattled enemy batters and pitchers, destroying their concentration, but other times it had the opposite effect, inspiring opposing players to greater efforts to defeat so vicious an adversary. The Cardinals Harry Walker claimed Durocher's abusive style actually cost the Dodgers at least one pennant because he made the Cardinals that much more determined to beat him and shut him up.

Another troubling Durocher trait was that he could be particularly hard on younger players. His 1946 squad was loaded with them, and already several, including Eddie Stevens, had gotten the notorious Durocher treatment. Stevens had been a promising minor league hitter but Durocher had so intimidated him in the spring of 1945 that when the Dodgers had called him up later that season, Stevens refused to report. When Branch Rickey Jr. at last talked him into going to Brooklyn, Durocher started in on him again, and this spring it had been the same. He was absolutely merciless, Stevens said. Once, he claimed, Durocher had gotten on him from the very first inning, standing on the top step of the dugout, pouring fiery abuse at the young first baseman until he gradually ran out of steam. Then Stevens saw him turn to Dressen and say, "Charlie, you take him for a few innings."

But Durocher was nothing if not contradictory, and another rookie, Dick Whitman, was having quite the opposite experience this spring. From the first day Durocher treated him well, overlooked his mistakes, and expressed confidence in him. In an exhibition game against the Phillies Whitman tried to go from first to third on a hit to right field, ignorant of the fact that Phillies right fielder Ron Northey had one of baseball's best arms. "I think the ball got to third base about the time I got to shortstop," Whitman remembered, "and when I looked up and saw the third baseman he had the ball and was just standing there as if to say, 'Well, when you get here I'm gonna tag you out.' Then I came back to the dugout and Durocher's standing there at the top step. He says, 'Son, this time you're going to get away with this because you're new, a rookie. Next time, we'll have a few words.' " In pinch-hitting situations Whitman said Durocher gave him the feeling that he had great confidence in his ability to deliver. "He'd come along the bench and stop at my seat," Whitman said, and say to me, " 'Now, you get up there, and you *hit that ball!*' " It gave Whitman the feeling that his manager thought he was the only batter in the world who could get a hit in this situation. "He thinks I can do this," Whitman remembered thinking. "He's chosen *me* to do this." Whitman said he learned more baseball that season than ever before or since, just listening as Durocher managed out loud. "He was always five batters ahead of everybody else," Whitman said, uncanny in anticipating events. Whitman thought Durocher was "just a great manager." If the writers were right and the Cardinals were as strong as they seemed to be, Durocher would have to be every bit of that.

8

*A*t the end of March the long training season came to an end, the last camp cuts were made, the equipment was packed, and the teams headed north to the baseball-hungry towns along their routes, bearing with them spring and spring's promise of summer. So broad and deep was the culture of baseball that the teams could take virtually any route north and be assured of an adequate park to play in and fans who would jam the splintery seats in Dothan and Valdosta, Augusta and Shreveport, Newport News and Evansville. Especially this spring when overflow crowds turned out everywhere the teams stopped. The Giants hooked up with the Indians for their barnstorming tour and played before standing-room-only crowds all along the way, beginning with a weekend series in Jacksonville, April 6 and 7. On the 8th they were in Hickory, North Carolina. On the 9th they played in Danville, Virginia, and the next day in Richmond. Then it was on to Bristol and Roanoke. On Saturday the 13th, the teams met in Cleveland for another weekend series. Then the Giants turned eastward, and on Monday before Opening Day they played the cadets at West Point in their final tune-up.

One-half of the Yankees split squad traveled north with the Dodgers through Georgia, the Carolinas, Kentucky, Ohio, and Maryland. The other half went west into Louisiana and Texas before turning north. In New Orleans on the last two days of March crowds of 9,000 and 13,000 turned out to see the Bronx Bombers against the hometown Pelicans, and in the Sunday game DiMaggio gave them what they came for when he hit a tremendous home run, his fourteenth of the spring. After the game, impetuous, high-living Larry MacPhail took the team to Arnaud's for a blow-out.

Meanwhile, the teams that had trained on the West Coast—the Cubs, White Sox, Browns, and Pirates—were making their ways east and then north. The Pirates and White Sox left San Diego for a sixteen-day train trip with three Pullman sleepers for each club, two baggage cars, and a diner— but no bathing facilities except washbowls. The teams pulled into Bisbee, Del Rio, El Paso, Houston, Dallas, Fort Worth, Oklahoma City, Tulsa, and Wichita, played their games, showered and changed, then got back on the train. The White Sox had arranged for air-conditioning in their coaches, but the Pirates hadn't, and since no laundry had been accepted at their San Bernardino base for several days before the team's departure, things became a trifle aromatic in the Pittsburgh sector, according to one writer.

But wherever they went, Ralph Kiner said, they played to overflow crowds. In Del Rio Kiner almost stepped on a rattler in the outfield. After the game in El Paso, some of the Pirates players went across the border into Juarez. When they came back to the train just before midnight there was manager Frisch, parked in a folding chair at the entrance to the track, checking on the condition of his tourists. With all the stops and the long hauls in between it was a demanding way to get ready to open the regular season, Kiner thought, but everybody—from players to fans—was fired with enthusiasm, and the hardships were taken in stride.

★ ★ ★

*K*iner had not only made the Pittsburgh team, he would be in the Opening Day lineup, batting third and playing center field when the Pirates faced the Cardinals in St. Louis. Joe Hatten, Hank Behrman, Hermanski, and Whitman were all going north with the Dodgers, and Hatten and Behrman were in Durocher's starting rotation. Marv Rickert had cooled off at the plate for the Cubs, but he still made the team, though Charlie Grimm was reluctant to give up on slugger Bill Nicholson. Gil Coan was going north with the Senators, but there were many who wondered why: he'd been a major training camp flop, and some thought rookie Ray Goolsby was a better-looking outfielder. Coan himself would later say he really should have been farmed out and would have been but for the bal- lyhoo. Dick Sisler had stuck with the talent-laden Cardinals, but Eddie Dyer was still waiting to see some of those long homers Sisler had hit in Cuban winter ball. Across town Bob Dillinger was wearing a Browns uniform and had played well enough to start, if not at his best position (third base), then at least somewhere in what was not an especially strong Browns infield. But Luke Sewell had decided to go with the experienced Mark Christman at third, and Dillinger would have to wait his turn. So, too, would infielder Bobby Brown and catcher Bill Deininger of the Yankees. Both would be doing their playing for the Newark Bears, the Yankees farm club in the International League. Brown would be back up at the end of the season, but Deininger, the "next Bill Dickey," would never play in a big league game.

A number of players had missed spring training while awaiting a service discharge. Just as the Reds broke camp they received word that Ewell Blackwell, their pencil-thin right-handed pitcher, had gotten his army discharge papers and would shortly report to the club. Manager Bill McKechnie was saddled with a very weak offense, so every live arm added to his pitching staff was welcome. Blackwell released his pitches side-arm, and with his long arms and legs right-handed hitters had the disquieting sensation that the ball was coming at them from somewhere behind third base. Phillies outfielder Del Ennis was awaiting his papers at the navy base in Bainbridge. Within a week the muscular youngster from north Philly would join his team and take a seat on the bench, waiting for his crusty manager, Ben Chapman, to notice him. Alvin Dark, a spectacular all-around athlete at LSU before the war, was still in the marines and a month away from discharge. Dark had excelled at every sport he'd ever tried— baseball, football, basketball, and track—and though he'd never played professionally, he thought he could make it in baseball. So did the scouts who'd been tracking him in the service. The Braves had a promising southpaw named Warren Spahn who had been a big winner in the minors before the war. Now he was a battle-tested hero of the crucial action at Remagen Bridge, and like so many others he was impatiently waiting his discharge. The Braves brass thought he could help the big club right away.

These were the young men for whom this spring had truly been a season of promise, though some, like Coan and Deininger, had fallen short of the high expectations set for them. Hundreds of others, too, had realized their dream of hooking on with a professional team as leagues dormant during the war years now sprang back to life. But there were other men, some of them young and some further along in years, for whom this spring had seen the blighting of once-bright hopes. They'd survived the war, as so many millions had not, but they had come out of it changed, some crippled in mind and body, some simply older and slower, their reflexes dulled. They weren't the boys they'd been before they'd changed uniforms, and they never would be again.

9

*A*ssessing the return of the players from the war, writers and management agreed that Jimmy Dykes had been wrong in his bleak prediction and that most players appeared to have resumed their careers with surprising ease. True, many had looked rusty at first, and there had been a rash of sore arms and other training camp injuries as the returnees tried to do too much too fast. Some ex-infantrymen complained that because of the change from combat boots to spikes their calves and Achilles tendons were sore, but considering the scale of the process of transition, things had gone far more smoothly than anyone had imagined, and on the eve of Opening Day the baseball world felt itself fortunate indeed. The game had survived the cataclysm of the war and now, with its stars returned, it was poised for what looked like its greatest season ever.

Of the more than 500 major leaguers who had gone into the service only two—outfielder Elmer Gedeon, who'd once played for Washington, and Harry O'Neill, a catcher for the A's in 1939—had been killed, remarkable considering the numbers involved and the ferocity of the fighting some of the players had seen. But the war had in fact taken something from baseball and its players, and virtually every one of the sixteen big league teams was affected by it. Some of baseball's casualties were spectacularly obvious like the one-legged pitcher who tried to make it back with the Senators, or Cecil Travis, moving gingerly about on his damaged feet with the same team. In other instances, though, the nature of the loss was more subtle but no less real. This was so with Billy Herman, Terry Moore, and Hank Greenberg, stars whose great days were now behind them, lost to the war, not through injury but simply through the passage of time. Others, who'd never been stars, just good ballplayers, came back and found they'd lost their edge in the service. Infielder Jimmy

Brown was like that, the Cardinals players said; nobody could figure out just why. Cub Hi Bithorn was another. And still others whose promise had been bright before entering the service suffered injury while there and couldn't come all the way back: Tommy Tatum, a fleet Dodgers outfield prospect before the war, suffered a serious arm injury in the service and was never the same player. This season he would occasionally substitute at second for Jackie Robinson at Montreal.

Bert Shepard was the one-legged pitcher, his right foot amputated by German doctors after his P-38 fighter was shot down over enemy territory in May 1944. Subsequently a fellow POW made Shepard a wooden foot, and the ex-minor leaguer began tossing a ball around in prison camp. In January 1945 Shepard was part of a prisoner exchange (the repatriated German soldiers got an apple and a picture of Hitler, he said) and weeks thereafter ended up at Walter Reed Hospital in Washington. There an assistant secretary of war heard about an amputee who dreamed of playing ball again. Robert Patterson placed a call to Senators owner Clark Griffith that began with Patterson telling Griffith, "We've got a guy here in the hospital who's got a leg off and an old wooden one made in prison camp. But he says as soon as he can get a new leg he thinks he can play ball again." Naturally, Shepard said, "Mr. Griffith was obligated in the spirit of the war effort regarding the wounded to offer me a tryout. I got a new leg at Walter Reed March the tenth, and four days later I tried out with the Senators." The team kept him as part of the war effort, and on those occasions when he did pitch (all but one were exhibition appearances), Shepard did well.* This spring he was a batting practice pitcher and coach, and a symbol of American sacrifice and sporting determination.

Herman, Moore, Greenberg, and the others weren't so obviously affected and so weren't seen as symbols. Besides, what were their losses of athletic skills compared to those who'd lost their lives, their limbs, their sight, homes, and loved ones? In the war-warped world of 1946, what did it matter that Billy Herman was slow around the second base

---

* One of Shepard's exhibition appearances in 1945 was against a crack team from the New London (Connecticut) naval base that included the young Yogi Berra. Several years later Shepard encountered Berra in the Yankees clubhouse and reminded him they'd faced each other back in '45. But by now Shepard was on crutches and without his artificial leg, recuperating from another of his many operations. Berra remembered him as a pretty good pitcher and said it was too bad he'd lost his leg. "Yogi, I had it off then, too," Shepard said. "No shit," Berra said in response. "I thought that was a pretty good compliment," Shepard said.

bag or that Terry Moore now had to go all out to catch up with fly balls he once could have put in his hip pocket? Within the world of baseball, however, it did matter that Herman's reactions in the field were slow and that his manager was beginning to look at him as a third baseman or possibly even as a first baseman. It mattered that Moore, once the league's finest defensive center fielder, was having trouble with his legs. "I knew right away in Florida I wasn't the ballplayer I'd been before the war," he said. And it wasn't just his legs. He now found that the fastball got on him quicker at the plate and that all the bases seemed to lie uphill.

Greenberg was discovering something similar. In his seven full seasons before entering the service (excluding 1936, which he'd missed with an injury) he'd compiled batting records that compared favorably with those established by the mightiest of the mighty—Ruth, Gehrig, and Foxx—averaging 35 home runs a season, 141 runs batted in, and hitting .325. Four times in those seasons he'd hit 45 doubles or more, and Greenberg was hardly a fast runner. Nor had he ever been much of a curveball hitter; Bob Feller said Greenberg couldn't hit his curve with a dining room table. But he'd murdered fastballs and curves that hung up in his eyes. This spring, though, even the fastball was giving him trouble. As usual, the big, Bronx-born slugger was still giving it everything he had, but so far, it didn't look like enough.

Cecil Travis was grimly giving it his all, too. He'd never had more than average speed, and now he had considerably less than that. Manager Bluege was thinking of shifting him to third where the range of plays was a bit less demanding, meanwhile waiting for Travis to regain that snap with the bat that had made him such a feared hitter before the war. And some days it was there, days, Travis said, when "it looked like it was back, but it didn't last very long." You might have two or three good days, he said, but then would come a string of bad days on which "pitchers you used to hit would get you out all the time." On the good days Travis permitted himself to hope his skills were slowly coming back to him, and he was still hoping so as the Senators prepared to open the season. He refused to blame his lusterless play on his physical condition, but teammates said they often saw the quiet Georgian on the trainer's table getting his feet worked on.

And there were players like Phil Marchildon and Charlie Wagner. Marchildon was still hobbled by his groin tear, but much more significant was his battle to regain the kind of concentration you needed out on the mound. This would take a good deal longer than healing a muscle. Then, to compound his problems, he was the victim of a freakish accident. The A's had an outfielder named Ford Garrison, a wartime fill-in who fancied himself an expert knife-thrower. One day in the locker room Garrison was practicing his act when he accidentally stabbed Marchildon in the hand. The Canadian tail gunner had been able to survive a crash landing and a POW camp—but not spring training. He was out indefinitely, and Ford Garrison was quickly dispatched to the minor leagues, never to return.

Broadway Charlie Wagner hadn't hit his stride as a pitcher until he was twenty-nine. Then in the 1941 season with the Red Sox he won 12 games and 14 the next. In 1943 he was gone to the navy for three years. "My best years were spent in the service," he said. "Now, if I'd been twenty-two coming back, it might have been different. But I was thirty-three, and it was a little hard to crack it again. To lose those three years when you felt yourself coming on was hard." Nor was it only age and rust with him. In the Philippines he'd contracted a serious case of dysentery and lost thirty pounds. When he arrived for spring training he was "just like a dishrag," and so weak he couldn't put anything on his pitches. While the other returnees were out on the field at Sarasota rounding into shape, Wagner said, "I spent most of my time on the can." He went north with the team, partly because the teams were allowed to keep thirty players on their rosters this season. And partly Wagner stayed with the Sox because he was so popular with everybody, including Tom Yawkey, Cronin, and Ted Williams, with whom he roomed. He threw batting practice, led the cheers from the bench, and waited for his condition to improve.

★ ★ ★

*A*mong those struggling to come back to the game from the war, none had a more affecting story than Lou Brissie. Brissie was a strapping left-handed pitcher from that fertile baseball garden of South Carolina. Nine of his uncles played textile ball in the Greenville area where Shoeless Joe Jackson was still a hero despite the Black Sox scandal. (Brissie knew Jackson and like so many in the area had strong feelings about his treatment by the baseball establishment.) Brissie's baseball apprenticeship was served as batboy on his uncles' team, meanwhile developing his own skills in sandlot games with his peers. The kids made their own bats and balls, the latter fashioned from parts of inner tubes wound with fishing line. The homemade balls were resilient and had a little give to them, Brissie said, "which was good because we didn't have any gloves."

In these Depression days Brissie's high school didn't have the money to field a baseball team, but from the time he was fourteen Brissie pitched and played first base for the Ware Shoals mill team. Even so early he threw hard, and the scouts began to come around; the day after he graduated in May 1941, Chick Galloway, who scouted for the A's, took him and another player to Philadelphia for two weeks where they worked out under the supervision of club officials. At the end of that time Brissie signed an agreement with Connie Mack that provided that Mack would send him to Presbyterian College where Coach Galloway could monitor his progress; when Brissie finished there he was to go into the A's farm system. But like millions of other plans, this one was altered by the war, and in December 1942, Brissie enlisted in the army.

In December 1944 Corporal Brissie was part of the 88th Infantry Division slugging its way slowly northward through Italy in some of the ugliest fighting of the European theater. Conditions were appalling. Famed war correspondent Ernie Pyle wrote back that "[o]ur troops were living in almost inconceivable misery. The fertile black valleys were knee-deep in mud. Thousands of men had not been dry for weeks. Other thousands lay at night in the high mountains with the temperature below freezing and the thin snow sifting over them. They lived like men of prehistoric times, and a club would have become them more than a machine gun."

At dawn on December 7, Brissie's squad had just returned to the front lines, having been sent to the rear for showers and a hot meal. Without warning, shells began pouring in. The first one exploded near Brissie, blowing open his left leg from knee to ankle. Hours later at a field hospital medics found more than thirty shell fragments in the shattered limb, mixed with bits of bone and mud. The decision was made to amputate, but Brissie begged the doctors to ship him on to an evacuation hospital. "Don't do this," he begged the doctors. "Send me to somebody who may be able to help me, because I wanna play baseball." The doctors complied, "red-tagged" Brissie for immediate evaluation, then shipped him to Naples.

The hospital there occupied a building that once had been a showplace of Il Duce's fascist regime, and one of its walls had been partly blown out in the fighting for the city; on a good day the convalescents could look out through the ragged hole and see Mt. Vesuvius. When they brought

Brissie in it was already evening, but almost immediately Dr. W. K. Brubaker was at his bedside. "The first thing I said to him was, 'I want you to save my leg,' " Brissie recalled. "He never looked up. He was looking at my chart, very business-like and serious. Then he said, 'We're gonna take a look at it right away. I'll see you tomorrow.' They operated the next day." It was the first of what would be twenty-three operations, but what Brubaker did that day in fact made it possible for Brissie to keep his leg.

In the spring of 1945 and with VE Day just weeks away, corporal Brissie was shipped home to begin an agonizing trip through army hospitals. In April 1946, he was released from the last of these and went back to Ware Shoals on a cane. The doctors had done what they could, and Brissie still had his leg, but no one believed he would ever play baseball again.

Brissie thought otherwise and sought out a doctor who worked with crippled children at the Greenville Shriner's hospital. "I showed him my injuries," Brissie said, "and explained to him what I wanted to do. I told him I needed some kind of support for the leg so that I could pitch again." Together, doctor and patient worked to devise a brace, and then Brissie began a regimen of calisthenics, running, and throwing. Up north, the new season opened with a thunderous fanfare of military bands, brass hats, and politicians tossing out ceremonial first pitches. In Ware Shoals, a big man hobbled along by himself through the crabgrass of a high school athletic field, trying valiantly to pull his past into his future.

PART 2

The Race

10

*W*ashington and Cincinnati were the traditional sites for the official opening of the season, Tuesday, April 16: Washington, of course, as the nation's capital, and Cincinnati because it was home to the game's oldest franchise. That morning Americans opened their newspapers and snapped on their radios to the unwelcome news that the government was reimposing wartime controls on meat and dairy products to help remedy world famine. Compounding this bad news was an announcement from Chester Bowles of the Office of Economic Stabilization that he could see no relief in sight from firm wage and price controls. These, Bowles said, were essential in the face of what he called "extreme inflationary danger." Five unions, however, were threatening a nationwide shipping strike in a move for higher wages, and fifteen railway unions that had just won a sixteen-cent hourly wage increase announced they would now begin pushing for an additional fourteen-cents-an-hour hike. Worse still, John L. Lewis had made good his threat and had taken his 400,000 coal miners out.

But for the moment Harry Truman was able to put aside these and other weighty problems (like the communists' latest victory in China's civil war) to attend the Senators opener against the Red Sox, resuming a tradition Roosevelt had discontinued in 1942. In the first days of his ascension to the presidency Truman had bewailed the stroke of fate that had thrust a manifestly mediocre man into the world's most important position, but lately, despite the enormous pressures of reconversion and the charting of a new world order, the president was looking more confident and even jaunty at times. Last week when Clark Griffith and National League president Ford Frick had called on him at the White House to present him with his season passes, the president had been in what Griffith said was "rare form" and had given his visitors a preview of his pitching form. This day he'd had lunch with some United States senators and then greeted a delegation of wounded vets from West Virginia before going to the park.

It was a chilly day there (as it was at the other parks on Opening Day), and the president wore a buff-colored fedora and blue-gray topcoat to his flag-draped box. With him were his wife Bess (black suit and furs), daughter Margaret, and a friend of hers from school. Others in the presidential party included Truman's chief of staff, Admiral William D. Leahy; Admiral Chester Nimitz, hero of the Pacific theater; House Speaker Sam Rayburn; Attorney General Tom Clark; and Captain Clark Clifford, a naval aide. As Truman took his seat a sixty-five piece army band struck up "Hail to the Chief," and then the band, led by Nimitz, Griffith, and the two squads, paraded out to the flagpole in center field for the raising of the colors, the players shuffling along out of step, as if deliberately putting the military era behind them. A crowd of 32,372 fans stood for the national anthem, and then southpaw Truman cranked up and sailed the ceremonial first pitch into a group of waiting Washington and Boston players, and the ceremonies were concluded. The photographers with their big box cameras moved away from the presidential box and took up kneeling positions near the on-deck circle, focusing on the old drama of peering pitcher and waiting batter. Roger Wolff of the Senators toed the pitching slab, took his sign from catcher Al Evans, and threw the season's first pitch to Dom DiMaggio. Baseball was officially back.

In a way familiar to Washington fans, the game that then unfolded was anticlimactic. Wolff dueled Tex Hughson on even terms into the seventh when the Red Sox pushed across three runs to clinch a 6-3 win. But Ted Williams brought the crowd, including the president, to its feet when he slugged one of Wolff's pitches 440 feet into the seats in center field. No ball, the writers agreed, had been hit that hard since the players went away to war and very few had ever been hit that far in Griffith Stadium. Ever the perfectionist, Williams said it hadn't felt as if he'd hit it *just* right. It had been his only hit in five at-bats, too, and some of his teammates kiddingly asked him how it felt to be a .200 hitter.

For the Senators, Cecil Travis had gone hitless against Hughson while first baseman Mickey Vernon, another returning serviceman, had doubled and singled twice to lead his team's offense. After the game the pervasive nature of the national housing shortage was made plain when it

Top: Jackie Robinson touches home plate at Roosevelt Stadium in Jersey City after hitting a three-run homer in his second at-bat in Organized Baseball. (UPI) *Below*: President Harry S. Truman, flanked by Admirals Leahy and Nimitz, throws out the ceremonial first pitch at Griffith Stadium to officially open the season. (*The New York Times*/Associated Press)

was revealed that ten members of the team were temporarily living in the Senators clubhouse. "If you possess an extra tent, igloo, or lean-to," a local paper said, "kindly get in touch with Clark Griffith of the Washington Baseball Club."

Commissioner Chandler attended the Cincinnati opener where professional baseball had been played for seventy seasons. At a team luncheon the day before Reds general manager Warren Giles reacted testily to those predicting a last-place finish for his team. Nobody could accurately predict where the teams would finish, Giles claimed; the postwar situation was simply too fluid. "But I know this," he said, "our team is a hell of a lot better than a lot of persons think."

Before the start of the game Chandler announced that since the Mexican jumpers had failed to return to their clubs by this date, they were all under a five-year suspension. Then, after the playing of the national anthem, Governor Frank J. Lauche, a former sandlot player, tossed the ceremonial first pitch to Cincinnati Mayor James Garfield Stewart, crouched behind the plate in mask and chest protector. The crowd of more than 30,000 settled down and cheered as the Reds took a 3–0 lead into the ninth inning against the Cubs. But the Cubs came up with four runs in their half of the inning, and the cheers turned to groans. For the moment, anyway, those who were disparaging the Reds seemed to be right.

In Detroit, the city settled a mass transit strike just in time for the opener, and a record crowd in excess of 52,000 turned out to watch the champions beat the Browns in classic fashion: Hal Newhouser stopped St. Louis, 2–1, striking out eight, and Greenberg provided the margin of victory with a line drive home run into the left field seats.

Newhouser's rival for American League pitching honors was even more impressive at chilly, wind-whipped Comiskey Park in Chicago where Bob Feller shut out the White Sox on three hits and fanned ten. A rookie center fielder named Bob Lemon saved Feller's gem of a game in the ninth inning when with one out and a runner at second he raced in, made a diving, skidding catch of a sinking line drive, then recovered and threw to second to double up the runner who'd been racing around to score what would have been the tying run. Lemon was coming back after three years in the navy and was only in center field because he'd failed previous trials at third base: his throws across the diamond from that position had a tendency to sink, making them tough for the first baseman to handle, and before this season was out manager Boudreau would begin exploiting this tendency by sending Lemon to the mound as a pitcher.* But for the moment the hero was most definitely an outfielder, happy to have saved the game for Feller and to pose, scraped and grass-stained, beside the great pitcher in the Indians locker room.

Over in the home clubhouse the White Sox hitters said they'd seen Feller faster before the war but never better. "He doesn't put everything he's got on all his pitches anymore," said outfielder Taffy Wright, "but he knows how to *really* pitch now." The fireballer himself scoffed at all the emphasis on his speed. He hadn't cut loose down in Florida, he said, because he'd been pacing himself for the long season. Today, he'd relied a lot on his curveball. It had deserted him in the middle innings, then had come back to him later when he'd needed it. As for his fastball, he claimed he was as fast as ever when he had to be.

In Boston, in pregame ceremonies a trio of musicians emerged from the grandstand in sombreros, and in a broad reference to the Mexican League took up a position in front of the Dodgers dugout and played "South of the Border." When they'd finished they tossed fake pesos into the stands. Major General Douglas L. Weart tossed out the first ball in newly renovated Braves Field on the banks of the Charles, and the new Dodgers outfielder Gene Hermanski dropped an easy fly in the sixth, allowing two runners to score. The next inning he threw to the wrong base, allowing another run. The Braves accepted Hermanski's charities and won—but lost the public relations game when hundreds of irritated fans showed up at the office afterward with green paint smeared on their clothing: the club had had the seats painted days earlier, but cold, wet New England weather prevented them from fully drying. Braves management issued a newspaper apology the next day, saying they would pay the cleaning bills.

In New York, baseball's unofficial capital due to its three clubs, Governor Thomas E. Dewey threw out the first ball at the Polo Grounds before more than 33,000 in heavy jackets and topcoats. The fans included delegates from the U.N., led by Secretary General Trygve Lie. Lie had never seen a ballgame before but said it certainly beat a Security Council meeting for fun, and he liked the hot dogs. Mexico's delegate, Dr. Castillo

---

* Once on the mound, Lemon's career as a position player was over: he was too gifted a pitcher and would eventually win more than 200 games and election to the Hall of Fame.

AN APOLOGY TO BRAVES FANS

The Braves management regrets the inconvenience to its patrons who sustained damage to their clothing at Tuesday's opening game due to recently applied paint in certain sections of the grandstand.

The management will reimburse any of its patrons for any expense to which they may be put for necessary cleaning of clothing as a result of paint damage.

For today's game the management assures its patrons that no section of the grandstand will be open for public sale where there is the slightest possibility of any similar damage occurring.

BOSTON BRAVES
JOHN QUINN, *General Manager*

When cold and damp New England weather prevented the fresh paint on the seats at Braves Field from fully drying, hundreds of Opening Day fans complained. The Braves management issued this newspaper apology the following day. (*The Sporting News,* April 25, 1946)

Nájera, knew the game, of course, and told a reporter he didn't expect to see the baseball dispute between his country and the United States brought before the international body. On the field, manager Ott and catcher Ernie Lombardi hit first-inning home runs as the Giants beat the Phillies.

Opening Day attendance figures for both leagues amply bore out the gleeful predictions of league officials and front office personnel that 1946 would prove baseball's most popular season yet. The American League set an all-time Opening Day record while the National League narrowly missed setting one of its own. There was a feeling of relief that the war was over, Branch Rickey told writers, and baseball was bound to benefit as the populace turned its attention to sports and kindred leisure activities.

★   ★   ★

A few days after the majors' openers the minor leagues got their seasons underway. Operating on much smaller budgets, the lower leagues had been hit hard by the war, and by its end a once far-flung network had shrunk to a skeletal twelve leagues. This year, however, forty-three were back in business from the high minors down to the Tobacco State League and the West Texas-New Mexico League with franchises in towns like Borger, Lamesa, Clovis, and Pampa.

No minor league opener was more closely watched than Jersey City's at Roosevelt Stadium against the Montreal Royals. Fans from as far away as Philadelphia, Baltimore, and even Pittsburgh came to see Jackie Robinson take the field for the Royals. He had not hit particularly well in spring training, and at times had looked awkward and uncertain at second base, an entirely new position for him. So the whispers had grown louder that Rickey's great experiment was a flop, that Robinson's thickly muscled body just wasn't built for baseball. If he'd been a white man, they were saying, he wouldn't even have made the Royals roster.

In Robinson's first at-bat he grounded out. But in the third inning with Royals runners at first and second and nobody out Robinson hit the first pitch on a rising line over the left field fence for a three-run homer. Then in the fifth he put on a demonstration of the flashy, daring, "tricky" sort of baseball that Negro league fans loved but that had long been disparaged by white critics who said you couldn't play that kind of ball and win in the majors. Some of the Negro players were undeniably great showmen, this argument went, but they couldn't stand up to the daily demands of serious professional play. Now Robinson showed the white players and the fans what he'd learned in his brief apprenticeship in the Negro leagues when he dropped a beautiful bunt down the third base line and beat the throw. At first base, he danced lightly away from the bag, then faked a steal. On the next pitch he took off and stole the base easily. When Tommy Tatum hit a grounder to third Robinson made as if to retreat to his base, but when the third baseman committed himself to throw to first Robinson whirled and raced for third, sliding in under the return throw. At third, Robinson began to rattle the Jersey City pitcher by feinting as if he were going to try to steal home, baseball's most daring play. Those who hadn't attended Negro league games had never seen anything quite like the man who now stopped and started with such quickness, his spikes digging up the dirt of the baseline but his feet hardly seeming to alight on the ground. There had been great baserunners in the majors who'd thrilled crowds through the years. Cobb, of course, had been the greatest, all blinding speed and menace; Max Carey of the Pirates; Pepper Martin, the Cardinals' immensely popular "Wild Horse of the Osage," who finished his steals with a trademark belly-flop slide that raised high the loose dirt of the old-time diamonds. More recently there was George Case of the Senators who'd led the league in steals five seasons in a row. But here was something quite different, and the man dancing off third was about to revolutionize more thoroughly than anybody since Babe Ruth the way baseball was played. Eventually his own stolen base totals in the majors would prove quite modest, but Robinson was the pioneer of a style of baserunning that would make speed and daring the offensive equal of the home run.

Disconcerted by Robinson's antics, the Jersey City pitcher now hesitated in his delivery to the batter, and the home plate umpire called a balk, bringing Robinson home with the run. Thus, without hitting the ball out of the infield and with only minimal assistance from his teammates, Robinson had manufactured a run. Nor was he through for the afternoon. In the Montreal seventh he singled, again stole second, and scored a moment later on a triple. In the eighth he put on his act again, bunting safely, taking two bases on an infield hit, then causing yet another balk. In all, he produced four hits in his debut, scored four runs, drove home three, and stole two bases. As a member of the black press corps happily reported to his readers, Robinson "did everything but help the ushers seat the crowd."

★   ★   ★

*H*ardly had the fans settled in to enjoy the delights of the new season when Bob Feller brought them to their feet to cheer his brilliance, hurling a no-hit, no-run game against the Yankees at Yankee Stadium, April 30. After his Opening Day three-hitter at Chicago Feller had lost his next two games, though he'd pitched well enough to win them both: the Indians got him a combined total of four runs against Detroit and Chicago. As the Indians came into Yankee Stadium for the first time there was more newspaper talk suggesting that Feller wasn't Rapid Robert any longer. Overlooking the fact that he might well have had a 3-0 record with a little more support, the writers noted that Feller seemed to be experimenting a lot this season, throwing more breaking pitches than he had before the war, a sign, it was said, that he knew he'd lost something off his fastball.

As he warmed up before a Stadium crowd that would be over 37,000 Feller knew he had very good stuff, better by far, he thought, than when he'd thrown his first no-hitter back in 1940. And when catcher Frankie Hayes caught Feller in the Yankees first, he knew Feller was really on and had all his pitches working. As it happened, the second batter Feller faced came closest to getting a hit when the speedy Snuffy Stirnweiss bounced a ball up the middle. Feller's powerful follow-through always carried him toward first base, and now he couldn't reach back across his body to field Stirnweiss's bouncer. Second baseman Ray Mack moved to his right for the ball, but his momentum would have left him in a poor position to try to throw Stirnweiss out. Then from his shortstop position Lou Boudreau cut the ball off in front of Mack and made a tumbling, off-balance throw that just caught the runner. It was a stunning defensive play that the big crowd loudly appreciated long before its eventual significance would become clear. Feller then walked right fielder Tommy Henrich before getting DiMaggio on another ground out. The inning thus ended without a strikeout, but beginning with the second inning Feller showed skeptics he hadn't lost his famed strikeout abilities. He struck out two in that inning, struck out the side in the third, fanned two more in the fourth, and two more in the fifth. Thus of the twelve outs in those four innings, nine had been recorded by strikeouts. Thereafter Feller eased off a bit, going more to his slider to get the Yankees right-handed hitters to hit ground balls.

Coming out to the mound to face the Yankees in the seventh, Feller could hear the building buzz of the fans and see the tense faces of his infielders. He knew he had a no-hitter going, but he was thinking about winning a game that was still scoreless. Keller led off and popped up to first baseman Les Fleming who temporarily lost the ball in the late afternoon sun, then recovered to make a lunging, one-handed catch. Then Feller got the next two hitters easily and the game went into the eighth. The Indians still couldn't do anything with Yankees right-hander Bill Bevens, so it was New York's turn again in the last of the eighth.

Boudreau, looking a bit tight, threw out Bill Dickey on a routine grounder, but third baseman Ken Keltner dropped Phil Rizzuto's foul pop-up, giving him another chance, and this time Rizzuto hit a hard grounder to the left of a diving Keltner that looked as if it would go through the hole between third and shortstop for a hit. Boudreau had less range than any topflight shortstop in the major leagues, but he was a better athlete than any of them and made up in instincts, agility, and baseball knowledge what he lacked in range. Now he saw Keltner wasn't going to get to Rizzuto's ball and raced behind him, gloved the ball at the edge of the outfield grass, and made a strong, quick throw. When Rizzuto flashed across first the ball had already socked into Fleming's mitt. It was the manager's second saving play of the game and illustrated Feller's frequent contention that no-hitters are largely luck: had Keltner gotten his glove on the ball, he might not have been able to recover his balance in time to throw the quick Rizzuto out; and if the ball hadn't come up in a true hop, Boudreau wouldn't have gotten him, either.

In the Cleveland ninth the Indians finally broke through against Bevens when Feller's batterymate Hayes swung just where Bevens put a 3-2 fastball and hit a line-drive homer into the left-field seats. That took some of the pressure off, but Feller would still have to get by Stirnweiss, Henrich, and DiMaggio.

As Feller walked resolutely to the mound with his slightly splayed, plowboy's gait, the New York crowd rose to cheer him, and even Larry MacPhail up in the press box was openly pulling for the Cleveland ace. But Feller's fielders continued to show they were tight as Stirnweiss dropped a bunt toward first and Fleming fumbled the ball. Immediately the public address announcer told the crowd the play had been scored an error, not a hit. Later, Frankie Hayes would say the Stadium almost shook with a roar of approval for the ruling, but the Yankees now had a runner at first with no one out.

Henrich, always a tough hitter for Feller, stepped into the batter's box. Feller's curve broke into the left-handed hitter's power zone, and Henrich was an excellent fastball hitter. "If somebody as much as says to me, 'Here's a fastball: let's see if you can get around on it,' I'm gonna do it," Henrich said. Yet in their prewar confrontations, Feller kept throwing him fastballs, and Henrich kept getting around on them. "Maybe he was a little bullheaded about it," Henrich said. "He just didn't believe I could hit them." Now, however, orthodox managerial strategy called for the home team Yankees to play for a tie, and McCarthy had Henrich bunting— something of a relief to Feller who would rather pitch to the right-handed hitting DiMaggio. Henrich got the bunt down, and Stirnweiss moved into scoring position.

Unlike the majority of batters, who hit fastballs much better than breaking pitches, DiMaggio was a very good curveball hitter. He also handled the ball that was away from him very well, Feller said. Feller thought the best way to work him was to crowd him with high fastballs. The trouble here was that if you got one too far inside, it might hit DiMaggio who was essentially immobile at the plate because he took such an exaggerated wide stance. Feller was no longer the wild man he'd been when he'd broken in, but because he threw all his pitches so hard his control was never fine, and so there was a risk in pitching DiMaggio close. DiMaggio worked the count to three-and-two, and Feller went to his slider, which broke away from DiMaggio. Trying to pull it, DiMaggio grounded easily to Boudreau with Stirnweiss moving to third.

Next it was Keller's turn, the hairy-armed, beetle-browed slugger who loathed his nickname, King Kong. And now for the first time Feller permitted himself to think about a no-hitter, partly because there were two outs in the last of the ninth, and partly, he said, "because Charlie could never hit me. Charlie couldn't hit me with an ironing board. He knew it, and everybody in the league knew it." Keller himself had once confessed to Henrich that when Feller threw that big curve he didn't have any idea how to swing at it. Nor did he this time, sending a routine ground ball straight at second baseman Mack. But to the horror of the Indians, as Mack came in on the ball, he stumbled and fell to his knees, the ball bouncing at him almost higher than his head. "There wasn't a damn thing I could do but stand there and watch him," Feller said. But Mack recovered, got off his knees, gloved the ball, and tossed Keller out to end the game.

Afterward, Feller told the writers he took a special satisfaction in the circumstances of the no-hitter: he wanted to put an end to all this speculation about his arm and his speed, he said, and what better place to do this than in New York? A jubilant Frankie Hayes joined in: Feller, he said, was just as fast as ever when he needed to be. The slightly slower fastballs he'd thrown today weren't fastballs at all but sliders. Echoing the White Sox, Hayes said Feller had learned to pace himself. Pitching this way would add five years to his career.

11

*U*nder the circumstances the Yankees loss to the Indians was hardly major: Feller was after all the dominant pitcher in the league, and when he had all his pitches working there wasn't much you could do with him except to hope he might beat himself through wildness. He'd walked five in the game, but as he'd pointed out at least a couple of those walks were given to batters Feller thought he had struck out. Then, too, it was far too early in the season to consider any single loss critical. Yet questions had begun to emerge about the Yankees.

They still had a formidable everyday lineup, led by DiMaggio, Henrich, and Keller. They had a good defensive club and a solid bench that was about to get better with infielder Billy Johnson due to get his service discharge soon and rejoin the team. The one area of concern coming out of Florida had been starting pitching. McCarthy had been counting on Spud Chandler to anchor the staff, and so far he'd done just that, tossing shutouts in his first two starts. Chandler was a tough-as-nails competitor whose career had taken off in 1941 when he'd perfected a slider. From that point on he'd been almost unbeatable, winning 48 against only 14 losses. "He was a bulldog," said Tommy Henrich. "He would *never* give a batter a good ball to hit, never give in to him." Along with Henrich, DiMaggio, and Bill Dickey, Chandler personified the Yankees tradition. He was thoroughly professional in every aspect of the game; he was both gifted and intelligent; and he radiated that cool, almost arrogant confidence that said to the opposition, "We're the *Yankees.*" He hadn't looked good late in '45 when he'd come back from the service at age thirty-eight, and the batters had hit him with an unaccustomed freedom. Now, though, those two shutouts said he was the old Spud, which was good news for McCarthy who needed the wins he would contribute as well as his locker room presence.

The rest of McCarthy's starting rotation was unproven. Bill Bevens, Joe Page, Randy Gumpert, and Al Gettel had never been big winners, nor had they been through the heat of a tight pennant race. Tiny Bonham had had some big years before the war but had slumped badly last year against a weakened league. Red Ruffing, age forty-two, had held out all spring, and McCarthy could hardly expect much from him. Relief ace Johnny Murphy was thirty-seven. It was an unusual position for McCarthy to find himself in since in prewar seasons he'd always been blessed with deep and experienced staffs.

And there were other concerns. Dickey, it was clear, could no longer be more than a part-time player and pinch-hitter. In that limited capacity he could still throw well enough and provide an occasional big hit, but Dickey would not again be a major player in a Yankees pennant, and McCarthy would have to turn instead to Aaron Robinson and Gus Niarhos. Niarhos had never been much of a hitter; Robinson had shown flashes of power but wasn't more than average defensively. Even together they didn't add up to Dickey in his prime.

McCarthy also had to be concerned about Flash Gordon. Gordon was one of his favorites because he was a consummate professional who put the success of the team far above his own statistics. He'd come back from his spring training injury quicker than anyone expected, but maybe he'd come back too soon: McCarthy had put him right back in the lineup, and at first Gordon looked as if he'd never been out, but then he began to experience leg troubles, and his hitting tailed off severely. He'd always been a big swinger with his share of strikeouts, but now the strikeouts were coming with a frequency that began to send little alarms through his manager.

Then there was DiMaggio. He'd had an outstanding exhibition season, hitting with his prewar power and consistency and fielding well, but then he'd hit a slump, both at bat and in the field, at one point going nothing for ten and four for thirty-five at the plate. On May 9 against the Browns, DiMaggio did the unimaginable, making two errors in one inning. Up in the press room Larry MacPhail growled that his big star had come out of the service over the hill. That, of course, was MacPhail, a hard-drinking hip-shooter whose every pronouncement was subject to later, sober reconsideration. Still, DiMaggio's play had people wondering: when was the last time the Yankee Clipper had gone four for thirty-five or made two errors in a single inning? Maybe it was DiMaggio's play, maybe it was

Dickey and Gordon, or the unproven nature of the pitching staff, but whatever it was the Yankees somehow seemed less than the invincible Yankees of old. And even McCarthy, Marse Joe, seemed in some indefinable way less confident than in the prewar days when he'd presided with a magisterial calm over clubs that had no real weaknesses, clubs studded with the likes of Gomez, Gehrig, Dickey, DiMaggio, Chandler, Keller, Ruffing, Gordon. . . . Dan Daniel, who covered the team for the New York *World Telegram,* tried to put his finger on what precisely was lacking in this 1946 edition and could only say that they lacked "bounce" and "lift" and that it remained for the manager to make the moves that would supply it.

Despite these questions, the men in the pinstripes were still the Yankees, still the team to beat, and none knew this better than the perennial pretenders from Boston. Some said, and not entirely facetiously, that the Sox had been laboring under a curse ever since they'd sold Babe Ruth to the Yankees prior to the 1920 season: the Red Sox had not won a pennant since, while the Yankees, with Ruth and after him, had won fifteen times. During that same span every other team in the league had won at least once, even the Browns. But some said it wasn't any curse of the Babe that was to blame for this Sahara-like drought. It was something far more tangible: that damned ballpark that inevitably warped all Red Sox teams into power-oriented outfits that played for big innings and emphasized slugging at the expense of better all-around play and consistency of execution.

If anything, matters in Boston had grown even more frustrating since 1933 when Tom Yawkey, a wealthy South Carolina sportsman, bought the club, because Yawkey had come on the scene vowing to spend whatever it took to bring a championship to Fenway Park. And spend he had, bringing to Boston such stars as Wes and Rick Ferrell, Lefty Grove, Jimmie Foxx, and Cronin himself, for whom Yawkey paid Washington the astounding sum of $225,000. Still the Sox failed to win and because of Yawkey's spending acquired the derisive nickname "the millionaires." Four times they finished second to the Yankees, and the team's New England fans developed a full-blown inferiority complex regarding the New Yorkers.

There were many in New England and elsewhere who thought the team's basic problem wasn't a ghostly curse or the configuration of its ballpark or its manager; it was Tom Yawkey, who had stamped his personality on the franchise. Nearly all of his players, almost to a man, swore by him. He paid them well by the standards of the day, readily came to their assistance in time of need, and seemed genuinely thrilled to be in their company. He loved nothing better than to come out to Fenway early on a game day, suit up, and practice with his boys. That was Tom Yawkey's version of heaven. "Tom Yawkey loved his ballplayers, and he would do anything for them," Joe Dobson said. "He was the best man that ever walked." Yet his critics wondered whether this very attitude wasn't part of the problem. Yawkey, they said, was too indulgent and too close to his players to encourage a hard-nosed competitiveness. Tommy Henrich suggested as much many years later to Bobby Doerr. Doerr had been wondering aloud why his team, with all the talent it had, hadn't won more pennants, whereas the Yankees with possibly no more talent had won so often, and Henrich had laconically said that maybe Yawkey liked his players a little bit more than the Yankees owners had liked theirs. Half-jokingly, Henrich added that when he used to exit Fenway Park and cross the lot where the Sox players parked their cars, he saw more Cadillacs than any other make.

The Red Sox players certainly weren't millionaires, yet they did seem to play with a kind of well-heeled complacency, as if winning wasn't everything. They were never known as "hungry" ballplayers, like the Cardinals or Durocher's Dodgers, or the Yankees, and, so the argument went, it was Yawkey's fabled generosity that dulled their edge. From this point of view even Yawkey's pregame practice sessions were harmful, since the players, subs mostly, who threw batting practice to him and fielded what he hit were the owner's pets and were often kept on the roster when their actual contributions to the team were negligible. The "ass-kissers squad" some of the regulars called them.

Away from the park Yawkey was a hard-drinking and almost hermetical loner, and his critics said his insularity had become over time part of his club's basic personality. *Globe* writer Clif Keane, who covered the team for decades, described Yawkey as a man who went to the park, took batting practice, had some drinks afterwards, then retired to his suite at the Ritz-Carlton. "End of the season," Keane said, "he'd go home to South Carolina. Never stayed around. You never saw him around town. Strange people, he and his wife: hid away from everybody." His players, too, had the reputation of being a bunch of individuals rather than a real team. Other players used to joke that on road trips when the Sox left their hotel for the ballpark, it was "twenty-five guys, twenty-five cabs."

Each spring of the Yawkey regime hopes were high in New England, and in a number of these springs the team had gotten off well, only to fall apart in August—or earlier. At that point, instead of going to Fenway Park, New Englanders went to the shore to grouse briefly about the "Red Flops" and to wait, again, until next year. This spring had been no different. Once again, the Sox had started well, hit with their expected power, and the pitching had been spotty—a familiar pattern. When the Yankees came to town for a two-game set, April 24 and 25, and hammered the Sox 12-5 in the opener, things seemed to be settling once again into the worn grooves. The next day, though, the millionaires turned around and hammered the Yankees by the identical score. The day after that, Dave Ferriss, who hadn't pitched well and had fans doubting he was the genuine article, shut out the visiting A's, 7–0. Hughson followed with a 2–1 win, and Harris completed the sweep with a 5–1 victory. "I don't have a thing," Harris crowed to a writer, "except a fastball that scorches their whiskers if they crowd the plate, a hell of a curve, and a damn good change of pace." Joe Dobson then closed the month by shutting out the Tigers and Newhouser, 4–0.

May began with the Sox behind Ferriss whipping Detroit, 13-1. The Sox completed a second consecutive sweep the next day when left-hander Clem Dreiseward got the win. Cleveland came in for two games, and the Sox won them both, stretching the winning streak to nine. This was more than the normal good start; this was looking like something more genuine. The Browns came in on Monday, May 6, for a double-header that drew 25,000, and the Sox made it ten in a row in the first game, 7–5, Williams driving in three runs with two doubles and a single. In the second game Williams scored the winning run in the ninth on DiMaggio's single as Dobson won his fourth without a loss. The next day it looked as if the streak would be snapped as the Browns hit Hughson hard early and held leads of 4–0 and 6–2. But the Sox came back and tied the game in the seventh, and it stayed that way until the last of the fourteenth when Leon Culberson hit a grand slam homer for the Sox, and the streak reached twelve.

Then it was Chicago's turn, and before the White Sox could get on the board in Wednesday's opener the Red Sox had nine runs. Though laced for 17 hits, Mickey Harris held on until two were out in the ninth when Cronin called on Ferriss to retire the dangerous Taffy Wright. On Thursday the Sox closed out the greatest home stand in team history when they beat Chicago 7–5, to run the streak to fourteen. Doerr's fourth-inning home run with a man aboard proved to be the margin of victory.

Even during the streak, though, there were doubters, and not only in New York. Tigers manager Steve O'Neill cautioned writers not to concede the pennant to Boston, pointing out that it was still early and that except for his Tigers, who weren't hitting yet, the teams the Sox had beaten in their streak were all mediocre ones that would probably occupy the second division in the final standings. "Wait until the Sox get away from Fenway Park," he said.

The wait wasn't long, for the Sox were on their way to New York for a weekend series with the Yankees that some writers were calling the "World Series in May." On the train down the Sox players scoffed at the notion that the series was that important. Sure, they wanted to do well, and anybody in the midst of a hot streak wanted to keep it going, but it was far too early to apply the term "crucial," much less the silly "World Series" tag. But beneath their dismissals their anxiety was clear: they had a lot more to prove than the Yankees, and everybody knew it.

Cronin's pitching rotation called for Dobson to face the great old-timer Red Ruffing in Friday's opener; ace Tex Hughson would go Saturday against Tiny Bonham; and on Sunday it would be Harris against Chandler. Friday was Ladies' Day, a promotional device clubs employed to broaden their fan base by admitting women for half-price, and a crowd of 64,183 was in the Stadium for a pregame style show that had models from a Manhattan department store strolling past dugouts filled with appreciative ballplayers. When the game began the Sox jumped Ruffing early, bunching singles by catcher Hal Wagner, Culberson, and Dobson, and a double by Metkovich for three second-inning runs. In the fifth Dobson ran into trouble when Rizzuto was awarded first base on Wagner's interference. Stirnweiss followed with a single, and then Dobson loaded the bases by walking Henrich. There was still nobody out and DiMaggio at the plate with the huge crowd roaring for the knockout punch.

Unlike Feller who with his great speed could pitch DiMaggio inside, Dobson had to pitch him away with curves. His strategy was to try to get him to hit the ball to center field, a vast area in Yankee Stadium that hitters referred to as "Death Valley" because so many long drives died in fielders' gloves out there. This time, though, his curve caught too much of the plate and Jolting Joe stepped into it and lined it hard and deep toward right field. Metkovich, playing DiMaggio slightly toward left cen-

With the red-hot Red Sox headed to New York for what the writers were calling the "World Series in May," the *New York World-Telegram* ran this item.
(*The Sporting News,* May 16, 1946)

STOP THESE MEN
—
Dangerous Characters
—
HEADED THIS WAY

Armed
with
Powerful
Clubs

A Menace
to Our
Fair
City

Johnny Pesky__ .430

Dom DiMaggio__ .397

Hal Wagner__ .390

For the May 10 game at Yankee Stadium a Manhattan department store brought some models to the park to show off its spring line. The Boston players appear to be appreciative enough. (*The Sporting News,* May 16, 1946)

ter, raced after it, but it was beyond him, carrying over the low wall and into the seats for a grand slam homer. Suddenly and decisively the Yankees had struck, taking advantage of their opponents' mistakes, as they so often had in past seasons, and the Boston lead was gone. Up in the press box when DiMaggio's drive disappeared into the reaching hands of the crowd, Boston writer Jack Malaney heard the New York writers crowing that with it went Boston's pennant pretensions. It "still was baloney no matter how you sliced it," Malaney had them saying: the Yankees were kings, and Boston had better get used to it, again.

Here Cronin made an uncharacteristic move. Often criticized for staying too long with his starters, Cronin relieved Dobson with Earl Johnson who all during the winning streak had been sitting idly in the bullpen. Johnson retired the Yankees without further scoring, and the Sox came in for their half of the sixth. Doerr began the inning with a walk. And now McCarthy, too, went to his bullpen, calling on right-handed fastballer Joe Page to pitch to York. The move backfired, however, as York smashed a high drive into Death Valley in left center for a triple that tied the game. Moments later, Dom DiMaggio singled home York, and that was the ball game: Johnson was untouchable the rest of the way, striking out four, and the Red Sox streak had reached 15. Far more important, though, they'd come back to win at the Stadium after DiMaggio had apparently floored them with his grand slam.

On Saturday more than 53,000 came out to see Bonham out-pitch Hughson. Hughson got Boston's first hit, a third-inning single, and Pesky got the second Boston hit in the same inning when he hit a ball off first baseman Nick Etten's glove. But those were the only hits Bonham gave up all afternoon. Henrich accounted for both Yankee runs. In the third Williams lost Hank Majeski's high fly in the sun, then made a less than spirited effort at retrieving it, and Majeski was credited with a triple. The crowd gave Williams a thorough going-over during Henrich's at-bat, and then cheered happily when Henrich capitalized on the mistake with a ringing double to right to score the run. In the sixth, Henrich ripped a homer off Hughson to close out the scoring, New York winning, 2–0. The Red Sox streak was stopped, and the Yankees, with their ace up for Sunday's game, were in a position to take the series and the psychological momentum from Boston.

Sunday's crowd of 69,401 was the largest ever in Yankee Stadium, as the teams set a major league attendance record for a three-game series.

Expecting to see Chandler and his mates coolly dispatch the pretenders, the crowd instead saw the Yankees play with uncharacteristic sloppiness in the first. Chandler got behind in the count to the first two batters and walked them both. Then Rizzuto booted Williams's double-play grounder, and Metkovich scored all the way from second. In the fifth inning it was more of the same when Metkovich walked, moved to second on an infield out and to third when Chandler threw a wild pitch. McCarthy ordered an intentional walk to Williams, and Metkovich scored as Doerr grounded out, Williams moving to second. York got an infield hit and when Majeski fumbled Dom DiMaggio's grounder, Williams scored.

The Yankees came back with a run in the sixth on Stirnweiss's triple and Keller's infield out, but that was all Mickey Himself would give them as he pitched a sparkling three-hitter. The Sox themselves had made but three hits off Chandler, but they'd capitalized on Yankee mistakes and had made none of their own. In other words, they'd played more like the Yankees than the Red Sox of old, who were supposed to lose the close ones when their power hitters were stifled. In these three games, though, the heart of the Boston batting order—Williams, Doerr, York, and Dom DiMaggio—had been held to a collective five hits in 39 at-bats (a .128 average), no home runs, and only three runs batted in. And yet the Sox had won two of three at Yankee Stadium and now went west with a five and one-half game lead over New York. It was still very early in the race, but suddenly it wasn't quite as early as the calendar indicated, especially as the Sox continued to win on their western swing.

In Detroit the Tigers made a move that indicated plainly that they felt the race was later than it looked, trading their popular outfielder Barney McCosky to the A's for third baseman George Kell. The trade was a shocker for Tigers fans. McCosky had been a star before the war and had played a major role in the Tigers 1940 pennant. Moreover, he'd grown up in Detroit where his father had moved the family from a coal mining town in Pennsylvania after his wife had died. McCosky grew up loving the Tigers and idolizing their great second baseman, Charlie Gehringer, whose batting stance and swing the boy copied. As a junior at Detroit's Southwestern High School, McCosky batted .448, and was even better as a senior when he hit .727. A natural right-handed hitter, he'd been converted to the other side of the plate by a ball-playing older brother who told him it would maximize the boy's already outstanding speed by starting him off two steps closer to first base. After that spectacular senior

After the Red Sox had won the May 10–12 series against the Yankees in the Stadium *The Sporting News* ran this front-page Willard Mullin cartoon in its May 16 issue. (Courtesy of Shirley Mullin Rhodes and *The Sporting News*)

year, McCosky signed with the Tigers in 1936 and two years later was their starting center fielder.

But McCosky was one of those who'd had trouble picking up where he left off before the war. His offensive game was based on speed, and this spring he'd been plagued by leg and ankle problems. On May 18 he was batting just .198, and his manager was desperate for some offense on a club where neither Greenberg nor Wakefield had started well. The Tigers had a surplus of outfielders and a weakness at third base, and with Connie Mack's team in town, McCosky was traded for Kell, a solid defensive third baseman and a line-drive hitter who currently had his average near .300. Mack had long coveted McCosky, whom he called "McClusky," and now he had him. "I went over to the Cadillac Hotel where the A's were staying," McCosky said, "and met with Mr. Mack. 'Well,' I says to him, 'You finally got me. Thanks a lot. This is my home town, and now I have to leave it.' " McCosky went back to Briggs Stadium, cleared out his locker, said his goodbyes, and prepared for life in the league's lower depths. Kell, overjoyed, moved right into the Detroit lineup and kept hitting, but the Tigers and their fans would miss Barney McCosky at the top of the lineup.

12

*T*hings were quite different over in the National League where no team had been able to establish an early dominance, and Durocher had his Dodgers alternating with the favored Cardinals for first place, just how no one was quite sure. On paper his club was no match for St. Louis, and yet here they were, in the lead, tied for it, or just a game back. His best position player, Reiser, was playing hurt and his best pitcher, Higbe, looked rusty after years in the service.

Reiser hit a phenomenal .652 in exhibition games, and Durocher, believing he still had the young man who could do anything asked of him on a baseball field, had shifted him to third base. But making a quick throw from there, Reiser separated his shoulder and missed the rest of spring training, as well as the regular season opener. When he returned to the lineup as the Dodgers opened their home schedule Pistol Pete stole three bases, including home, but his arm was plainly in very bad shape. Whether at third or in center field he had to throw sidearm; his throws didn't have much steam in them, and now the injury appeared to be affecting his swing as well. In the first week of May with the Dodgers in St. Louis for games that would be rained out, agents for Jorgé Pasquel came looking for Reiser. Even with his serious injury, he represented the sort of marquee player Pasquel coveted, and by the time Rickey learned the Mexicans were talking with Reiser, their offer was up to $100,000 for three years with $50,000 of that up front. Rickey hopped a plane for St. Louis, then went directly to Reiser's hotel room where he talked with him for several hours. After Reiser affirmed his loyalty to the Dodgers Rickey left. Afterward Pistol Pete denied to beat reporters that the subject of a new contract had ever been raised. Considering Rickey's debating skills and his wiliness in money matters, Reiser may have been telling the truth.

Kirbe Higbe began experimenting with a hard knuckleball when he managed the service team he called the Manila Dodgers. In 1946 Hig used the new pitch to win seventeen games for Durocher's Dodgers. (National Baseball Library and Archive, Cooperstown, N.Y.)

As for Higbe, he'd missed the past two seasons in the service, though he had played some baseball in the South Pacific where he managed a team he called the Manila Dodgers. There were only two rules on that club, said Joe Garagiola, who played on it. One was that the batter was always hitting away, the bunt and the take sign being outlawed. The other rule, Garagiola said, was that "nobody hits a triple with Kirby on first because he's not gonna run all the way around. He's gonna stop at third." Other than these regulations, the players did pretty much as they pleased. Manager Higbe requisitioned the living quarters designated for the umpires, and from there he and Senators pitcher Early Wynn sold Filipinos beer that Higbe got from the Seabees.

In his early days in the majors Higbe had been a hard—and wild—thrower who'd led the National League in walks and strikeouts. But in 1943, his last year before entering the service, he'd lost velocity on his rising fastball and in the Philippines began experimenting with a knuckleball that he was now trying to throw with the same motion and speed as his fastball. So far the results hadn't been especially encouraging, and Durocher was beginning to wonder what kind of pitching staff it would be that was anchored by rookies Hatten, Behrman, and twenty-year-old Ralph Branca. True, he did have veterans Hal Gregg and Vic Lombardi to use as starters, but Gregg's arm was bothering him considerably, and while Lombardi was a gritty little battler, he wasn't the sort a manager could send out there every fourth day or who could stop losing streaks and win the big ones. Durocher needed Hig, and everybody associated with the team knew it.

At other positions Durocher had thus far succeeded in disguising weaknesses through adroit juggling of his personnel. He was using the veterans Herman, at second, third, and first, and Galan, in the outfield, first base, and third base.* In addition to Herman's and Galan's occasional turns at first base, Durocher was using a small committee there but would finally and reluctantly settle for Eddie Stevens and Howie Schultz. The latter was a 6'6" sometime pro basketball player who'd filled in

---

* Galan had held out during spring training, threatening to retire to his lucrative liquor business in his hometown, Berkeley, California. Rickey eventually agreed to a small raise but stipulated that Galan would have to play all the positions except catcher. Galan countered by saying he'd play anywhere except second and shortstop. He'd broken his knee running into an outfield wall in 1940, and he feared that as a middle infielder his career might quickly be ended in one hard take-out slide by an enemy baserunner.

during the war years and had survived the off-season overhaul, mainly because Durocher never believed the left-handed Stevens could hit southpaws.

In the outfield, Durocher was using the kids—Whitman, Furillo, and Hermanski—along with the veteran Dixie Walker and Reiser, when he wasn't at third or on the bench resting his arm. Behind the plate Durocher definitely missed Mickey Owen, despite whatever he and Rickey were saying publicly; and he was currently trying to get by with Don Padgett, overweight and unproductive after his years in the service, and Ferrell Anderson, a beefy twenty-nine-year-old rookie. Eventually Rickey would help his manager here by bringing up Bruce Edwards from Mobile of the Southern Association.

At least Durocher could now devote his full energies to managing since at the end of April he'd beaten the assault charge that had been hanging over him since last summer. In what was clearly a hometown decision, an all-male Brooklyn jury deliberated less than half an hour before returning "not Guilty" verdicts for both Durocher and Joe Moore. The jurors told the judge their verdict had been unanimous on the first ballot, and the only reason they'd stayed out as long as they had was because they'd lingered for a smoke in the jury room. Durocher had testified that plaintiff Christian had called his players crooks and bums (in the non-honorific sense). "One thing I won't stand for, and that's to have my boys called bums and crooks and accused of throwing games," Durocher said, artfully deflecting the thrust of Christian's heckling from himself to his boys. From the bench Judge Louis Goldstein made quite clear the significance of the verdict when he thanked the jurors for their fairness and added that personally he was happy with the disposition of the case "for the sake of the Brooklyn baseball team." Here was further proof, the judge said, that "justice could be expected from American juries." Outside the courtroom fans of baseball and justice mobbed the exonerated Durocher, ignoring the fact that earlier he'd settled a civil suit by paying Christian $6,750.

★   ★   ★

*T*he louder the drums beat for the Cardinals, the more Eddie Dyer tried to muffle them, pointing out that despite a deep and star-studded roster, his team, too, had its share of problems and question marks. Few listened, preferring instead to dismiss his bland pessimisms as a first-year manager's understandable efforts to keep public expectations at a reasonable level. He was in a hot spot, writers and fans agreed, because if he failed to win with the team he had, the blame would land squarely on him.

Dyer had been an outstanding pitcher in the Cardinals organization before hurting his arm. Thereafter he turned to managing, winning nine minor league pennants, then overseeing all the Cardinals minor league operations before getting Sam Breadon's call to manage the big club this year. It was, to be sure, a great opportunity, but it was also fraught with a good many more problems than outsiders supposed, and like many others in the game Dyer was discovering that the big crowds turning out all around both leagues were impatient for instant success and would tolerate nothing less. When his Redbirds dropped a Sunday double-header to the visiting Reds early in May, Dyer was relentlessly booed whenever he stuck his head out of the dugout. Even the popular Stan Musial, close to the top of the league in batting, was the target of fan hostility, and on that same Sunday a fan was arrested and fined for throwing a beer bottle at him.

Dyer tried to shrug off the booing, saying it was all part of the game, but managers and players in both leagues agreed they'd never experienced the volume and viciousness of the abuse that now rained down on them from stands packed with ex-GIs. A mood of irresolution and unfocused resentment seemed to characterize many of these former servicemen, and they were taking it out on their erstwhile diamond heroes, whom they appeared to regard as officers in flannels. "If you had been in prison for four years saying 'Yes, sir' to a lot of guys you'd like to spit on," one ex-GI said, "would you start cheering everybody the moment you got out?" He and his buddies, he concluded, were going to give the players, managers, and umpires hell whenever they made mistakes. So Dyer and the Cardinals got it, and when they failed to put daylight between themselves and the rest of the league they heard themselves referred to as overpaid bums.

In fact, though, Dyer spoke truthfully when he said his team had too many problems and question marks to be considered such overwhelming favorites. No team in the major leagues had been harder hit by the war than the Cardinals, and a month into the season this was becoming evident.

They'd gotten back Moore, Musial, Slaughter, and Walker for their outfield; Johnny Beazley, Ernie White, Howard Krist, and Alpha Brazle for their pitching staff; and utility player Frank "Creepy" Crespi for their infield. Moore, though, wasn't what he had been and Dyer couldn't play him regularly in center field. Left-hander Ernie White, a World Series hero in 1942, had been pinned down in icy water for most of a day during the Battle of the Bulge and had reported to spring training with a dead arm that he traced back to that incident. Dyer had been counting on White to resume his spot in the starting rotation, but almost from the beginning of spring training White's prospects looked grim. At the end of the exhibition season he had six teeth extracted, hoping that this was the source of his problem. It wasn't, and on May 14 Breadon gave up on him and peddled him to the Braves for cash.

Krist, a reliever and spot starter before the war, had rung up a record of 34–8 in the 1941–43 seasons before entering the army. In 1944 in France he badly injured a leg while carrying ammunition and spent much of the following year in an army hospital. After his discharge, he'd suffered additional injuries in an auto accident near his upstate New York home. Dyer had hoped Krist would fill the vital if unsung role of the "swing man," moving from the bullpen to the starter's slot as situations required, but Krist was giving up more than a hit an inning, and after May 5 Dyer lost faith in him after he entered a game in relief and gave up a homer on the very first pitch to light-hitting Skippy Roberge of the Braves.

The Cardinals had also been disappointed in their hopes for right-hander Red Munger whom they'd expected to be released from the army in time to start the regular season. But the big Texan, an All-Star before entering the service, was still in occupied Germany, and now no one knew when to expect him.

By far the most serious of Dyer's problems was Johnny Beazley and his aching shoulder. In 1942, before entering the army, Beazley had been one of baseball's best pitchers, winning 21 games and two more in the Series. Stationed in Texas, Beazley had pitched some for the base team but not regularly enough to keep in good shape. When his old team came through for an exhibition game Beazley's commanding officer wanted him to pitch against them, even though Beazley told him he really wasn't in condition to get major league hitters out. When the Cardinals began to hit him freely in the game, Beazley reached back for something extra, and the result was this lingering pain. Dr. Hyland's examination of the handsome Tennessean revealed no sign of injury other than a knotted muscle behind the shoulder, which, Hyland said, should disappear with regular throwing and stretching.

Dyer, of course, had been counting on Beazley to be the big man on his staff, just as his counterpart in Brooklyn had been counting on Kirby Higbe. But Beazley's spring showing had been poor, and in the one game he pitched well an observer said he'd thrown so softly he could have been caught barehanded. Still, Dyer gave him the honor of opening the season, and Beazley was hit hard by the Pirates. Thereafter he sat around, watching his manager try other pitchers in his slot. His teammates from the '42 champions shook their heads, for this Johnny Beazley bore little resemblance to that season's confident, dominating performer. "He'd had that *good* overhand curveball," Joe Garagiola said, "but now it was a shame to watch him try to pitch. You could catch him with a Kleenex."

For Frank Crespi the outlook was even bleaker. Like Garagiola, a native of Italian Hill, Crespi before the war had been a scrappy and versatile performer at second base and shortstop. But Crespi broke a leg in a tank training accident at Fort Riley, then suffered even more extensive injury to the leg in two separate freak mishaps in the hospital. He had hoped to rejoin the team in spring training, but by the time the Cardinals went north he still hadn't practiced, and the doctors were saying he needed another operation. Once Dyer got Kurowski back in the lineup, he could put young Schoendienst at second and use Lou Klein as his utility man. For the moment, the loss of Crespi looked less important, but it left the Cardinals a thinner squad than the manager had anticipated, and it reduced some of Sam Breadon's maneuverability in the trade market.

These war-related problems were substantial, but they weren't the only ones the club had suffered, for they had also lost two of their brightest minor league pitching prospects in Hank Nowak and Johnny Grodzicki. Nowak had posted impressive statistics on his way up through the St. Louis chain, and in his last season before entering the army he'd won 13 games at Houston, including three consecutive shutouts. On New Year's Day 1945, Nowak, by then an infantry sergeant, was killed in action in Belgium.

Grodzicki at least made it home, though he did so on crutches. He'd been raised in an orphanage in the tough coal-mining town of Nanticoke, Pennsylvania, and by the time he was in high school had attracted the attention of the scouts. He was big, he threw very hard, and he had a mean streak that scouts like to see in a pitcher. The Cardinals signed him and sent him to New Iberia in the Evangeline League where Grodzicki began his professional career at $60 a month. As hard as he threw and as mean as he was, minor league hitters weren't eager to dig in against him, and one player recalled that after someone had hit Grodzicki for a homer the pitcher followed him around the bases, swearing at him all the way. The next time that batter came up, Grodzicki threw at his head and sent him spinning into the dirt.

The making of Grodzicki as a pitcher was his mastery of a change-of-pace pitch made the more devastating because he threw it with the same arm speed as his fastball. "Where I learned it," he said, "was from Dizzy Dean," the Cardinals's famed fireballer who'd had to learn guile after injury had taken the heat from his best pitch. Dean taught the youngster to keep his fingertips off the ball and to lead slightly with his elbow when releasing it, thereby greatly reducing the ball's velocity. Primed for Grodzicki's outstanding fastball, the batter started his hands and hips too early and so was well out in front of the pitch by the time it actually arrived in the hitting zone. Armed with these two pitches, Grodzicki achieved an astonishing 31–9 record for the Columbus Redbirds in 1941, prompting his manager, the veteran Burt Shotton, to call him the best minor league pitcher he'd ever seen. Writer Bob Broeg said that prior to his induction Grodzicki had been universally regarded as the organization's best pitching prospect, and that, Broeg added, "was really saying something because you have to remember that at that time the Cardinals' system was absolutely *loaded.*" One of the players in that system, Joe Garagiola, said simply, "Grodzicki was a legend. You heard about him everywhere."

Immediately after Pearl Harbor Grodzicki was drafted and sent to paratrooper school in Georgia where an older brother was an instructor. But Grodzicki got no special favors from his brother who arranged to have Johnny in his plane for the first jump. "If you don't jump, I'm gonna kick you out," Grodzicki's brother threatened him. When his basic training was completed Grodzicki was shipped to the European theater and, at the end of March 1945, was dropped across the Rhine River near Wesel as part of the massive Allied drive on Berlin. On March 30, just as he and three other paratroopers had scaled a village wall, a German shell exploded in their midst, killing the others and tearing a jagged hole in Grodzicki's right buttock. Examination at a field hospital revealed extensive muscle and nerve damage; the sciatic nerve had been completely severed.

After an operation in Germany, Grodzicki was evacuated to England where he spent months in convalescence and physical therapy. Earlier in the war a wound of this type routinely resulted in amputation, but by this point surgical techniques had advanced considerably and doctors were able to save the leg, though Grodzicki had only limited use of it. When he began to walk again, the big ex-pitcher found he had no control of his foot, which dropped limply toward the ground with every step he took. Despite this, Grodzicki was determined to resume his baseball career, and in the winter of 1945–46 he was fitted for a brace and went to Panama to pitch in a semi-pro league. It was a rough reentry: he had no strength in the leg, and on the mound his balance was badly off. Nor could he field his position or get over to cover first base on balls hit to the right side. Still, when the Cardinals opened their spring training in St. Petersburg Grodzicki was there. During the practices he threw on the sidelines or tossed a little batting practice. Afterward the famed Cardinals trainer, Harrison (Doc) Weaver, worked extensively on the leg. "Old Doc Weaver," Grodzicki recalled, "he had me in the whirlpool all the time. 'John,' he used to say to me, 'I don't think you're gonna make it.' But he worked on me all the same." At night Grodzicki tossed and turned, haunted by thoughts of a career that might well be over and made physically uncomfortable by the leg which dripped with sweat all night long.

When the team went north for the season Grodzicki went along as a batting practice pitcher, and Dyer, who knew how good this man might have been, watched daily for signs that he might be regaining strength and mobility, that he might yet help the team sometime down the road.

★   ★   ★

/n the middle of May the Cardinals swung east for games with the Dodgers, Braves, Phillies, and Giants. On May 14 Brooklyn had a two-game lead when the Cardinals came into the organized bedlam that was Ebbets Field.

In an era when there were a number of cozy parks—Wrigley Field, Crosley Field in Cincinnati, Fenway Park—Ebbets Field was the coziest, its stands seeming to hang out almost into the field of play. Dodgers shortstop Pee Wee Reese once spoke about the phenomenon of playing in what felt like a neighborhood setting, of going out to his position and looking up into the grandstand to see the same faces, game after game, all of them hollering encouragement, waving scorecards, some even tossing out tiny vials of holy water or religious medals. Those fans, said Kirby Higbe, were so much a part of games at Ebbets Field that "they were just about on the roster."

Of course, the sensation was quite different for visiting players, especially members of the hated Giants and the feared Cardinals, who had to endure that cauldron of partisanship. Brooklyn-born writer Donald Honig said there was something both exotic and menacing to Brooklyn fans about the Cardinals. Dodgers radio announcer Red Barber always reminded his listeners that the Cardinals were the only National League team west of the Mississippi, Honig recalled, so that they seemed almost like frontiersmen in flannels. "We had tremendous respect for and fear of the Cardinals," Honig said. "Batting practice would be over, and there'd be that moment, that great moment before the game starts, when they play the National Anthem, and you'd see them in the dugout, and you'd think, 'These guys are here to *kill* us.' No other team inspired that sense."

The Brooklyn fans would throw anything at you, according to Terry Moore. "Firecrackers, bottles, anything they had handy. And it seemed like every time we'd come in there something would happen. The umpires would get us together before the first game and say, 'Boys, let's have a good series.' Then, sure enough, all hell would break loose." The umpires themselves were scared to work those Dodgers-Cardinals series in Ebbets Field, he claimed. And it was certainly no picnic for the Cardinals players, either, even after the game was over, for then they had to run the gauntlet to the subway they took back to the Hotel New Yorker in Manhattan. Jeff Cross, a Cardinals utility infielder, said they used to button up their jackets, duck their heads, and make a run for the subway, surrounded by fans trying to pull off their tie clasps, grabbing at their hats, even squirting ink at them from fountain pens. "They were great baseball fans, I guess," he said, "but they were crazy, nutty people. Going to play at Ebbets Field with all those people, the band they had there in the stands, cowbells ringing—it was like going to a circus." A Colombian immigrant to Brooklyn recalled how astonished he was by the depth and even ferocity of Dodgers culture in the borough to which he'd come to live with relatives. You didn't have to actually go to the games to follow the team, he said. Just walking the streets during a game would keep you abreast of their every deed, for everywhere there were people sitting on stoops cheering the play-by-play that came from their radios and standing on street corners discussing strategy. When the team lost, a gloom descended over Brooklyn—until the next day's game.

In the Cardinals-Dodgers game of May 14 nothing untoward happened, and it appeared that for once the umpires would be blessed by an uneventful series. Lanier, long the Dodgers's nemesis, went all the way against four Brooklyn pitchers and Marty Marion drove in two St. Louis runs in the eleventh to break a 5–5 tie. Thirty-one thousand were in the little park, some of them lured by the 500 pairs of nylon stockings the Dodgers gave away before the game. In the series' second game, though, there was the traditional bit of trouble as Dodgers starter Les Webber began throwing well inside to the Cardinals batters. When he gave Slaughter a close shave, the fiery right fielder bunted up the first base line and as Webber came over to field the ball Slaughter crashed into him at full speed. Webber made the tag but the two squared off as their teammates raced from their dugouts and the fans howled for satisfaction. Dyer got between the main belligerents and calmed Slaughter. He had great influence with Slaughter who always credited Dyer with having lit the fuse under him that saved his career.

This was back in '36 when both men were at Columbus of the South Atlantic League and Dyer and the Cardinals had a question mark next to the name of their young outfielder who ran flatfooted and lacked that all-out hustle they wanted to see. "I had a habit," Slaughter recalled, "of running in from the outfield, and as soon as I'd crossed the third base line, well, I walked from there to the top step of the dugout. One day Dyer says to me, 'Son, if you're tired, we can get some help for you.' Well, from then on I ran straight from my position to the top step of the dugout, and I ran all the way out to my position. I ran everywhere. I never walked on a ballfield again." Now Dyer got Slaughter back to the St. Louis dugout and the game resumed. When he ran out to right field at the end of the half-inning Slaughter got it from the crowd, but before the inning was over he'd silenced them with two marvelous catches and a throw that doubled up Carl Furillo at first base. The Cardinals went on to win the game behind Howard Pollet, 1–0, and went into first place by percentage points.

From Brooklyn they went north to Boston, always something of a relief, said Stan Musial. Musial enjoyed playing in New York, partly because he hit so well in both the Polo Grounds and Ebbets Field, and partly because in New York he got the kind of media attention he couldn't get out in the midwest. "We were the western-most club," he said, "and people in the east didn't get our box scores in their morning papers, so they didn't know what kind of a year I was having." In New York, though, with all the writers and the radio shows Musial's exploits were fully covered, particularly this season with his average near .400 and people beginning to talk about him the way they talked about Ted Williams. Still, it was a relief to leave all the heat and hoopla of New York behind and head to Boston. "It was quieter up there," Musial said, "the weather was usually a little cooler, the lobster was good—and the pitching staff was weak." In the two games at Braves Field Jeff Cross stole home to win one of them but Beazley was hit hard again in the second, and the team turned south again with a split.

They were scheduled for a doubleheader with the Phillies on May 19, but barely arrived in time for the games: while the team was in New Haven the engine crew of their train walked off the job as a major rail strike loomed. Hours later when Truman struck a temporary deal with union leaders the crew returned, but the Cardinals didn't get into their hotel rooms in Philadelphia until almost 3:00 A.M. Scant hours after that they took the field in front of the largest Phillies crowd of the season and won both games. In the opener Lanier staggered through to his sixth win without a loss, though for the second successive game he was hit freely. In the nightcap Harry Brecheen shut out the Phillies and sent his team back into first place in their seesaw battle with Brooklyn. As the Cardinals came back to New York for two games with Mel Ott's lackluster Giants, they were looking to open some daylight between themselves and Durocher's Dodgers. This seemed like the opportune moment to do so, considering the quality of Cardinals opposition and the fact that the Dodgers were hurting: Hal Gregg had been sidelined with a worsening arm injury; Rex Barney, newly returned to the club from the service, had arrived out of shape; and Reiser had hit an outfield wall once again, aggravating his shoulder injury. But the Cardinals were about to experience troubles of their own.

13

*T*he Cardinals' problems surfaced on May 23 when Lanier, right-hander Freddie Martin, and infielder Lou Klein failed to report for that day's game at the Polo Grounds. Amid rumors the three had gone to play for Jorgé Pasquel, Johnny Beazley took the mound against the Giants and threw a four-hit victory. But the win was greatly overshadowed by the absence of Lanier and the others, and when Red Schoendienst got back to the room he shared with Lanier he found the pitcher's luggage gone and a note on the bureau. "So long, Red," Lanier had written. "Keep hitting those line drives. I'll see you next winter, and we'll go hunting."

The players' decisions had been some time in the making. Martin and Klein, both coming back from the service, had played winter ball in Cuba to regain their edge and had been approached there by Pasquel's agents. As early as February Martin's name had come up in rumors of players who might jump their American contracts for bigger money in Mexico, but when Martin reported to St. Petersburg that particular rumor died. The lean Oklahoman had been in the St. Louis organization since 1935 and until 1941 had enjoyed only moderate success. In that season, however, Martin began throwing a sinker and with it compiled a 23–6 record for Eddie Dyer and a remarkable 1.52 earned-run-average. Then, even before Pearl Harbor, he'd been drafted and had spent the following four seasons in the South Pacific. When he reported to the Cardinals in Florida Martin was a thirty-year-old rookie trying for a spot on a deep and talented team. He had, however, an ace in the hole, or rather in his pocket—a $3,000 check from Pasquel, earnest money if Martin would sign with him. But Martin had worked and waited a long while for his chance with the Cardinals, and now apparently he was to get it with his old manager

The story of the Mexican League and its raids on Organized Baseball began in the winter of 1945–46 when Jorgé Pasquel, a wealthy and politically well connected Mexican, encountered Giants outfielder Danny Gardella at a Manhattan gym. Subsequently Gardella became the first prominent American to "jump" his contract for the bigger bucks in Mexico. *Top left*: Pasquel, and on his right, Gardella, and ex-Dodgers catcher Mickey Owen. Pasquel went after the roster of St. Louis Cardinals owner Sam Breadon (*top right*), and got three players from it (*bottom right*): from left, infielder Lou Klein and pitchers Freddie Martin and Max Lanier, a star left-hander. Breadon's tight-fisted fiscal policies saw him dispose of the Cooper brothers, Walker and, on his left, Mort (*bottom left*) and cost him the loyalty of Lanier. (Top left: Okrent and Lewine, *The Ultimate Baseball Book*. Upper and lower right: Broeg, *Redbirds*. Lower left: AP)

running the big club. During spring training he'd pitched brilliantly in spots and easily made the team, but then it appeared that Dyer was uncertain how best to use him, and Martin began to wonder what his role would be, if any. Both wartime winner Barrett and Johnny Beazley had flopped as starters, yet Dyer still hesitated to insert Martin in the regular rotation. In this hiatus the Pasquels came calling again and found him receptive.

With Kurowski a holdout, Dyer had used Schoendienst at third in the early going, opening up second base for Klein, but with Kurowski back, Dyer had been using Schoendienst more and more at second. He was five years younger than Klein, much faster, and a line-drive switch-hitter. Moreover, he hadn't been away from the game as Klein had. The more Dyer looked at Schoendienst at second, the more he saw to like, and by mid-May it was apparent the Redhead was settling in for a good, long run as the Cardinals starting second baseman. When the Pasquels came back to Klein with an even sweeter offer than the one they'd made in Cuba he took it. He could see his future with the Cardinals was a limited one, and as Schoendienst said many years later, "When somebody comes up to you with a suitcase full of cash, that can catch your eye in a hurry. That's like a hanging curveball."

When both Martin and Klein decided to go south, they knew from the Pasquels that the Mexicans were pressuring Lanier to join them. They knew, too, that Lanier was still resentful of his treatment by Breadon. What neither man knew, however, was that the star left-hander couldn't have been in a more receptive mood than he was in just then because, despite his 6–0 record, Lanier was worried about the condition of his pitching arm and thought he might not be able to finish the season. He traced the trouble to his service ball days at Fort Bragg. In a situation tellingly similar to that of Johnny Beazley, Lanier had been pressed into pitching against a squad of touring major leaguers even though he knew he wasn't in condition to do so. He hadn't pitched in a month when the big leaguers came through, Lanier said, but the officers told him the soldiers wanted to see him pitch, and so Lanier went out, pitched, and hurt his arm. His last two starts told him his arm might be giving out, and the game against the Phillies had been particularly rough as he'd battled the pain and the Phillies hitters before that big crowd. He'd had pain in the spring, but not like this, particularly when he tried to throw his big-breaking curveball.

While the team was in Philadelphia Bernardo Pasquel made his offer to him, and Lanier remembered thinking, "Shucks, if I have to put up

Top: A white-suited Jorgé Pasquel attends the opener of his league in Mexico City, March 21, with Mexico's president Manuel Avila Camacho. (*The Sporting News,* March 28, 1946) *Below*: Babe Ruth, the symbol of the national pastime, surprised everybody by flying down to Mexico with his wife (*left*) and adopted daughter, May 15. While there, the Bambino hit a home run in a batting exhibition and played golf as the guest of Pasquel. (*The New York Times,* May 16, 1946)

with this pain, I might as well get paid some money for it." The pain and an uncertain baseball future were not all that Lanier was thinking about now. He was thinking also of the clause in the Uniform Player's Contract stating that a player could be released by his club ten days subsequent to being notified in writing. That meant, of course, that from the moment of his release the player was off the payroll without being given so much as rail fare home. Lanier knew well enough that once Breadon realized he couldn't pitch, he would drop him—though Lanier's prominence meant that Breadon would likely first try to realize some cash by peddling him to another team, as he had Ernie White. And then there was the vivid memory of the sale of Walker Cooper to the Giants, a transaction that made no sense to the pitcher except as a pure business deal. The players of Lanier's day were well aware that in many ways professional baseball was a rough way to make a buck, but most of them hadn't yet come to the awareness that baseball really was after all a business. At contract time they recognized that they were at a great disadvantage in the negotiations, and afterward they might grumble about how unfairly they'd been treated, but then they pulled on their heavy flannels and went out and played the game as hard as they could, because to them it still was a game—America's game—and they loved it.

But now Bernardo Pasquel was talking big money to the man who was concealing a sore arm from management while his teammates Martin and Klein were urging him to get smart. If baseball was a business to Sam Breadon—and the owner's dealings with Johnny Mize and the Cooper brothers strongly suggested this—why shouldn't he make a business decision, too? He told Bernardo Pasquel he'd think it over and talk some more when the team got to New York.

But when the team checked into the New Yorker Lanier still hadn't made up his mind. He was not a worldly man, and he knew nothing about Mexico and what life would be like there. This was a big step, especially since Chandler's ruling made it clear there would be no coming back. But the money was big, too, bigger than what the thirty-one-year-old could hope to make at his current salary, even if he pitched another ten years: the Pasquels were offering $20,000 a year for five years with a $35,000 bonus for signing.

Finally, he agreed to go, called Bernardo Pasquel, and the three players went over to see him at the Roosevelt Hotel on the morning of May 23. They discussed details and schedules, and then Pasquel opened his suit-

A few days after jumping the Cardinals on May 23 Martin and Lanier packed up the latter's brand-new Chrysler and departed from Mexico, having heard nothing from Breadon. (*The Sporting News,* June 5, 1946)

case full of hundred dollar bills and paid the players their signing bonuses. Outside, the city was bedlam with the rail strike really on this time and rumors flying that Truman would call out the army to run the lines. Klein caught a bus for his native New Orleans, where he would collect his things and get to Mexico City the best way he could. Lanier and Martin went back to the New Yorker, took the guts out of Lanier's large shortwave radio, stashed their money inside it, and caught a bus to Washington, D.C. "We had that radio up there above us in the luggage rack," Lanier said, "and one of us would watch it while the other one tried to sleep for a while." There were no flights the two could get from Washington to St. Louis, but they got rail seats to Chicago. However, with only skeleton crews operating the trains and all flights overbooked, it seemed as if the players might be stranded in Chicago. Lanier called Jorgé Pasquel and told him they would get to Mexico City as soon as they could make it to St. Louis and collect their belongings. Take a cab, Pasquel told them, and bring the bill with you. It amounted, Lanier said, to more than $300.

Meanwhile, behind them, their ex-teammates were having their own troubles getting from New York to Cincinnati for a night game on May 24. In 1946 only the Yankees regularly rode planes on their road trips, and they had just begun the practice. Now, though, all the teams found they had to scramble to book charter flights to make their next road games, and Cardinals traveling secretary Leo Ward was able to get only nineteen players on a DC-3 for Cincinnati. At Columbus thunderstorms forced the plane to land before flying on to Cincinnati. When they arrived, they were already late as they piled into cabs for the final hop to Crosley Field where a crowd of more than 26,000 waited in the stands. On the way to the park the hood latch of the cab in which Musial, Slaughter, Moore, and Buster Adams were riding gave way, and so with Musial at the wheel and the reluctant cabbie stretched out across the hood to keep it down they whirled into the parking lot and ran to the clubhouse to suit up.

Any hope that the team's missing players might turn up in Cincinnati was quickly dashed, but Sam Breadon was there to meet the team, having flown in from St. Louis to assess the damage and try to anticipate what further losses his club might sustain. Now there were strong rumors that offers were about to be made to Kurowski and to all three starting out-fielders. In fact, Kurowski had already been approached by a Mexican agent while the third baseman waited in a New York barbershop for a haircut. The man said he was authorized to make Kurowski an offer and

When 250,000 union members struck the nation's railroads May 23 the teams had no way to get to their games on the 24th. Here members of the Cardinals wait for a plane to Cincinnati. Standing from left are Ken Burkhart, Harry Brecheen, Ted Wilks, Stan Musial, and Johnny Beazley. Whitey Kurowski is seated at left. (*The Sporting News,* June 5, 1946)

asked how much it might take to get him to sign with the Pasquels. Kurowski wrote down a figure on the newspaper he'd been reading. The man tore off the page and said he'd get in touch at a later date.

When the team returned to St. Louis the Mexicans paid Musial a visit at the Fairgrounds Hotel where he was living with his wife and infant daughter while they tried to find private housing. This time Alfonso Pasquel, accompanied by Mickey Owen, came to make the pitch. Musial was making $13,500 this year, the final one of a three-year deal he'd signed before entering the service, so when Pasquel laid $65,000 in cashier's checks out on the table, Musial suddenly had a lot to consider: the checks, he was told, represented half of what would be his annual salary in a five-year deal. Owen was along to tell Musial that the Pasquels had followed through on every one of their promises and that if Musial moved his family to Mexico, he wouldn't be sorry. Owen said Jorgé Pasquel was building him a house and that he and his wife liked things in Mexico so well they were considering making it their permanent residence. Here was a hard sell, but Musial, though he was one of the most genial, affable men in the big leagues, was also a fairly shrewd negotiator. He'd been raised in a tough town that turned out nails and wire, and he'd learned early in life the value of a dollar earned. He told his visitors he couldn't make so momentous a decision on the spot, but would have to think it through with his wife. That evening when Pasquel called back, Musial said he'd discussed it with his wife and realized this was a great deal he was being offered, but he was going to honor the final year of his contract with Sam Breadon. However, he seemed to leave the door slightly ajar to further talks, perhaps after the season had ended.

There had been an almost palpable tension in St. Louis over Musial's intentions. Photographers staked out the Fairgrounds, and after Pasquel and Owen had called on Musial they followed the pair to a restaurant and snapped away while Pasquel and Owen tried to eat dinner. When the Musials suddenly found housing and moved out of the Fairgrounds, news hawks were certain that all their luggage meant Mexico, so when Musial announced he was going to play his baseball in St. Louis, the city and the midwest sighed with relief.

In the Cardinals clubhouse the next day Whitey Kurowski decided the time was right to clear the air and refocus the team's attention on the most important matter. He, too, had been approached by the Mexicans, he told his teammates, and he believed in getting all the money he was worth, something, he knew, that wouldn't be news to any of them. But, he continued, he'd signed with Sam Breadon for this season, and he felt honor-bound to play in St. Louis. Let's put this Mexican business behind us, he urged his teammates, and concentrate on winning the pennant.

Coming from Kurowski the speech had an impact: the players knew he'd waged a bitter holdout this spring, yet here he was, telling them that they had a job to do right here in St. Louis, whatever private misgivings some of them might harbor about the way Breadon ran his club. The job was to win the pennant. That was the way Rickey had schooled the Cardinals players, from Class D to the major leagues: not just to advance up the ladder, not just to be good and to win, but to win the championship. That was the way, Rickey had taught them, to make real money, to make

In the uneasy aftermath of the departures of Lanier, Klein, and Martin, Alfonso Pasquel and Mickey Owen paid a call on Stan Musial at his St. Louis hotel. Later they ate at a restaurant, watched by scribes. When Musial and his wife and infant daughter moved out of the hotel into private housing, writers and photographers were sure their packed bags meant Musial was going to Mexico. (*The Sporting News,* June 19, 1946)

up the difference between what they were actually drawing in salary and what they thought they were really worth. Kurowski was from that old school, and so were most of the others in the clubhouse, but it wasn't easy to shrug off the losses of Lanier, Martin, and Klein, however much they might want to. The loss of Lanier, Red Schoendienst said, hurt the Cardinals terribly, and it was going to take them a while to adjust. While they did so Breadon himself tried to help by privately giving substantial bonuses to Musial, Slaughter, and Moore. All the same, team morale was affected, while over in Brooklyn the Dodgers got a big boost from Lanier's defection, for no other pitcher in the league was tougher on them. In June as the Cardinals tried to regain their stride, the Dodgers sprinted to a lead and then began steadily to lengthen it.

14

By June even the most stubborn and traditional owners had come to realize that the postwar world of baseball wasn't quite the same as the prewar one, that it wasn't exempt from the forces and pressures at work in the nation, and even in the world for that matter, as the Mexican challenge was revealing. But because for so long they'd enjoyed a special and protected status as custodians of the national pastime the owners were slow to understand the nature of the challenges to the game, and in general their response was to stall for time and hope they would go away.

In the Mexican matter, for instance, the New York area teams failed to see it as symptomatic of longstanding player grievances now brought to the surface by the end of the war. Instead, the Yankees, Dodgers, and Giants simply obtained restraining orders in American courts forbidding further raids on their rosters by the Pasquels. But in doing so, the clubs had invited legal attention to the potentially explosive issue of the Uniform Player's Contract with its reserve clause and ten-day severance provision. In the hearing for the injunction sought by the Yankees the Pasquels' attorney argued that Organized Baseball constituted an illegal monopoly, but he also raised the issue of the player's contract and characterized it as a form of peonage. New York State Supreme Court Justice Julius Miller eventually granted the injunction the Yankees sought, and he chastised the Pasquels for seducing employees to break contracts they'd voluntarily entered into. But before he made his decision, Miller asked what were to prove troubling questions about the contract and whether in its present form it was absolutely essential to the continued health of the game. He was assured by the Yankees attorney that the "great American game, as we know it, will be destroyed if the present contract were declared illegal." The major issue before Miller was the sanctity of the contracts signed by the players and their American clubs, not the equity of those contracts, and it was on that issue that he found for the plaintiff. Immediately afterward the Pasquels' attorney announced he'd seek a separate trial on the legality of the contract, and even before he did so some in the baseball world were saying it hadn't been a good idea to seek these injunctions, precisely because in doing so the issue of the contract was bound to be raised. These observers felt that the Mexican challenge, though vexing, would eventually go away; the issue of the contract wouldn't. White Sox executive Leslie O'Connor put it baldly when he said that he and the late Judge Landis had worked for twenty-five years to keep baseball out of the courts. O'Connor meant, of course, that the game was far better off policing itself and enforcing its own regulations than having others step in.

The lawyers for the Yankees, Dodgers, and Giants had been speaking truthfully in their pleas before the court when they argued that baseball, "as we know it," was founded on the standard contract with its reserve clause. If a club's exclusive rights to a player's services were ever to be successfully challenged, the traditional structure of Organized Baseball with its scouting systems, its signings, its farm systems, and its player transactions would topple, leaving the chaos of free agency and an open market. But even as the "magnates," as the owners were described in the sporting press, worried about the Mexicans' threatened legal challenge to the contract there arose the cognate specter of unionization.

The would-be organizer of the players was Robert Francis Murphy, a Harvard-educated lawyer who'd worked for the National Labor Relations Board in Washington and now was back in his hometown of Boston. It was there in April that he formally established an organization he was calling the American Baseball Guild. He had talked to enough players, Murphy told the press, to satisfy himself that they operated at a gross disadvantage in labor relations with their employers. His American Baseball Guild, he said, stood for a minimum salary of $6,500, arbitration of all salary disputes, and a player's right to half the price in the event he should be sold.

At first, Murphy's new union was regarded merely as a sign of the times in this period of postwar reconversion. The owners and the sporting press dismissed it out of hand, as did many players who were inured to what they'd been taught to consider the necessary conditions of Organized Baseball. Baseball, they said, was not Ford Motors or Bethlehem

Steel. Baseball was, well, different. And even if it was true that the owners often gypped the players, this wasn't a situation an outsider, a union agitator, was likely to remedy. Many of these scoffers came from southern mill towns where anti-union sentiment had always been strong—one reason northern manufacturers had relocated there. Bill Voiselle was typical of them: in his hometown of Ninety-Six, South Carolina, the mill workers had fought through the 1920s and '30s to keep the unions out. Voiselle's father and brothers had worked in the mills of Ninety-Six, and the pitcher himself had literally grown up in the long shadows of their smokestacks. A baseball union was simply a deeply unappealing idea to a man like him, however unfairly he felt treated by the Giants.

Other players said they knew that owners like the grand old men of the game, Clark Griffith and Connie Mack and Sam Breadon, weren't getting rich off the players' hides: historically these clubs had drawn modestly, and the money simply wasn't there. What would a players' union profit men who played for these owners? The dues would just be another bite out of an already meager monthly check. And even if the money were there, all previous attempts to organize players had failed, including those initiated by former players like David Fultz whose Fraternity of Professional Baseball Players flared briefly around World War I, and then fizzled out, leaving a very few players richer but the essential conditions unchanged. Baseball, these players said, simply wasn't by its nature amenable to unionization. Finally, there were the many players who might not have strong feelings on the issue but who were either just beginning their big league careers or who knew themselves to be marginal and felt lucky to be in the majors at any price and had no inclination to rock the small, tightly-rigged boat that was keeping them above the uncertain waters of the workaday world. For such men the status quo was far less of a problem than the possibility of losing their place as big leaguers in some murky and dubious battle over unionization.

Despite these hurdles, Murphy was convinced the players' grievances were real and that the time for organization was right. As visiting clubs came through Boston, he canvassed them, enduring the ridicule and the incredulity, patiently asking the players whether at some future point they might join his Guild if they saw it might substantially improve their condition. On so conditional a basis Murphy was able to announce that a "majority" of big leaguers now favored a player's union; how firm that sentiment was, he didn't say.

His strategy, as it developed through the early weeks of the season, was to target the Pittsburgh Pirates and try to force the club to recognize the Guild as the players' legitimate bargaining representative. Pittsburgh was a union town in an area that hadn't forgotten the bitter, violent Homestead strike of 1892 when Henry Frick called in the Pinkertons and the Governor called out the militia to break the strike at Carnegie Steel. Murphy met with Pirates players at the Kenmore Hotel during their first trip to Boston and told them of his plans for a players' union. Ralph Kiner said the team was splintered: there were those with a strong union bias; those who were equally committed to management; and those like himself who were youngsters, just trying to stick with the big club. And the best way to stick with the big club in those days, Kiner said, "was to keep your mouth shut and keep out of sight." Referring to the almost invisible young officer of the popular novel *Mr. Roberts,* published that year, Kiner said the young player had to be "sort of an Ensign Pulver type." In his own case, Kiner was advised by veteran catcher and team captain Al Lopez to stay completely out of all union discussions. It could ruin your career to get mixed up in this thing, Lopez told him. Personally, Lopez felt a union would never work in baseball and would be bad for the game.

When he felt he had sufficient backing on the team, Murphy went to the club's management requesting that an election be held to determine whether the players wanted the Guild to represent them. The principal owner of the Pirates was William Benswanger, a member of the Dreyfuss family that had run the franchise since 1900. He was along in years and by this point somewhat removed from the club's daily operations, but he was kindly in an aloof, patrician way and was genuinely liked by some of the team's older players. Besides, Benswanger was trying to sell the Pirates, and his player partisans felt a unionized team would seriously jeopardize his chances of doing so. Benswanger's chief counsel tried to stall Murphy, claiming the season was the wrong time to try to schedule so epochal an event as Murphy had in mind. It would be far better, he argued, to wait until the season was over and then have a meeting to discuss whether and when such an election might be held. Murphy recognized the tactic for what it was, and the pro-union players were resentful of its transparent motive. After consulting with them, Murphy set a deadline of June 5 for the club to notify the Guild whether it would consent to the election. At the same time he notified the National Labor Relations

Board and set about drumming up support for the Guild among players of other teams.

Once they got wind of his plans, much of the sporting press and all of baseball's brass blasted the idea of a union. The *Sporting News* caricatured the idea in articles, editorials, and cartoons. How could such a thing hope to work, the paper asked, in so highly individualized a sport? Was there to be a certain wage standard set for infielders and another for pitchers? If all infielders were to be paid a scale wage, would Tiger Eddie Mayo (a light-hitting utility man) be guaranteed the same wage as slugger Hank Greenberg? Would players take their orders from their manager or from their shop steward? If a pitcher didn't want to come out of a game, could he refuse the manager's order to do so on the grounds that it was manifestly unfair to organized labor or was abridging his rights as a worker? And when the five o'clock whistle blew, would the players lay down their mitts and bats and walk off the field? Franklin Lewis in the Cleveland *Press* and longtime St. Louis writer J. Roy Stockton were about the only prominent writers at the time who took Murphy and his Guild seriously. Lewis wrote that a union of some sort was inevitable, even if it should not turn out to be the one Murphy was now heading. And Stockton wrote that Murphy and his Guild were exactly what the owners deserved for their "smugness" and their "everybody-but-us-be-damned" attitude.

For the owners, Clark Griffith and Larry MacPhail led the way. Griffith, whose beginnings were almost coeval with those of the game itself, flatly predicted that a union—any union—would wreck baseball. MacPhail, who could be as disingenuous as he was impetuous, suggested the players ought to revive David Fultz's old players' fraternity rather than form a union. In fact, MacPhail went on, he himself would help them do this and would encourage his fellow owners to grant the fraternity representative a place on baseball's executive council to chart the direction of the game. That way, MacPhail said, baseball could guard against the threat of rank outsiders like Robert Murphy coming along and trying to tell the players what to do.

As Murphy's deadline approached, journalistic and executive scorn for him and his target team intensified. When the Pirates were walloped by the Dodgers in a game in which they committed six errors, Les Biederman wrote that "members of Pittsburgh Local No. 1, American Baseball Guild, acted like men who had been barred from the big league union, rather than

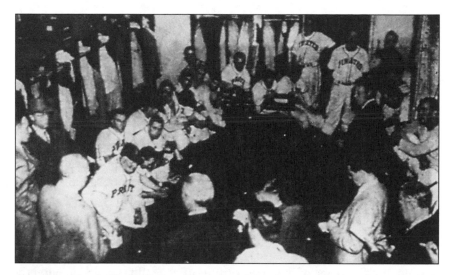

American Baseball Guild founder Robert Murphy talks to the Pirates in their clubhouse prior to their June 5 game with the Dodgers at Forbes Field. The more militant Pirates wanted to strike, but eventually the team took the field, though vowing to strike two days hence if management failed to recognize the guild. (*The Sporting News,* June 19, 1946)

the pioneers of the movement." Front office personnel said the game was about to flirt with extinction if Benswanger should give in to Murphy or if the players made good their threat to strike. Good faith and sportsmanship were the twin pillars of the national pastime, not unionization and job actions, of which, it was said, America already had far too much.

On June 5, the Pirates were scheduled to play a night game at Forbes Field against the Dodgers, and Murphy announced they wouldn't take the field unless management allowed the Guild to hold an election, one that he was confident he would win. That afternoon he met with Benswanger and other club officials and was told the club needed more time to study the Guild's proposals. Murphy went down to the clubhouse, informed the players of the official response, and listened as they reacted. The more militant of his Guild members wanted to strike immediately, but after some deliberation, Murphy told them he thought they ought to give management one last chance and sent a message up to Benswanger that he must come down to the clubhouse immediately if he wished to avoid a strike. Benswanger did so, something he hadn't done since 1934, and spoke briefly to the players, reminding them that his door had always been open to them and that it had always been his intention to treat them fairly and with respect. When he'd finished and left, the players conferred once again, deciding finally to take the field against Brooklyn, but vowing that unless management agreed to the election, they would definitely strike the game against the Giants two days hence. Meanwhile, management was rounding up a group of minor leaguers and semi-pro players in the event the regulars did strike.

For a while it appeared they would. Management gave no sign it was about to make any concessions, and Frankie Frisch made out a lineup for the Giants game that included himself at second base and the seventy-two-year-old coach Honus Wagner at shortstop. When Murphy and the writers and photographers showed up in the Pirates clubhouse a little after five o'clock, Frisch was waiting for them and ordered everybody not connected to the club to leave. Clearly, Murphy and the media would have to, but Bob Rice of the Pirates front office could stay and apparently took part in the often heated debate that ensued while up above the Giants took batting practice and then infield practice and the fans waited. In the corridor outside the locked clubhouse door, Murphy paced and talked with the media.

Inside, the debate was confused because, unaccountably, Murphy had failed to make clear the perimeter of the proposed job action: if the players did strike tonight's game, was it for this game only, or were they to stay out until management capitulated? The failure was a crucial one, for if management feared a protracted strike, the prospect of one for the players was even more fearsome. Many of them felt underpaid, but how would they get along without any pay at all? How would they even get home or, if they had families living with them in town, arrange to get them home?

Pitcher Rip Sewell and former Cardinals infielder Jimmy Brown, both Southerners from mill towns, led the opposition to the strike. Sewell, Kiner recalled, vigorously argued for management and for the game itself, telling his teammates, "You just can't do this!" He supported most of the Guild's proposals, Sewell said, but he was unalterably opposed to a union and especially to a strike. Brown echoed him as did outfielder-third baseman Bob Elliott. Sewell, Brown, and Elliott drew the team's top three salaries, a fact not lost upon the militants. When the vote was taken, it went 20-16 in favor of striking, but this was well short of the two-thirds majority required to take the action. Bob Rice then cracked open the

Top: Robert Murphy talks to an unconvinced looking group of Pirates executives, including club president William Benswanger (*left*). *Below*: Rip Sewell, left, who led the opposition to the strike, leads the team onto the field. (*The Sporting News,* June 19, 1946)

clubhouse door, told Murphy and the others, "No strike," and closed it again. The Pirates belatedly took the field to the boos of the fans who well knew the reason for the delay, and then the Pirates jumped on the Giants pitchers and beat New York, 10–5. After the game Benswanger again came into the clubhouse and addressed the players, thanking them for their wise decision and suggesting that whatever differences existed between management and the players could easily enough be worked out through the formation of a players' committee that he and his assistants would be happy to meet with.

For his part, Murphy claimed he wasn't at all disappointed in the outcome and that he regarded it as only the first battle in a war. He said he was filing a grievance with the National Labor Relations Board, charging that Benswanger's clubhouse visits as well as the presence of Bob Rice both during the debate and the vote constituted unfair labor practice. But that already terrifically overburdened board shortly notified Murphy that it was dismissing his grievance. Undaunted, Murphy also petitioned the Pennsylvania Labor Relations Board on the same grounds. Here, at least, he got some satisfaction as the PLRB ruled that the Pirates players were entitled to hold an election—but not until the end of August. Murphy said he'd use the intervening weeks to map strategy with the Pirates Guild members and to step up his efforts to organize the two clubs in his hometown. The other owners who had watched all this, while thanking providence it was Benswanger and not themselves who had to face this problem, now sent him telegrams of congratulations. Even though the Guild had been stymied in Pittsburgh, all the owners saw the event as an ominous sign, and they began to lay plans for a hush-hush meeting during the upcoming All-Star Game where they would work at devising some strategy of their own to meet these clustering challenges.

$\mathcal{C}$oming at what was traditionally regarded as the season's halfway point, the All-Star Game provided the baseball world an opportunity to take stock of its season and to look ahead to the World Series. And despite the Mexican League, the American Baseball Guild, and the player unrest these phenomena symbolized, baseball had reason to congratulate itself, for it had made a remarkable resurgence. Riding a mounting wave of relief at the war's successful conclusion and a concomitant desire to turn away from death and toward the pleasures of the sun, baseball in 1946 had already achieved an unprecedented popularity, whether measured in the number of players involved, leagues in operation, or in attendance figures. During the off-season of 1945–46 the want-ad spaces of the *Sporting News* had been filled with notices placed by ballplayers looking for teams, and with the resurgence of the minors and the renovation of farm systems by the big league clubs more players than ever before were playing professional baseball. There were more teams than ever before, too, and from the majors to Class D, attendance was booming with several leagues already approaching all-time figures. Even tiny towns in the lowest reaches of Organized Baseball were benefiting from this postwar enthusiasm. Newnan, Georgia, a town of 8,000 in the Georgia-Alabama league, was a spectacular example. Playing in a park that seated four thousand, the Newnan Brownies were regularly filling the place to the exits, had smashed all previous attendance marks, and even organized motorcades to accompany the team on their road trips to towns like Valley, Carrollton, and La Grange. When a Brownies player distinguished himself on the field the hat was passed through the stands, and the collections were substantial. And Newnan wasn't even leading the league. Neither were the Chattanooga Lookouts in the Southern Associa-

Want-ads in *The Sporting News,* March 21, 1946.

tion, but such was the fan hunger to follow them that the team began broadcasting their road games. In the Pacific Coast League attendance records were falling everywhere with Oakland, Los Angeles, and San Francisco leading the way. San Francisco, with a beautifully refurbished park seating 18,600, was on a pace that would bring in nearly 700,000 to Seals Stadium, breaking the all-time minor league attendance figure.

Along with the crowds came the same rowdiness that had been so conspicuous a feature of the first weeks of the big league season. Everywhere
in the minors observers commented on the unruly, occasionally violent
behavior of the fans and the players as well, on the vicious baiting of
umpires and opposing players, on the showers of beer bottles, debris, and
firecrackers that greeted unpopular decisions. Assaults on umpires were
especially common in the lower minors where some leagues were finding
it difficult to keep their umpires because these officials were so intimidated by the threatening atmosphere in the parks. One umpire in a Border
League game literally took matters into his own hands when he held up
play, went to his car, and returned to the field with a wrench for protec-
tion. Often enough players and management joined in the umpire-baiting,
and when players were fined by league officials for on-field brawls or for
tangling with umpires, collections were taken up in the stands to pay the
fines. One club president was suspended for two years for slapping an
umpire, after which five of the league's umpires resigned in disgust.

★   ★   ★

*O*f those players who'd starred during the war years and of the rookies
who had shone so brightly in this year's spring training there was almost
no evidence on the All-Star squads. Last season's game had been canceled because of transportation restrictions, and many said it was just as
well since the level of play was so clearly down. Had there been a game,
Johnny Dickshot, Chuck Workman, Red Barrett, Ken Burkhart, Roger
Wolff, Dave Ferriss, Mickey Haefner, and the Tigers pitching tandem of
Newhouser and Trout would surely have been present. This year, only
Newhouser and Ferriss were All-Stars. The only rookies to make the
teams were Reds' Ewell Blackwell and Phillies outfielder Del Ennis, and
neither had been a spring training standout since both were then still in
the service. Gil Coan was struggling badly for the Senators and looked
overmatched against big league pitchers. Bob Dillinger was playing well
enough for the Browns, but Luke Sewell still wouldn't start him regularly.
Frankie Frisch had slugger Kiner hitting cleanup, but Kiner had virtually
no offensive support around him in the Pittsburgh lineup; and the
league's veteran pitchers had already seen enough of his tremendous
power to prefer the risk of walking him to giving him anything good to
hit. As a result, Kiner was drawing a fair number of walks, but, green and
aware that he was his team's sole source of power, he also was striking out

With the Ware Shoals Riegels, a semi-pro textile mill team, lefthander Lou Brissie begins his long comeback from wounds suffered in the Italian campaign. (Courtesy of Lou Brissie)

a lot, especially on outside breaking balls. Down in the International League, the spring's other heralded rookie was proving to even the most benighted bigots that he was a rare talent. Jackie Robinson was at or near the top of the league's batters in average, runs, hits, and stolen bases and was fielding with a grace that bordered on brilliance. Wherever the Royals played, big crowds turned out, though the team as a whole was also outstanding, and some meanly said Robinson wasn't their main attraction. In some places, notably Baltimore, the big crowds came out to jeer him and even threaten him. Montreal was a far more restful, tolerant environment for Robinson and his wife, but there was no doubt that he played everywhere under a tremendous, relentless pressure that had already gotten to his teammate John Wright. Wright cracked under it and was demoted, replaced by another graduate of the Negro leagues, Roy Partlow, a superior if undisciplined talent for whom this revolution had come at least ten years too late.

Even farther down than the lowest of the minors, down where the factory hands played textile ball and dreamed of making the leap like Gil Coan all the way to the majors, Lou Brissie took his braced and mostly immobile leg out to the mound again and tried to pitch. It was a disaster. "I don't know how many pitches I threw," he said of that first appearance, "but it couldn't have been too many. Before I could turn around they had something like five or six two-base hits and two or three home runs: I was trying to drive off the leg, and I couldn't. It just wasn't there." Brissie left the game and the park and went off by himself to shed some tears of pain and fear that for him the dream of making that big leap to the majors might well be over, left behind in the mud and shell craters of the Italian campaign.

★   ★   ★

*T*his year's All-Star Game would be played at Fenway Park, which was fitting since the Red Sox dominated the All-Star selections just as they'd dominated the league, placing eight men on the squad: pitchers Ferriss and Harris; infielders York, Doerr, and Pesky; Williams and DiMaggio in the outfield; and catcher Hal Wagner. Many thought Tex Hughson should have been named to the squad as well. Thus, the Red Sox resembled an all-star squad by themselves and so ruled the league that, barring some cataclysmic collapse, the outcome of the race was no longer in doubt. The only question that remained to be answered was just how good this team was: was it to be ranked with the great teams of the past like the '27 Yankees or Connie Mack's A's of 1931? Or were the Sox instead a good team having a great year when the Yankees and the Tigers weren't? However fans and writers answered this, there was no question that from the top of its lineup to its bullpen this was a strong squad.

As the teams broke for the All-Star Game the Red Sox record stood at 50-20, a .714 pace that exactly matched what the Yankees had maintained over the course of the 1927 season. Their four regular starters—Ferriss, Hughson, Harris, and Dobson—had a combined record of 38-13, and in Earl Johnson and Bob Klinger they had a better than average bullpen. As was traditional with them, they had a strong offense, with Williams leading the way and getting support all around him in the lineup from Pesky, DiMaggio, Doerr, and York, all of whom were hitting .300 or better except York. Williams and Doerr were tied for the league lead in hits, and Pesky was only two behind. The Sox weren't a great defensive club, and with the exceptions of DiMaggio and Doerr they had no standouts at any position. The catchers, Wagner and Roy Partee, were both better than average. Pesky was an average shortstop; his range and his arm weren't first-rate, but he was quick and got to the ball well. Cronin had plugged a hole at third with the acquisition of Pinky Higgins, who'd become expendable in Detroit after the arrival of Kell. Williams had his well-publicized lapses in left, and of York's defense it was sometimes said that he was "part Cherokee and part first baseman." In right field Cronin was shuffling Leon Culberson, Rip Russell, Catfish Metkovich, and Tom McBride. Later the Sox would add still another man there when the veteran Wally Moses moved over from the White Sox. This wasn't a team that was going to win many games for you with their gloves, said Dave Ferriss, but they were steady, and this year they were playing heads-up baseball. Put another way, this Red Sox team wasn't going to lose games with their gloves that their pitchers ought to have won.

Part of that heads-up play, the Sox felt, came from the presence of York, despite his occasional defensive lapses. Part of it came from the confidence they developed in their starters, the feeling they had when they took the field behind any of the four that the man on the mound was going to keep the team in the game and give the hitters a chance to win it. This was a feeling Red Sox position players hadn't enjoyed in the past, but now they felt free to play the whole game of baseball—batting, fielding, and baserunning. For the first time almost within living memory Red Sox base runners took intelligent gambles, forcing the opposition into mistakes, creating runs without extra base hits. Doerr, one of the baserunning gamblers, said the Sox never ran the bases better than they did this year. Several times, he pointed out, when the Sox had runners at first and second with none out, the lead runner scored while the opposition was completing a double play, rather than complacently stopping at third. Pesky and DiMaggio were the only regulars with true speed, but by being so much in the game the Sox found they could get along without it.

The intangible factor in the team's success was its spirit, which had been sky-high since the first day of spring training down in Sarasota. It was a hard thing to analyze, the players said, but they had no doubt that for whatever reasons a spark had been struck when they'd come together in Florida, and now it was a fire fueled by success. "I can't explain it," Broadway Charlie Wagner said. "It was like when you've been away from each other for fifty years since high school. There was such enthusiasm from Doerr and Williams! That was when it started, and it just continued right through the season." Doerr said the team had more spirit than any he could remember, and they had more fun, too. "There were a lot of funny guys on that team," he said, a lot of clowning around on the bench with "guys putting baseballs in the shoulders of their uniforms, tossing a loaded sponge around, making moustaches out of horsehair upholstery stuffing." Of course, he added, "when you're eight, nine, ten games out in front you can do those kinds of things."

Early in the season Dom DiMaggio predicted it would take 105 wins to clinch the pennant, and after each Red Sox victory he'd announce in the clubhouse how many they had left to win. By the All-Star break the Red Sox were nearly halfway home by his calculations, but most people thought they were a good deal farther along than that.

★ ★ ★

The Yankees hadn't given up; they had too much pride for that. But the outlook for them at the break was bleak enough: they were seven and one-half games back. "We were playing almost .600 ball, and we still couldn't gain any ground on the Red Sox," Tommy Henrich said. "When you play that well and don't close the gap it kind of breaks your heart."

One who had apparently conceded was their owner, Larry MacPhail. MacPhail said early in the season he didn't like the way the team was playing. His attitude and several offhand remarks he made to writers indicated that he thought with all the talent he'd provided his manager, Joe McCarthy ought to be getting more out of the team. He and McCarthy were temperamentally incompatible under the best of circumstances, and these weren't, with the Red Sox threatening to run away from the rest of

With the Red Sox threatening to turn the race into a rout, the Yankees's Larry MacPhail panicked and fired Joe McCarthy who had managed the team since 1931. Here his successor, the great catcher Bill Dickey, meets with the press in Boston, May 24. (*The Sporting News,* June 5, 1946)

the league. Near the end of May MacPhail, angry at what he evidently considered a lost season, forced McCarthy to resign.

The precipitating incident occurred on the Yankees flight from Cleveland to Detroit, May 21. After beating the Indians in the first two of the four-game series, the Yankees dropped the last two, and now McCarthy, his stomach in revolt and his nerves frayed, got into a verbal fracas with pitcher Joe Page. Normally, McCarthy handled what disciplinary problems there were in private, yet now he gave Page a very public tongue-lashing for womanizing and late-night carousing, two activities McCarthy detested. Amazingly, Page answered his manager back, and word of the incident was quickly relayed to MacPhail in New York. Evidently, it was the excuse he'd been looking for, a further confirmation that McCarthy wasn't in control of this team, and after the Yankees had swept two from the Tigers and gone on to Boston MacPhail announced McCarthy's resignation and his replacement by Bill Dickey. Then

MacPhail watched his team lose to the Red Sox as Ferriss chalked up his seventh straight win.

The managerial change was largely cosmetic, as MacPhail must have known it would be. Under Dickey the team played only a little better than it had under McCarthy, though they did take two games from the Red Sox at the Stadium just before the break. In the first of these Spud Chandler gave a classic illustration of his obdurate refusal to give batters anything good to hit. Pitching against Harris before a crowd of better than sixty-eight thousand, Chandler walked a whopping nine batters and threw a wild pitch. But he also struck out nine and carried a no-hitter into the eighth inning, finishing with a two-hit, 2–1 victory. It was a bit trying, standing out there in the field behind him and watching him nibble at the plate all night, said his right fielder, Tommy Henrich, but you had to admire the results.

Chandler was named to the All-Star team, but no other Yankees pitcher was having an outstanding season, and only Charlie Keller was having one at bat. Joe DiMaggio was on the All-Star squad, too, an almost obligatory selection, but he wouldn't be going to Boston for the game: the Yankee Clipper was sidelined with a partial cartilage tear in the gimpy knee that had bothered him since his minor league days. Dickey planned to use Johnny Lindell in center field after the break, but if DiMaggio was to miss a substantial amount of playing time, then the team's real concern would not be whether they could catch Boston but whether they could beat out the Tigers for second place.

The Tigers situation was in many ways like that of the Yankees: they were playing well enough but couldn't pick up any ground on Boston. Both Greenberg and Wakefield had gotten off to slow starts, and Wakefield remained cold. Of late, Greenberg had begun to hit for distance and drive in clusters of runs, but he wasn't getting much help except from Roy Cullenbine. Prewar sensation Pat Mullin remained in a slump and was having shoulder problems. On the mound, Virgil Trucks and Dizzy Trout had pitched well at times but had been inconsistent during the first half. Newhouser, though, had been magnificent.

Early on he'd erased all doubts as to what those wartime records had really meant: here was a great pitcher at the peak of his form. Batters who'd faced him before the war and remembered his lack of control now saw him getting his first pitch over for a strike; instead of hitting ahead in the count, they now found themselves hitting 0–1, 1–2, or 0–2.

Feller pitching to Joe DiMaggio in Yankee Stadium, in his April 30 no-hitter. (Courtesy of Bob Feller)

Those same hitters who recalled Newhouser's fine fastball now learned—too late, often—that he'd mastered a baffling change-of-pace that he threw with the very same motion. "He drove a lot of guys on our ball club crazy with that," Red Sox catcher Roy Partee said. "You'd be looking fastball, and he'd take about eight inches off with that changeup, and you're waiting and waiting: *geez!* where the hell is it?" Earlier in the year Newhouser had lamented that 1944 had probably been his best chance to win 30 games when he'd just missed, winning 29. But this year, he said, with the Tigers' pitching staff back at full strength he couldn't expect to pitch as many innings or to get some relief appearances where he might pick up a few "cheap" wins. But at the break Newhouser's record was 16–3, and he stood a solid chance to win his 30.

So did Feller. On a bad ball club Feller had won 15 by All-Star time, six of them shutouts. The Indians had the worst hitting in the league, and with a little more support in the right spots Feller's record would have been even more impressive. But perhaps more exciting than his chances of winning 30 was the possibility he might break Rube Waddell's single-season strikeout mark, currently figured at 343. The mark had stood since 1904, despite the efforts of fireballers like Walter Johnson, Dazzy Vance, Dizzy Dean, and Lefty Grove. At the break Feller had fanned 190 in 180 innings, and Feller's consistency had fans and writers thinking about Waddell's record: in every one of his starts he was getting seven, eight, or nine strikeouts, and there were those games where he simply overpowered the batters and rang up whiffs in the double figures.

A recent off-field development looked as if it might be of some additional help to Feller in his quest for the record. Bill Veeck had finally succeeded in buying into a big league club when he headed a syndicate that bought the Indians. A combat veteran who'd been badly wounded in the South Pacific, Veeck was a showman who believed fans came out to the park for spectacle as well as sport. In his prewar days when he'd operated the minor league Milwaukee Brewers Veeck had arranged plenty of spectacles—various special "nights," giveaways, giant birthday cakes set up at home plate and out of which popped newly acquired players—and his clubs had been successful on the field as well as at the box office. By and large baseball owners were a conservative and stuffy lot, and earlier they'd thwarted the brash and breezy Veeck when he'd tried to buy the Phillies. Now he was in the door of their exclusive fraternity, and soon enough they would deplore his Barnum-style promotional efforts. But as Veeck took stock of what he had on the Indians as gate attractions, he saw only Bullet Bob Feller and his heroic quest for the ancient record. Whatever he could do to throw the spotlight on this, he would.

★   ★   ★

In the National League no team had been able to establish a dominance like that of the Red Sox over their American League opponents, but the Dodgers had a five-game lead over the Cardinals, and a few days before the break it had been as much as seven as Durocher deftly shuffled his squad like the playing cards of which he was so fond. The All-Star Game manager, Charlie Grimm of the defending champion Cubs, picked four Dodgers for the team: Higbe, Reese, Reiser, and Dixie Walker.*

After his rocky start Higbe had settled in to provide that staff anchor Durocher so needed. Here was a genuine character who recognized few limits in life and transgressed even those. Boisterous, hard-drinking, and a womanizer of prodigious proportions, Higbe was so profane some teammates referred to him as "Kirby Fucking Higbe" because of his incessant use of that word. Infielder Spider Jorgensen said that when Higbe used to get to his hotel room on the road, he'd call room service with an order that must have shriveled many an ear. "This is Kirby Fucking Higbe," he'd say, "and I'm in room two fucking fourteen, and send me up a tube of tooth fucking paste, one of those bristle fucking tooth fucking brushes, and a carton of Lucky fucking Strikes." Howie Schultz, the tall and pious first baseman who took his turn as the pitcher's road roommate, said when Higbe got to the room he routinely ordered two BLT sandwiches and two shots of Southern Comfort whiskey. Higbe was broke most of the time because of his gambling losses, Schultz said, and had to borrow money from him and other teammates.

Out on the mound Higbe had the kind of competitiveness Durocher liked in his players: he wanted the ball and was convinced that if he got it, he'd win. Nature had blessed him with an outstanding arm, but Higbe's head wasn't quite equal to his physical talent, even in this year when he'd succeeded in making an important adjustment and was relying more and more on his hard knuckleball. "Jeeminy!" exclaimed Billy Herman, "what an arm he had! He should have won twenty every year, but he lost a lot of games he ought to have won because of careless mistakes." Higbe was in fact still mostly a thrower rather than a pitcher like Spud Chandler or Harry Brecheen of the Cardinals who had a plan for every game, every batter. Higbe went out there to win, his teammates said, and gave it everything he had. But if he lost, he lost, and he lost little sleep over it.

---

* The squad Grimm picked was an unintended tribute to Branch Rickey's ability to recognize talent and develop it. He had, of course, built both the St. Louis and Brooklyn farm systems as well as the big league teams, and in addition to the four Dodgers, Grimm chose six Cardinals for the team. There were five ex-Cardinals, too: the Cooper brothers, Johnny Mize, outfielder-first baseman Johnny Hopp, and infielder Emil Verban. Walker Cooper, Hopp, and Verban had all been Cardinals when the year began, and Breadon had dealt them all away for cash.

Willard Mullin's tribute to the great Dodgers veteran Dixie Walker who led his team's charge to the top through the middle of the pennant race. Written off many times in his career, Walker had a knack of bouncing back. In the last days of the race, though, he tired badly. (Courtesy of Shirley Mullin Rhodes and *The Sporting News,* July 17, 1946)

Durocher's offensive anchor had turned out to be Walker, not Reiser. The latter was hitting above .300 and leading the league in stolen bases, but he wasn't driving the ball deep into the outfield gaps any more, and he was out of the lineup so frequently with injuries that he couldn't establish a hitting rhythm. In truth, what the fans were seeing of Pistol Pete was the quick fading of a great talent, not its efflorescence. Walker, on the other hand, was in the Indian summer of a long career that had seen its full share of injuries and mishaps.

He'd been written off by the Yankees, White Sox, and Tigers before the Dodgers took a chance on him. He would turn thirty-six before this season was over and looked it, his long Scots-Irish face weathered and creased from thousands of hours of squinting into the sun on hundreds of ballfields. He was slow on the base paths, and in the outfield, said one of his teammates, he went after balls like a man stepping on egg cartons. But Walker could hit; he was at his best in clutch situations, and he was an inspirational force in the dugout and clubhouse. Brooklyn, a community that loved figures elsewhere disparaged as "losers," took the well-traveled Dixie to its heart. The "People's Cherce," they called him in the local dialect, and Walker responded, both on the field and off: he made himself the People's Cherce, Eddie Stevens said, by his unfailing willingness to attend borough events from bar mitzvahs to bingo games. He even sang with the ragtag ballpark band, the Dodger Symphony. Over the winter Rickey had scoffed at the fact that in 1945 Walker had led the league in runs batted in, and even Durocher, who certainly knew better, had said all during spring training that he wasn't counting on Walker at his age to be a big part of the Brooklyn attack. In Rickey's case the claim was doubtless another of his efforts to deflate a player's sense of his worth to the team. But Durocher, who preferred veteran players and had seen what Walker could do under pressure, was merely mouthing the Rickey line while waiting to see what he could expect from the youngsters Whitman, Hermanski, and Furillo. They were certainly contributing, particularly Whitman and Furillo, but they weren't Dixie Walker, and early on Durocher abandoned any pretense of platooning Walker and was sending the old man out there every day.

And Dixie was doing it, every day. Through his years of bouncing around the leagues he'd learned what he could and couldn't do at the plate and had changed from a hitter who tried to pull pitches to right and over the wall to one who picked his spots to pull but more often went with the pitch. He'd made himself into an excellent contact hitter, almost never striking out: in 1945 when he'd driven home 124 runs he'd struck out only sixteen times. Many of his hits flared into the off-field, but when a pitcher tried to overpower him inside, Walker was quick enough with the bat to make him regret it.

Durocher had also come up with an effective replacement for Billy Herman in Eddie Stanky. Durocher had wanted to go with the old star at second, but Herman had returned from the service "fifteen pounds late and thirty-eight years old," as he himself put it, and after watching him in spring training, Durocher reluctantly concluded that the war had finished Herman as a first-string player. He could still handle the bat and execute the hit-and-run with the best—one of his manager's favorite plays—but on the bases Herman was now a liability, and he simply didn't have the range any longer to play a topflight second base. As his longtime teammate Augie Galan dryly put it, "You have to be able to do more than just wave at those balls."

But since Herman could still hit, could play a little at second and third and even at first, and because he knew how to win, Durocher was inclined to keep him as a valuable reserve. Rickey wasn't. Because he'd been a star over so many years Herman had worked his salary up to $20,000, far too much for the utility player he now would be with Brooklyn. Rickey would in all probability have traded or sold him at some point, but Herman himself greased the skids for an earlier departure by being associated with a bit of hotel room vandalism near the end of spring training. Herman's room was extensively damaged in an after-hours party (there were shards of glass deeply embedded in the ceiling plaster, arguing for major league arms at work), and Dodgers traveling secretary Harold Parrott claimed Herman had been the instigator, motivated by his resentment of Rickey's behavior in salary negotiations. Herman wanted to wreck the room, Parrott said, and stick Rickey with the bill. The charge was not altogether implausible, given the fact that it was Herman's room and that he had a well-earned reputation as a "night crawler" who had raised his share of hell through the years. But Herman denied he'd even been there, claiming he'd switched rooms to accommodate a friend. Whatever the case, the incident made Rickey that much more determined that Herman had to go, and at the June trading deadline Herman went—to the Braves, where he joined Mort Cooper and Johnny Hopp who'd been exiled there for the same basic reason: money. In return Rickey got catcher Stew Hofferth, who was supposed to plug the hole Rickey claimed wasn't there with the departure of Mickey Owen.

Herman's departure made Durocher's squad that much thinner than it might have been, but it cleared the way for Eddie Stanky who had been a wartime fill-in many doubted had the talent to play regularly once the

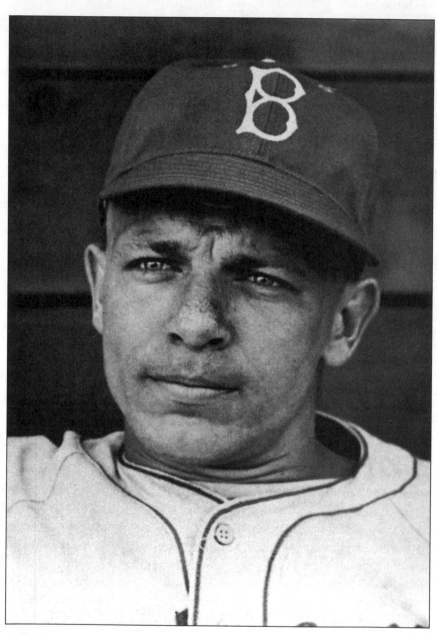

Eddie Stanky, Leo Durocher's kind of guy. (National Baseball Library and Archive, Cooperstown, N.Y.)

boys came back. Small in stature and lacking in real speed and fielding range, Stanky's arm was no more than adequate, even for second base. Both Rickey and Durocher liked to disparage his physical skills, but they always ended up praising his contributions as a player. Stanky, they said, couldn't run, throw, or hit very well but was a valuable player nevertheless. This was a sort of con job, because in fact, while Stanky certainly wasn't as physically gifted as this year's All-Star second baseman, Schoendienst, he was hardly a second-rate talent, either. Alvin Dark, who would spend the last part of this season with the Braves and later play shortstop alongside Stanky on two pennant winners, knew the truth about Stanky's talents. A shrewd, hard-headed judge of players and later a successful manager, Dark said Stanky had "great hands, soft hands." You threw the ball to him, he said, he always caught it. You hit it to him, he gloved it. And as the years went on, Dark pointed out, Stanky made himself into a pretty good hitter.

He wasn't that yet. What he could do at bat, however, was get on base, a leadoff man's main job. Assessing his offensive talents, he'd concluded he wasn't going to get aboard enough through pure hitting and so would have to draw a large number of walks. He became a master at it and in 1945 had drawn a record 148 walks that helped translate into a league-leading 128 runs scored. This season he was on a pace to surpass both totals.

The strike zone in 1946 was generally considered to extend from the uniform's letters to the batter's knees, and Stanky did everything he could to shrink it. He would roll his pants practically above the knee, Augie Galan said, and assume an exaggerated crouch with his shoulders hunched, his head pulled down between them, and his arms hanging out over the plate. In that stance, Galan estimated, Stanky shaved almost a foot from his strike zone. Unless circumstances called for it or the pitcher delivered a fat, easily hittable pitch, Stanky didn't start swinging until he had two strikes on him. Then, still looking for a walk, he would foul off strike after strike until the pitcher lost patience or control and threw him a fourth ball, whereupon Stanky would flip his bat toward the catcher's ankles—a nasty habit, they said—and take his base. A baseball axiom applied to base stealers who couldn't hit much was that "you can't steal first base." Stanky's act came as close to succeeding at that as you could get.

Off the field Stanky was quiet, polite, and well spoken, "one of the class men of baseball," as Dark put it. A clean-living, church-going gentleman himself, Dark appreciated these qualities in his double-play partner. "You could go to church with him," he said, "or family meetings, golf, just about anything. He was wonderful." His dislike of profanity made him the natural target of the often rough-spoken men he associated with in the game, and Billy Herman loved to taunt him with particularly profane outbursts. "He'd try to get away when I'd talk like that around him," Herman laughed. "He was just like a priest." Once he put his spikes on, however, and stepped on the field of play Stanky underwent a transformation of almost Hyde-like proportions, becoming as Dark said, "just an altogether different person": relentlessly competitive, confrontational, angry. No colder pair of eyes ever appraised an opponent, probing for his weakness, than Eddie Stanky's. The nicknames he acquired through the years attested in a kind of shorthand to the players' dislike of his on-field personality: Stinky, Muggsy, and the Brat.* But these traits were precisely why his manager loved him so. Durocher's most famous line, which he uttered this season in the midst of a lengthy tirade, drew on the playing personality of Stanky as a classic illustration of the difference between winners and nice guys.

It happened one day at the Polo Grounds when Dodgers broadcaster Red Barber was needling Durocher about some homers the Giants had hit off his pitchers the previous day. Durocher snarled that the hits were cheap pop flies that in an honestly configured ballpark would have been routine outs. "Why don't you admit they were real home runs?" Barber asked. "Why don't you be a nice guy for a change?" That set Durocher off, as Barber had known it would.

"A nice guy!" Durocher screamed. "A nice guy! I been around baseball for a long time . . . but I never saw a nice guy who was any good when you needed him." The nasty guys, he said, the tough guys, the guys who would "put you in a cement mixer if they felt like it," were the ones you could count on in a pinch. "Nice guys," Durocher said again, pointing over at the Giants dugout and Mel Ott. "Look over there. Do you know a nicer guy than Mel Ott? Or any of the other Giants? Why, they're the nicest guys in the world! And where are they? In last place!" Then Durocher pointed to Stanky, taking his cuts in the batting cage. "Look at that little [expletive deleted]," he said. "Think he's a nice guy? The hell

---

* Stanky's own teammates often disliked him. At Boston, the Braves star right-hander, Johnny Sain, ordered Stanky never to come near the mound when he was pitching.

he is! He'll knock you down to make a play if he has to. He can't hit, he can't throw, he can't do nothing. But what a ballplayer! I wouldn't give him for any second baseman in the league. Or any two second basemen."

Despite Durocher's high regard for him, Stanky wasn't the kind of player who got picked to start an All-Star game because inevitably other men with more obvious talents stood out. Charlie Grimm especially wasn't going to choose Stanky. He'd never liked him, and earlier this season Stanky had brawled with Len Merullo of the Cubs, emptying both dugouts and occasioning the presence of policemen on the field the next day. Grimm's second baseman was Schoendienst who joined Kurowski and Marion to make up three-quarters of the All-Star's infield. In addition, Grimm picked Musial and Slaughter for the outfield and left-hander Howie Pollet. His selections reflected league consensus that the Cardinals still had more individual stars than any other team. But the Cardinals had been badly hurt by the departure of Lanier, Martin, and Klein; the ensuing uncertainty surrounding the intentions of Musial, Slaughter, and Moore; and the inability of so many of their prewar players to come back and make significant contributions. June hadn't been an outstanding month for the team, certainly not the sort that won pennants, and July wasn't looking much better.

On the plus side, they had finally gotten Al Brazle and Joe Garagiola back from the service, and the addition of the young catcher was particularly welcome since that position was proving a real headache for Dyer. The manager had been counting on veteran Ken O'Dea to fill Walker Cooper's big shoes, but O'Dea's back was so bad he couldn't play regularly at that demanding position. That left untried rookie Del Rice and journeyman Clyde Kluttz to carry the load. But now Garagiola returned with all the glowing press clippings preceding him.

The young man himself wasn't at all sure what he could do at this level. After all, he had but 148 professional games under his belt when he joined the Cardinals in May, though he had played a lot of amateur ball and had been seasoned even further by playing for Kirby Higbe's Manila Dodgers. Still, those experiences were hardly the equivalent of a pressure-packed pennant race, and many years later Garagiola would say he should have been farmed out. Instead, because of the team's catching problem, he was ordered to report to the team in Philadelphia. When he arrived at the hotel the desk clerk assigned him to a room with Marty Marion. Ordinarily, Marion roomed with trainer Doc Weaver so that

Weaver could work on Marion's chronically aching back, but tonight Marion was alone. For the awed rookie, however, the very idea of awakening Mr. Shortstop was unthinkable, and so he paced the corridor outside the room, eventually sitting down on the floor with his luggage. When Marion came out for breakfast, there was Garagiola, asleep.

The incident illustrated Garagiola's—and the Cardinals's—problem: it was going to take some time for him to fit in and to gain the confidence of his veteran pitchers, all of whom were still regretting the absence of Walker Cooper. But Garagiola was only part of a larger problem, for the Cardinals as a team hadn't quite come together. The war had created as-yet-unresolved gaps and dislocations, added to by the Mexican business. But those who knew the Cardinals well were far from counting them out, because this was a hustling indomitable bunch that prided themselves on tough and selfless team play. They had come up together through the Cardinals system, thoroughly schooled in Cardinals baseball. The players not only knew each other through long association on the field, but they and their families socialized together off it. Long before a Pirates team of the late 1970s popularized the slogan "We are family," the Cardinals really were that, and this gave a cohesiveness to their play that was both impressive and effective. They encouraged and goaded each other, and held each other up to the highest standards.

The inspirational force and the standard bearer of the Cardinals tradition was Terry Moore. He wasn't having a good year, either in the field or at bat, but Moore was still a presence, and when he told the team just before the break that they could overhaul the Dodgers, the players listened. Moore in fact was the team's acknowledged "second manager." It was to him, not to Dyer, that the players came with their problems, and it was he who meted out discipline when anyone, from star to seldom-used sub, failed to play the Cardinals way. If you failed to get from first to third on a single, "you heard about it from Terry," Harry Walker said. If you didn't get a bunt down or move a runner up a base when the situation demanded that, Moore told you "you shouldn't be picking up your check if you can't do your job." And if you didn't make a real effort to take out the enemy middle infielder on a force play at second, Walker said, "you better not come back to that dugout, because he was gonna be on you. He'd come up and rap you on the back of your hand with those big, hard hands he had, and brother, that *hurt!*" In losing Walker Cooper to the Giants and Lanier to Mexico, St. Louis had lost two keepers of the Cardinals flame, and when he was interviewed at the All-Star Game, Dixie Walker pointed to these losses as crucial ones. But the Cardinals still had Terry Moore, they still had a lot of talent, and they still had time.

★ ★ ★

*T*he All-Star Game itself turned out to be Ted Williams's show: he hit two homers, two singles, drove home five runs, and scored four as the American League crushed the National, 12–0. No other player had so dominated this game since its inception, and the Kid's performance both capped his remarkable first half and provided a spectacular illustration of just why the Red Sox were headed for the pennant. Clearly, Williams was the greatest hitter now active, and he might just be what he aspired to be: the greatest who ever swung a bat.

When he'd reported to Sarasota in February he'd said it might take him as long as three months to get everything in synch after his long layoff—probably more honest guess than spring training hyperbole—and by May he had everything working smoothly. He was a compelling sight in the batter's box (except if you were looking at him from the mound), digging in with the toes of his left foot, pumping his elbows and flexing his fingers; then cocking his right knee inward in his stride, his bat whipping through the strike zone on a slightly upward arc that produced those soaring drives to right and right-center. His home field was hardly designed to accommodate his power, for although it was very short to right field at the foul pole, it quickly receded to 380 feet in straight-away right and then 420 in right-center. The hitting style Williams had perfected through thousands of hours of practice, thought, and observation called for him to pull everything and to swing for distance. In Fenway Park this meant he hit a lot of very long outs. "No telling how many I saw caught in front of the bullpen gate [in right-center]," said the longtime Fenway groundskeeper Mac McCarthy, "but of course he hit a lot of balls over it, too—way over." One time in '46, McCarthy remembered, Williams hit one so high over the bullpen, it sailed through a fan's straw hat and bounced off the floor, thirty-four rows up from the fence. "The guy was half-asleep when Ted connected," McCarthy went on, "and when the fans started yelling and he saw the ball heading toward him, he stuck out his hat, and the ball went right through. He said, 'Hey! I sat way up here to get away from all the excitement!'" Williams probably never hit a ball any harder.

He didn't go for a home run on every swing, of course, but his thinking was that his best chance of getting a hit was to swing hard at balls in the strike zone and pull them. Through the development and exercise of tremendous mental discipline he'd blocked out the zone where he could "get a good ball to hit" (his succinct summation of his theory of hitting), and he stuck to his regimen with a fidelity some thought fanatical and others said was sheer stubbornness. He would not deliberately hit to left field, nor could he bring himself to swing at a pitch he didn't think was in his zone, even when it was close enough for him to have hit it hard somewhere. When there were runners on base and he took a walk rather than swing at what he thought was a bad pitch some said this wasn't discipline or stubbornness, it was selfishness. And some who said this were his teammates. "Some of us used to get mad at him in that situation," said Roy Partee, "where possibly he might have hit some of those balls to the left and driven the base runners in. But you had to understand Ted: it was something he'd trained himself to do, and he was in a pattern he couldn't change." Partee once took advantage of Williams's plate discipline to win a bet. Williams liked the catcher to throw batting practice to him because Partee could throw hard and put the ball where Williams wanted it. One day Partee bet the Kid fifty cents he wouldn't hit a single pitch out of the batting cage in his next ten swings. Naturally, Williams took the bet, and then for ten consecutive pitches Partee threw Williams balls he wouldn't have swung at in game situations. Swinging at them now, Williams either fouled them off or missed them altogether. "He got so mad at me he wouldn't pay me," Partee said, then added that years later at a Red Sox reunion he'd reminded Williams of the bet, and Williams had laughed and handed over two quarters wrapped in a napkin on which he'd scrawled, "Debt Paid."

Generally, Partee said, "if Ted didn't swing, the umpires wouldn't call it a strike," and league pitchers routinely complained that Williams got four strikes. Virgil Trucks concurred. You might get a called strike on him, Trucks said, "and occasionally even strike two. But never strike three: he always got the benefit of the doubt." His eyesight was reputedly so keen that umpires trusted his reaction to a pitch rather than their own judgment of its location. Williams preferred to attribute his strike zone judgment to discipline plus intensity, rather than X-ray vision. He didn't want to be thought of as some kind of freak but instead as an athlete who'd taught himself a difficult skill. He did in fact have 20-10 vision, but it was as much his intensity of concentration as it was his eyesight that made his plate judgment so keen, he said, and Trucks agreed. "He could see a nit on a telephone pole five hundred yards away," Trucks claimed, "and he just *concentrated so much!*"*

In his first at-bat in the All-Star Game Williams took another walk, which was probably all right with National League starter Claude Passeau. (Back in 1941 with the National League but one out from victory, Williams had slugged one of Passeau's pitches for a three-run homer that brought the American Leaguers a dramatic victory.) Then, in the fourth inning Williams got going against Kirby Higbe by hitting a tremendous drive into the center field bleachers. As he came around second in his characteristic head-down jog, Williams shot a glance and a wink at Marty Marion and asked, "Don't you wish you could hit like that, kid?"

Subsequently Williams added singles off Higbe and Ewell Blackwell before coming to bat against Rip Sewell in the eighth. Prior to the game Williams and Bill Dickey had watched Sewell throwing his notorious "eephus ball," or blooper pitch, a lob that Sewell threw in a high arc that dropped it down into the strike zone where batters futilely lunged at it. Dickey's view was that the way to hit it was to take a couple of steps forward, sort of running up under it, and meet it in front of the plate. Williams asked Sewell if he dared throw the eephus in the All-Star Game, and Sewell replied, "I'm gonna throw it to you, Ted. So watch out." Now as Williams faced Sewell with the outcome of the game no longer an issue, the pitcher smiled at him, and Williams shook his head ever so slightly, as if to say, "Don't do it, Rip." But Sewell did it, and Williams, overswinging, fouled it straight back. When he stood in again, Sewell nodded and once more threw the eephus. This time Williams let it go, and umpire Larry Goetz called it a ball. Then Sewell came back with a conventional fastball, and Williams, unable to unload, took it for a strike. "Now," said Sewell, "I had him one ball, two strikes. I wound up and threw him another blooper. It was a good one. Dropping right down the chute for a strike. He took a couple of steps up on it—and he hit it out of there. And I mean he *hit* it."

---

* Stan Musial, Williams's only contemporary rival for all-around batting prowess, felt concentration at the plate was as important to his success as eyesight and reflexes, and that it was the loss of the ability to shut everything out but the pitcher and the ball that was the root cause of his own decline as a batter, not simply advancing age. "Instead of being able to lock in on the pitcher and shut everything else out," he said, "I'd find my mind kind of wandering. Then after I'd swung at a bad pitch, I'd be back on the bench, wondering, 'Why did I swing at that?' "

Game films subsequently showed Williams out of the batter's box when he caught up with the blooper. (Larry Goetz had seen this at the time but hadn't called it: "We're not really playing for blood," he said.) The ball sailed high over the Boston bullpen, a majestic drive, and Williams, grinning broadly, toured the bases. As he passed Marion he asked once more, "Don't you wish you could hit like that, kid?"

16

*W*hen Sam Breadon returned to St. Louis from the All-Star break he was not in a good mood. As a National Leaguer he'd been embarrassed by the 12–0 debacle of the game, and at the hush-hush meeting of the owners he'd been cold-shouldered by commissioner Chandler. Breadon had disobeyed Chandler's order that owners not have individual contact with Jorgé Pasquel by meeting with him in June in Mexico City. Breadon had gone there in secret but had been recognized by an American sportswriter who subsequently broke the story, and Chandler had publicly made clear his great displeasure with Breadon's behavior. The commissioner at first threatened a large fine and when Breadon appeared unrepentant even muttered about suspension. Eventually he settled for a severe reprimand.

The other owners, though, had been eager to hear Breadon's firsthand assessment of the Mexican situation. What he told them was that in his opinion the Pasquels were in baseball to stay, that they in fact had all the money behind them that they claimed, and that politically they were very well connected. Moreover, he'd found that Mexicans were much more avid baseball fans than he'd supposed; he'd attended a game in Mexico City and found the fans enthusiastic and knowledgeable. In short, Breadon's view was that the Mexican challenge was to be a more substantial and durable one than some had been led to believe.

In light of Breadon's sobering report, Robert Murphy's continuing activities, and a recent ruling in the Al Niemiec case, the owners spent their time in Boston talking about ways to make their ballplayers happier. Clearly, there was no escaping the fact that salaries would have to rise, a prospect that made an owner like Sam Breadon wince. Breadon told the others he was convinced the Pasquels meant to keep coming after American players with offers that beggared what the owners had thus far been willing to pay. The only question was, how high would the owners have to go to keep their biggest stars? And if they had to greatly boost these players' salaries, might they then have to accept the sacrifice of lesser players to Mexico in order to keep their payrolls within acceptable limits?

There was also the question of the owners' legal claims to any of the players, stars or benchwarmers. In the aftermath of the Mexicans' contention that the reserve clause amounted to a kind of peonage, it seemed likely that the Uniform Player's Contract would be challenged in court. That seemed even more likely after the Niemiec case, for in finding for the player in his suit against Seattle, Federal Judge Lloyd L. Black had excoriated the terms of the contract on the same grounds as had the Mexicans. Robert Murphy hadn't directly attacked the contract in his statement of the Guild's position, but the drift of developments since then suggested that at some point he might well make it part of his campaign.

Nothing was decided in Boston except that these matters needed study, and a subcommittee was formed for that purpose. The best answer to the Pasquels and Murphys, it was felt, was a happier ballplayer. But how could you make him happier without in the process surrendering anything vital to your own interests? You might be able to give him a few more dollars, but Larry MacPhail spoke for the majority of the owners when he said that the reserve clause was the game's foundation rock.

Back in St. Louis, Breadon was being given the needle by fans and the press for having in one way and another so squandered his team's talent that they were going to have a hard time catching the Dodgers. Looking at the depleted Cardinals pitching staff, fans wondered why Breadon hadn't been able to keep Max Lanier. And looking at Dick Sisler's failure to play up to expectations, the writers pointed out that Johnny Hopp over in Boston was leading the league in batting and was running the bases with the daring usually associated with the Cardinals. When Dyer shifted Musial to first base and benched Sisler after the All-Star Game the St. Louis *Post-Dispatch* ran a front-page photo in its sports section, showing the former Cardinals player sliding into third base.

When the Giants opened the Cardinals second half by walloping them 13–3 at Sportsman's Park, the loss pointed out the team's critical pitching problems as well as the fact that Dyer wasn't any closer to solving them. In that game Dyer had used the newly activated Johnny Grodzicki and injury-plagued Howie Krist in an effort to stop the Giants hitters; neither was effective. The next day the Cardinals snapped back to win a doubleheader from New York, but to do so Dyer had been forced to use Howie Pollet in relief in the second game after the ace southpaw had gone the distance in the opener. Was the manager panicking, fearing to lose any more ground to the Dodgers? Using your best pitcher that way with the stretch run yet to come was buying future trouble. In the last game of the Giants series still another of Breadon's moves came back to haunt the Cardinals as Walker Cooper got the Giants off quickly when he hit a three-run homer off Ted Wilks in the first inning. In a real sense this was a kind of two-fold haunting since Dyer was trying to fill Lanier's slot in the starting rotation with Wilks, who really was a reliever. It wasn't working: in 16 innings as a starter, Wilks had given up 11 runs (a 6.18 earned-run-average), whereas in his more natural relief role he'd given up but 14 runs in 43 innings (2.93). After Wilks failed again in this game Dyer went to Grodzicki in relief, and he, too, was ineffective, and in the New York third, trying to pivot on his game leg, he threw wildly to second, allowing another run to score.

After the Giants left, the Dodgers arrived for a four-game series generally recognized in St. Louis as crucial. All Brooklyn really needed, it was said, was a split; if they were to win the series or even sweep it, they could dash the Cardinals's hopes. St. Louis needed to close ground now on the Dodgers; if they could, they wouldn't have to watch the scoreboard later and depend on other clubs to beat Brooklyn in the stretch and help the Cardinals cause.

The setting for the showdown couldn't have been more advantageous for the Cardinals: on their home turf in the midst of a Mississippi Valley summer and the whole midwest excited about the clash with Leo the Lip's invaders. Visiting teams didn't relish coming into St. Louis, even when they were in the driver's seat. The weather was one thing. The Cardinals were accustomed to the heavy heat and the corn-belt humidity, but for visitors these conditions could be like playing against a squad with a tenth man on the field. John McGraw used to say that visitors had to play anywhere between 10 and 20 percent better than the Cardinals to beat them at home because of the weather, and the Cardinals players themselves occasionally would play up the local conditions: in the 1930s visiting players stepping out into Sportsman's Park, where the ground might still be steaming slightly from a morning's downpour, were sometimes greeted by the heartbreaking sight of pranksters Dizzy Dean and Pepper Martin huddled under a blanket in front of the home dugout, feigning a chill.

Sportsman's Park itself was another factor. The Cardinals never had the kind of rabid fans the Dodgers did in Ebbets Field, so there wasn't that kind of home-field advantage for them. But Sportsman's Park was a kind of advantage nonetheless because its playing surface was the worst in baseball, and the Cardinals were used to it, whereas visitors were always far less so. The problem stemmed from the fact that both the Cardinals and the Browns played there, and from the first day of the season until the last the field never got a rest. By June most of the infield grass had been worn away, with the area between home plate and the pitcher's mound bare, and the outfield had begun to look as if it had mange. Cardinals infielders and outfielders had a sort of joking competition as to which area was the more difficult to play on. The infielders referred to the park as the "Rockpile," in part because the infield surface became so hard after a summer thunderstorm and in part because of the many pebbles that somehow could never be groomed out of the skin area. Playing his home games there through the years, Marty Marion developed what amounted to a tic, constantly bending over at his position to pick up pebbles, then tossing them over his shoulder. He did it even when on the road. But Marion learned to play the crazy hops that so often came his way, staying with balls where lesser shortstops gave up or misplayed them. He had superb range and a strong, accurate arm that delivered the ball to his first baseman in a light, easily-handled fashion. Still, the "Rockpile" had its effect on Marion's fielding, and coming into this season he'd been averaging better than 27 errors a season.

Cardinals outfielders said the hops out there were even tougher to predict. Enos Slaughter called Sportsman's Park "Hogan's Brickyard," and said that most of the season the outfield grass survived only in clumps that caused all manner of uneven caroms. "That ball would come out to you ever' which way," he said. "Sometimes you'd get hit in the throat, sometimes in the leg, sometimes in the stomach. You'd try to get in front of it and stop it, but, boy! it was tough." Like Marion, Slaughter made his share of errors—and he rarely made any after the Cardinals traded him away. But he, Musial, and Terry Moore had developed techniques for handling the peculiarities of their home field that were a combination of defensiveness and daring, learning when they could charge a ball and anticipate its hop and when they had to simply try to block one to prevent its skipping past for extra bases. "You couldn't just charge that ball, glove it, and come up with it, expecting to nail a guy," Terry Moore said. "You had to field it with both hands and watch it all the way into your glove. I don't know how many times I came in on a ball, expecting it to go into my glove and found it bouncing into my bare hand. And I remember many a time the opposing center fielder would be coming past me as I'd be going out to my position, and he'd be mumbling something like, 'I wonder when they're gonna fix this field so you can field a ball on it?' "

★   ★   ★

*W*ith Red Barrett and Ken Burkhart completely ineffective, Wilks sent back to the bullpen, Lanier gone to Mexico, and Munger still in Germany, Dyer decided to go with Beazley and Murry Dickson in the Sunday doubleheader, July 14, then follow with Harry Brecheen and Pollet Monday and Tuesday. Durocher was countering with Higbe and Lombardi in the doubleheader and Hugh Casey and Joe Hatten in the single night games. Sunday morning was bright and warm, promising to be another scorcher in the nineties. The front pages of the morning papers were filled with reports of the upcoming Paris peace conference where the nations would gather to try to resolve the lingering questions of the war: reparations, standing armies, boundary disputes, and the repatriation of displaced persons. Outside the park at Dodier and Spring, scalpers were doing a good business as an overflow crowd streamed in from all over the midwest.

Dyer was, of course, taking a big gamble in sending Beazley out against Higbe in the opener, but then he had few options. Beazley had only recently rejoined the team after a spell on the sidelines resting his aching shoulder, but he'd looked a trifle better with more zip on his pitches since his return, and Dyer had decided to try to "steal" a win behind him. It didn't look like a good gamble as the Dodgers got good swings against him in the first and came up with a run. But then the Cardinals came in and quickly scored twice off Higbe with Slaughter singling in the second run. With Musial at second and Slaughter at first Dyer called for a double steal with Buster Adams at the plate, clearly hoping to turn this into a big inning that would take some of the pressure off Beazley. Dodgers catcher Bruce Edwards went to second with his throw, but the rookie rushed it, and it sailed high. With a right-handed batter at the plate, Stanky had the coverage at second, and as he leaped for Edwards's throw he left himself vulnerable to the onrushing Slaughter. It was an opportunity no one would miss in this bitter rivalry, least of all Country Slaughter for whom baseball was a species of combat and Stanky one of the more odious enemies. He crashed into the little second baseman and knocked him sprawling, but Stanky held on to the ball and prevented Musial from scoring. But even the tough Muggsy couldn't shrug off Slaughter's hit, and Stanky had to be taken from the game to the hospital for X rays. But two runs were all the Cardinals could get in the inning as Higbe wriggled out of the jam. In the third, however, when Slaughter drove in his second run with a single, it became obvious that this wasn't going to be Higbe's day, and Durocher yanked him and replaced him with Rube Melton who got out of the inning without further mishap. Beazley, though, was proving no puzzle for the Dodgers hitters: they scored a run in the fourth and tied it up with another in the fifth, and Beazley still hadn't retired anyone in that frame when Dyer came out to get him and brought in Wilks. Wilks went to his heavy sinker, got out of the jam without giving Brooklyn the lead, then settled in for a stretch of scoreless relief work.

But the Cardinals were having their troubles with Melton, too, and the score was still 3-3 with two out in the eighth when Musial singled, bringing Slaughter to bat. After a slow spring that had people muttering that Slaughter was an old man who'd left his best baseball in the service, Country had started to hit. He now had his batting average up over .300 for the first time this season, and, more important, he was driving in big runs, as he'd already done today. Though Dyer often had him hitting in the cleanup slot, Slaughter never thought of himself as a slugger. He took a flat, compact swing, aiming to hit the ball hard somewhere: if it went over the fence, fine, but he didn't swing for the seats. But now against a tiring Melton he hit a high, rising drive that cleared the tall screen in right, scoring Musial ahead of him. When Wilks set down the Dodgers in the ninth the Cardinals had a 5–3 win—and a big boost in morale.

Dickson went out in the second game against Lombardi, and as with Beazley it looked as if Dyer had guessed wrong in his choice of starters: the Dodgers scored in the first and had threats in both the second and third. But Dickson escaped both times and then began to settle down. On the deep and talented pitching staffs of the 1942 and '43 pennant winners, manager Billy Southworth had used Dickson in relief, though he'd been a starter in the minors. Then he'd gone away to war and heavy combat duty in Europe, and when he returned Dyer had him scheduled again to work primarily out of the bullpen. But events had forced the manager to send Dickson out as a regular starter, and the results so far had been encouraging.

In an important sense Dickson was a manager's dream: he had what the players called a "rubber arm" and could literally pitch every day. In fact, he once told roommate Harry Brecheen he thought he might be a more contented player if he could pitch every day, and later in this season he would volunteer to pitch a doubleheader. But in two other ways Dickson caused his manager to pace the dugout in exasperation. For one, Dickson was a tireless and compulsive experimenter on the mound. Garagiola nicknamed him "Tom Edison" and said he didn't have enough fingers to sign for all the pitches Dickson threw. He threw a slider, a curve, a knuckleball, a changeup, and a fastball, and he threw them all at different angles—straight overhand, three-quarters overhand, sidearm, and even with a slightly submarine release. "That guy could pitch a whole inning," said an admiring Brecheen, "and not throw all his pitches." The problem here was that there were times when Dickson lost sight of his main objective, getting batters out, and appeared to focus on inventing novel ways to pitch. Instead of pitching to a batter's known weakness, Dickson occasionally seemed to want to find some surprising way of retiring him. Then there was his peculiar theory of pitching. "Dyer just couldn't understand it," Garagiola said, "but Dickson always felt that he was a better pitcher if he got *behind* the batter. His thinking was, 'If I can get behind them, then they're looking for a particular pitch—and I'm not gonna give it to them.' " This theory and its practice was a source of anguish for Dyer, but, as Garagiola said, in this season when he'd come up short of starters Dyer had to grit his teeth and go along with it.

On this afternoon, Dickson kept his concentration and as the game progressed he got stronger and steadier. Lombardi was throwing well, too, though the Cardinals were picking up hits in every inning. But Lombardi was a gritty little man, and he got the outs he needed. Like a lot of second generation immigrant kids who became fascinated with baseball, Lombardi had parents who never really understood the game or how a healthy boy, raised with a strong work ethic, could devote his energies to a silly game played in flannel knickers. Neither parent ever saw their son pitch in the big leagues. Despite his lack of baseball background and diminutive stature (he was 5'6"), Lombardi was a fine all-around athlete and threw a surprisingly live fastball, which he mixed with a good curve, and a sinker. Durocher and Rickey liked him because he got the most from his talents with a bulldog's mentality on the mound.

One thing Lombardi couldn't do, however, no matter how hard he tried, was to get Stan Musial out. "He shoulda married me," Lombardi said of Musial with bitter asperity. "Couldn't get him out. I never could understand it. He hit way over .400 off me. Some of the other guys used to tell me not to worry about it, that he hit .400 off a lot of pitchers. He was just a great hitter, that's all, especially against me." Now in the St. Louis eighth Musial struck against him once again, lashing a triple off the screen in right, then scoring the tying run on Kurowski's fly ball. It stood that way until the twelfth, Dickson matching Lombardi pitch for pitch, and the big crowd tense and hoping for a Cardinals breakthrough. As Dickson went out for the Brooklyn twelfth he'd shut them out since the first inning, and he set them down again this inning.

Now it was Musial's turn again against Lombardi. This time he belted a pitch over the screen and into the seats, and the Cardinals had a doubleheader sweep on the two late homers by their big hitters. Thus when Durocher's boys trooped into the visitors' clubhouse they now had to think about a series split instead of a win or a sweep, and Dyer had his left-handed aces ready for the last two games. At least the Dodgers wouldn't have to face the other lefty, Lanier. But in fact Lanier was in town, and in the second game of the doubleheader a heckler leaned over the roof of the Cardinals dugout and hollered to Dyer that he'd just seen Max, and wouldn't Dyer just love to have him ready to face the Dodgers? Dyer worked up a wan smile over that, the best he could manage under the circumstances.

Lanier had come to St. Louis for the funeral of an old hunting buddy, and while he was there he confided to a few close friends that Vern Stephens had been right: conditions in Mexico were a long way from those the expensive imported ballplayers had been led to expect. Lanier's Vera Cruz team played its home games in Mexico City because it was simply too hot and muggy down in Vera Cruz during the summer months. When Vera Cruz was at "home" Lanier lived well at the Reforma Hotel, the best in Mexico City. The ballpark there was decent, too, and had grass on both the infield and outfield, something Lanier could appreciate after his years in Sportsman's Park. But road conditions were something else. In one park, Lanier recalled, "they had goats out there in the outfield, and they had to round 'em up before they could start the game." In another

Mexican League president Jorgé Pasquel being told to leave the field by umpire Amado Maestri after Pasquel had sought to intervene in a dispute. Such scenes as this soon convinced Max Lanier and Mickey Owen that they'd made a mistake in coming south of the border. (*The Sporting News*, June 19, 1946)

park a train track ran across the outfield and at a certain time in the after-noon play was suspended, the left and right field gates were opened, and a train rumbled through. Where locker room showers existed, they were one-man affairs, and players had to wait their turns. Hotels seemed prim-itive by the standards of the American players, and Lanier was particu-larly bothered by those without window screens: the bugs, he said, were awful and kept him awake half the night. But the most difficult part of the adjustment to Mexican life was the food, and by the time Lanier arrived for the funeral he had pretty much stopped eating in restaurants, except where there was simply no other choice. At the Reforma he'd taken to eat-ing canned tuna fish that he mixed with mayonnaise and onions. It was a bland, monotonous diet, but easier on him than the local fare he just couldn't digest. To him, even the Mexican beer tasted bad.

★   ★   ★

*M*onday night was Red Schoendienst Night as a delegation from his hometown of Germantown, Illinois, showed up to honor him and present him with a shotgun. The honored one responded quickly by leading off the Cardinals first with a double off Hugh Casey, an old Cardinals antag-onist and veteran of the prewar battles between the teams.* Like Dyer, Durocher was beginning to scratch around for starting pitchers, and play-ing one of the hunches he was famous for, he started his ace reliever for the first—and only—time this season. Even for the canniest of hunch players the odds are always against him, and this hunch proved wrong as the Cardinals quickly scored twice, drove Casey out, and went on to a lopsided 10-4 win. But even in so one-sided a Cardinals-Dodgers game something was likely to happen, as Terry Moore said, and in the third inning it did when third base umpire Al Barlick ruled that Reiser, playing left field, had trapped Slaughter's sinking line drive. In one sense, Bar-lick's call was academic since the Cardinals runner at third would have scored even if Reiser had been ruled to have caught the ball on the fly (spectators in the left field stands later said he had). But with the run scor-ing and still only one out Durocher could see the game slipping away, and he tore from the dugout screaming obscenities and for the next five min-

---

* Casey once threw at Marty Marion when Marion wasn't even in the batter's box. While Casey took his warm-up tosses, Marion moved near the catcher to see what he was throwing, and the Dodgers pitcher hurled one at him and told him to get away from the plate area.

utes followed Barlick around the third base area, thrusting his hands in the umpire's face and kicking dirt on him, Reiser alongside. Finally, Barlick had had enough and threw both men out of the game. Afterwards, when Barlick filed his report to the league office, Ford Frick notified Durocher that he was suspended for five days and fined $150.

No sooner had he heard this than Durocher packed his bags and took a plane to Brooklyn to confer with Rickey. What the two discussed specifically will never be known, though in general it was clear they talked about where the Dodgers might get some help, both in pitching and at first base where Durocher was increasingly unhappy with Schultz and Stevens: in the 10–4 loss he'd resorted to faded outfield slugger Joe Medwick at first, and Medwick had committed two costly errors. Later, some would speculate that Durocher had asked Rickey to let him have Robinson from Montreal to play first. If he did, Rickey would have turned him down flat. The Robinson experiment was too important to Rickey and he'd spent too much time carefully planning it to jeopardize it by bringing Robinson into so precarious a situation: a suddenly tight pennant race in which a rookie, the sole member of his race in the majors, would be asked to save a team while playing yet another unfamiliar position. This year's potential pennant wasn't worth that kind of risk.

On Tuesday night in Brooklyn Rickey and Durocher listened to Red Barber's account of the match-up between left-handers Pollet and Hatten with all the pressure now on the latter to keep his team from being swept. Hatten had thus far proved a disappointment, but tonight he looked more like the pitcher who'd starred in service ball. Going into the ninth he clung to a 4–2 lead, the Dodgers offense provided by the veteran Dixie Walker and Stanky's replacement, rookie Bob Ramazzotti. The Cardinals had their seventh-, eighth-, and ninth-place hitters due up, and it was looking very much as if they'd have to settle for three out of four in the series, especially when Hatten got ahead of Marion, 1–2. He'd been struggling all night with his control and had walked five, allowed a run to score on a wild pitch, and hit a batter. Now he hit Marion in the back, and there was a rustling in the packed stands and along the Cardinals' bench. Clyde Kluttz stood in and promptly whistled a single into left, Marion stopping at second. Dyer looked along his bench for a right-handed pinch-hitter for Pollet and stopped at Erv Dusak. When they were coming up together through the St. Louis system, Stan Musial said, Dusak had been more highly regarded than he had. He was big, fast, had an out-

Leo Durocher arguing with his customary vigor to umpire Al Barlick in the Cardinals game of July 15th. Durocher lost, the Dodgers lost, and Ford Frick suspended the Dodgers manager for five days. Durocher immediately left St. Louis to confer with Rickey, and some suggest he asked Rickey to let him have Jackie Robinson from Montreal. (*The Sporting News*, July 24, 1946)

standing arm, and he could hit for distance. But in this, his first full major league season the pitchers had discovered he couldn't consistently hit a curve, and by now Dusak was being fed a steady diet of them. Dyer flashed him the bunt sign, willing to trade the out for moving the runners into scoring position while at the same time minimizing the double-play potential. The Dodgers anticipated the strategy and brought their infield in, but Dusak missed the bunt attempt. Now Dyer switched signs and called for Dusak to swing away, hoping that with the infield still in Dusak might skip one past them. But again Dusak missed a big curve. Hatten threw wide on his next two pitches, then came in with one on the inner half of the plate, and Dusak got around on it with the fat part of the bat, sending it deep to left. Reiser broke back on the ball but quickly ran out

of room and could only look up as it disappeared into the crowd. What had a moment before appeared to be a 4–2 Brooklyn win was suddenly—and sickeningly, for the Dodgers—transformed into a 5–4 Cardinals victory and a series sweep that brought them within a half-game of a shaken Dodgers team. Afterward, in a noisy Cardinals clubhouse Dyer said he expected the two teams to go right down to the wire, just as they had in '41 and '42.

★   ★   ★

*T*he Dodgers continued to stumble in Cincinnati under acting manager Dressen who some felt had blundered in staying with Hatten in the disastrous ninth in St. Louis. But when they got back to their adoring faithful in Brooklyn and Durocher had served out his suspension they recovered their poise and began to win again while their archrivals went into a batting slump. From Dixie Walker to Dick Whitman, Durocher had instilled his combative spirit into the team, and they resolutely refused to acknowledge the evidently superior talent of St. Louis. Except for the punchless Braves, no team in the league had hit fewer home runs than the Dodgers, and they were in the midst of a power outage that would see them go an entire month without hitting one. And the Dodgers starters had the fewest complete games of any staff in the league; in one stretch in late July through early August Durocher used thirty-two pitchers in 13 games. Despite the fact that the Montreal Royals were burning up the International League, Rickey for some reason refused to bring anybody up from that squad. The only help he gave Durocher was to sign outfielder Joe Tepsic to a hefty bonus and place him on Durocher's roster, but this was a bizarre move that was no help and instead created considerable friction.

Tepsic was a swift, muscular man, a veteran of Guadalcanal and the Pacific theater and was best known to sports fans as a football player at Penn State, but the contract he signed with Rickey not only paid him a bonus but contained the unheard-of clause that prevented Tepsic from being sent to the minors without his consent. He had no professional baseball experience and was clearly a raw, unrefined talent, and Durocher refused to use him. So, Tepsic simply took up a roster slot and gathered splinters on the bench. Finally, Durocher, desperate for additional batting punch, asked Tepsic to consent to a demotion to Montreal, but he refused. Durocher wanted to replace him with Chet Ross of the Royals, who had put in parts of six seasons in the majors, but Tepsic told Durocher in a private meeting that he wouldn't go down until Durocher could prove to him that he couldn't play up here. "He started bullshittin' me to go down," Tepsic said, "and I said, 'A contract's a contract. I don't have to go, and I ain't going. *You* can go to hell. You don't want to play me, that's your business.' " Durocher said that it would be Tepsic who would get the blame in this situation, that he would look like the selfish one. Tepsic replied that he didn't care what it looked like, and in a subsequent clubhouse meeting he announced that he knew he was a better ballplayer than fifteen other men on the team. That hardly sat well with anyone, especially the veterans Walker, Cookie Lavagetto, and Reiser.*

It must have been particularly upsetting to Reiser who with swiftly eroding skills was playing his heart out for Durocher and the team. The longer the season went on, the less he was able to do. His shoulder was now so bad he could no longer throw overhand, and Durocher had moved him to left and was using the strong-armed rookie Furillo in Reiser's old spot. Reiser now played so wrapped in tape he could only chop at the ball at bat, and his offensive production declined alarmingly. Favoring the shoulder, he developed such a pronounced hitch in his swing that on several occasions he asked the plate umpire if the catcher had tipped his bat as he started forward with it. Durocher still had him hitting third in the lineup, partly because he hoped Reiser might get hot, and partly because he had no one else who was more of a threat there. The one thing Pistol Pete could still do when he was in the lineup was run. He could no longer hit the ball against the wall or over it, but he had been able to leg out three inside-the-park home runs, and he still led the league in stolen bases. Five of his steals had been of home, a dead-game competitor's way of producing some runs when other means had failed him.

---

* Shortly thereafter, when it was time for the pennant contenders to vote on individual shares of the potential prize money, the Dodgers showed their contempt for Tepsic by voting him only a twelfth of a share, less than they gave the departed Tommy Brown who hadn't played a game and less than they gave the bat boy. Recognizing a potential legal grievance, team officials subsequently convinced the players to vote Tepsic an eighth of a share.

In retrospect, the Tepsic signing might be seen as the first sign of the decline of Rickey as the most astute judge of talent of his time. In the years to come, still convinced of his fabled powers of assessment and intuition, Rickey would make a series of odd, costly mistakes with the Pirates, where he signed to huge bonuses All-America football player Vic Janowitz, high school pitcher Paul Pettit, and the identical twins double-play combination of Johnny and Eddie O'Brien. All were major busts, and so were the Pirates who finished dead last every year of Rickey's tenure but one.

But Reiser's style of play and what can only be called his bad luck continued to cut into his playing time. On August 1 with the Cardinals leading 1–0 in a game at Ebbets Field, Reiser gave his characteristic head-long chase to Kurowski's long drive to left-center and again collided with the wall. Kurowski ended up with a double, and Reiser ended up in the hospital with another concussion. Then, while convalescing at home, he suffered burns to his hand and arm while lighting the kitchen stove for his wife. In a burst of what might have been unconscious irony, he told reporters he'd been lucky to escape with only superficial injuries.

The Cardinals-Dodgers series that saw Reiser injured again and the Dodgers top the million mark in attendance also brought into the open the bad blood that had so long existed between the teams. Tempers flared as Dodgers pitchers persistently threw inside to Cardinals batters, hitting several and bringing matters to the boiling point. As always, the focus was Durocher.

He had long been baseball's leading advocate of the bean ball or "purpose pitch," a pitch deliberately thrown so close to a batter that he had to dive out of its path. The point of the tactic was twofold: to establish the pitcher's right to the inside part of the plate, thereby keeping the batter from crowding it and getting better plate coverage with his swing; and to intimidate him with the threat of being hit by a ball coming in at speeds upwards of 80 miles per hour. No batter who ever stepped into a batter's box was entirely without fear of being hit, not even the monumentally phlegmatic Johnny Mize, who never said anything when he was hit or spun into the dirt by a high, tight fastball, or Ted Williams who'd become such an icon that no pitcher dared throw at him. And all the players knew the dark legend of Ray Chapman, killed by a pitched ball in 1920 in baseball's only on-field fatality. Though illegal, the purpose pitch was a standard tactic, and players expected to be thrown at in certain situations. There was even a catcher's sign for it, said Joe Garagiola: if one finger pointing down meant fastball and two meant curve, the thumb held under the first two fingers, then flipped upwards meant just that—let's flip this guy.

The situations that called for it were following a home run and as retaliation when the opposing pitcher had hit one of your men. In the first instance, the purpose pitch was the angry pitcher's way of saying to the batter, "You'd better not try crowding the plate to hit another off me." In the second, a pitcher who was throwing at batters could expect to have the favor returned. Alvin Dark, who learned his baseball under Durocher, told a story that illustrated the practice. When he was managing the San Francisco Giants in the early 1960s Dark became exasperated as the opposing pitcher kept knocking his hitters into the dirt. Finally, he told his pitcher Billy O'Dell he'd buy him a new suit if O'Dell could hit his opposite number when he next came to bat. O'Dell did it. "Well," Dark said to him when he'd returned to the bench at the end of the half-inning, "I owe you a new suit, big man." "Forget the suit, Skip," O'Dell came back. "Just send up a pinch-hitter when it's my turn."

Since his first years as the Dodgers manager Durocher hadn't hesitated to instruct his pitchers to throw at enemy batters, and in any game against his team hitters could expect to hear his foghorn voice cutting through the noise of the crowd and the chatter of the players, *"Stick it in his ear!"* He thought it gave his pitchers an edge for batters to know they might well be knocked down: they might be a bit more nervous and shifty of foot up there, he thought, and his pitchers might then be able to work the outer portion of the plate more effectively. Under his leadership there had been some memorable "throwing contests" between the Dodgers and the Cardinals, including the near-tragic one in 1940 when the Cardinals' Bob Bowman beaned his former teammate Joe Medwick and blighted his career.* There were plenty of players still on both squads who had vivid memories of that incident, and now as matters threatened to get out of hand again, league president Ford Frick was notified of the situation and showed up at the final game of the series to see for himself what was going on. Subsequently, he issued a strongly worded memorandum to the league in which he ordered managers to put an end to the practice of throwing at batters and also deplored the kind of gutter language he'd heard from the players at Ebbets Field. Though ostensibly directed to the league as a whole, everybody knew the memorandum's real targets were Durocher and his Dodgers, and shortly Frick would admit as much, telling a reporter that it was the number of hit Cardinals batsmen that brought him out to the park. Nobody got hit with the league president at ringside, but evidently Frick didn't like what he saw—and heard. Of the on-field language, Frick observed that the composition of baseball

---

* The Cardinals players claimed this was an accident, though some said it was a consequence of Durocher and Dressen trying to call the Cardinals pitches and making a crucial mistake. Both men, particularly Dressen, prided themselves on being expert sign-stealers, and on this day they were whistling to the Dodgers hitters when they believed a curve was coming. They whistled "curve" to Medwick, but Bowman threw a fastball, and Medwick couldn't get out of the way.

crowds had dramatically changed since the prewar years when the great majority of the spectators were men. There were too many women and children now attending games, he said, to tolerate the kind of talk he heard at Ebbets Field.

Durocher didn't care about the language business: Frick wasn't going to put an end to the traditional profanity that went with ball games and ballplayers. But he screamed on the subject of purpose pitches. The league was in a conspiracy against his boys, he said: they were the only ones singled out for a practice that was widespread and that, in any case, was a time-honored and legitimate baseball tactic. Dyer was a crybaby for running to Frick with his complaints. As for himself, Durocher claimed he never went to anyone when pitchers threw at his boys because he understood that was how baseball was played and always had been. Besides, there were ways of taking care of such matters, and you didn't need league officials to interfere. Baseball was a tough game, he said, and harkened back to that mid-July series in St. Louis when Slaughter had, as he put it, "almost cut Stanky in half." Did he "yammer" about that? No, because he knew teams didn't get to the top by being nice guys. Why, in his own playing days, he went on, he went down in the dirt many a time and never thought anything of it.

Dyer claimed it wasn't he who'd gone to Frick, and Frick backed him up, but Dyer did go on record as saying Dodgers pitchers had been throwing at Cardinals batters all season. Durocher snarled back that, regardless of what was claimed now, he knew it had been Dyer who'd set the league president on the Dodgers, just as he knew that memorandum hadn't really been addressed to anybody else but himself and his players. But nobody was going to stop him and the Dodgers from going all-out to win, least of all the Cardinals. They weren't the team to beat, anyway, he said. It was the Cubs he was really worried about.

★   ★   ★

*O*n the night of August 13 Dave Ferriss became the first pitcher since the great Wes Ferrell in 1929–30 to win 20 games in his first two big league seasons as he beat Philadelphia, 7–5. It was his eighth straight win and had baseball people talking about Ferriss in the superlative terms usually reserved for the greats of the game. Maybe this young man was one of them. While he wasn't a dominating pitcher and there was nothing spectacular about him, all he did was win. If the game was close, he pitched tough; if his teammates were scoring bunches of runs, as they had tonight against the A's, then Ferriss relaxed a bit and let the opposing batters hit the ball.

But the big story that night was in Cleveland where more than 65,000 turned out at the brand new Municipal Stadium to see Bob Feller duel Dizzy Trout. Feller had been so spectacular lately that he seemed a good bet to pitch a no-hitter every time he went to the mound. And he was going to the mound often, not only as a starter but in relief roles as well. Lou Boudreau had talked with Bill Veeck and then with Feller, and since it was clear the Indians weren't going anywhere in this year's race, it was decided Feller might as well go after 30 wins and Waddell's strikeout record, which was now being variously figured at either 343 or 347. For Feller, there was an added incentive to go for the record: General Mills had offered him $5,000 if he broke it.

The way he was throwing and the frequency of his appearances made it look as if he had a shot. On July 28 he'd shut out the Senators on four hits and fanned ten. Three days later Bobby Doerr's second-inning single was the only hit the mighty Red Sox had managed as Feller won his twentieth, and he added nine strikeouts. On August 4 his offense was shut out, and he lost to the Yankees. Four days later he pitched yet another one-hitter, this one against the White Sox. The only Chicago hit in this gem was a fluke single by Feller's former batterymate Frankie Hayes whose homer had won the game when Feller no-hit the Yankees back in April. Earlier in his seventh-inning at-bat, Hayes had lifted a foul fly that Indians right fielder George Case just missed getting to after a long run. Then Hayes hit a pop fly toward shallow left that Boudreau called for. Normally, a ball in such a location would have been the left fielder's, the assumption being that a fielder coming toward the ball has a better view of it than one going backward, but Boudreau's left fielder Pat Seerey was an indifferent defensive player and slow afoot, so Boudreau called for it. It was hit farther than he thought, however, and by the time he realized it would have to be Seerey's play, it was too late, and the ball fell safely. Two days later Feller came back in relief, pitching three hitless innings against the Browns and striking out four. The next day he appeared again in relief and saved a win for teammate Allie Reynolds.

This night before the big Cleveland crowd Feller had another no-hitter going through six innings, but his weak-hitting teammates hadn't done anything against Trout, either, and in the Tigers eighth a walk and two singles produced the game's only run, and Feller lost, 1-0. He struck out seven to run his season's total to 262, breaking by one the personal high he'd set in 1941 before he went away to war.

On August 20 the Indians opened a series at Washington with a night game that matched Feller against knuckleballer Mickey Haefner. In an effort to generate some fan interest in another of his poor teams, Clark Griffith, the Old Fox, had arranged for a pregame exhibition of Feller's spectacular fastball. The only trouble was that he hadn't asked the star attraction to participate but had simply made the arrangements and advertised the event in the daily papers. Griffith had gotten the army to set up a photographic device behind home plate that would clock Feller's fastball. The device had originally been created to measure the velocity of shells and was accurate to within .0001 second; the idea was for Feller to throw his fastball through the device's aperture. When Griffith came down to the Cleveland clubhouse to tell Feller it was time to take his warm-ups, Feller told him he wasn't going to participate since Griffith hadn't had the courtesy to ask him. Besides, he said, it was he who had brought in all those extra fans, and surely he was due some money if he were the feature attraction. With the device already in place, the army technicians standing about, and the fans gathered to see the show, Griffith had little room to move and asked Feller how much it might take to get him out on the mound. They settled on $700. "He went out and got back with that check so fast I couldn't believe it," Feller recalled with a chuckle. Then Feller went out, took his warm-ups, and went to the mound.

The aperture he was to throw through was slightly smaller than the strike zone, and while he was by no means the kid who'd led the league in walks three times—and terrorized batters—Feller was no control artist, either, and Gil Coan said he and his Senators teammates were a bit surprised when Feller fired his first pitch right through. He did the same with his second, third, and fourth pitches as well. On his fifth and last throw Feller's fastball hit the device's wooden frame and splintered it. The crowd oohed when his speed figures were read out, and Feller's second pitch was clocked at 98.6 miles per hour as it crossed home plate. Subsequent calculations showed that when leaving his hand the ball was traveling at 107 miles per hour.

No sooner had Feller thrown his final pitch than Bobo Newsom burst from the Senators dugout and ran out to the mound, broadly pantomim-

August 20, Griffith Stadium: Rapid Robert Feller, on his way to breaking the single-season strikeout record, throws his famed fastball through a military device designed to measure shell velocity. Feller's fastest pitch was clocked at 98.6 m.p.h. as it came through the device, 107 as it left his hand. (Courtesy of Bob Feller)

ing that he, too, wanted to be clocked. While he was a talented pitcher, Bobo was also a well-known clown and hardly a fireballer in Feller's class. The crowd roared with delight as he took an exaggerated wind-up, then threw a Rip Sewell–type blooper pitch and scurried back to the dugout.

Then Feller took the mound again, this time in earnest—and lost as his team committed four errors. But he did strike out seven more to run his total to 275, and the league's chief statistician announced that the best research into Waddell's record season had been unable to authentic the higher figure of 347. Therefore, he ruled, the record would belong to Feller if he were to top 343. The writers went to work then, trying to figure out how many more starts Feller would get in September and how many relief appearances he might make. The latter figure was the more uncertain, of course, but figuring on ten more starts, it looked as if Feller would have to average around 6.8 strikeouts per outing to break the record. There was no doubt that this late in the season and with so many innings already behind him, his velocity had fallen off a bit, and his strikeout totals in his starts had decreased considerably since April, May, and June. Then, too, batters had begun to adopt a blatantly defensive attitude when hitting against him, and instead of swinging away had begun chopping at the ball in an effort to avoid a strikeout.

On September 5 against the Tigers Feller showed the first clear sign that he was wearing down as the Tigers gave him the worst beating of his career, chasing him in the fourth inning with a nine-run burst. And the surest sign of the accumulated strain was that Hank Greenberg had capped the Tigers big inning with a three-run homer (his thirtieth), for throughout their careers Feller had paralyzed the Tigers slugger with his sweeping side-arm curve. Then working with just two days' rest, Feller came back against the Browns and threw a strong six-hitter, striking out eight to go over the 300 mark. The record was by no means surely within his grasp, but with three weeks of the season to go, what had once looked impossible no longer did.

★ ★ ★

While Feller rocketed toward Waddell's record another sort of pitching drama was unfolding in Philadelphia where Lou Brissie had begun to work out with the A's. After what he called the "shattering" experience of trying to pitch again Brissie regained his confidence and his resolve and two weeks later took the mound again, this time with markedly better results. And with each time out after that he got better, learning what he could and couldn't do with the brace, beginning to learn, too, that he'd lost a lot of velocity off his fastball because he couldn't drive off the leg when delivering it. Shrapnel fragments in his pitching hand began to hurt him when he'd turned over a number of curveballs, and he had to begin learning to dole these out. But all the while he was gaining in arm strength and control. During his convalescence, both overseas and back in the States, Connie Mack had stayed in touch with him and now invited Brissie to Philadelphia. He jumped at the chance and went to work out before Mack and his coaches, running in the outfield and throwing some batting practice. "I think he really wanted to get a look at me to see what was left," Brissie said.

Osteomyelitis is a very volatile condition that can flare into full infection again with only the slightest accidental bump or bruise, and in his workouts as he landed repeatedly on his braced leg, Brissie indeed saw the infection return. "One day I just noticed a long red streak running down the leg," he said, "and so off I went to Valley Forge Hospital where they put me on a heavy dosage of antibiotics." When the A's left town on a western swing, they left Brissie behind at Valley Forge, where after several weeks he was released. Club officials told him he might as well go back home since the season was winding down, and it had become clear to everybody that Brissie had tried to do too much too soon. To Mack, Brissie's situation was one of the minor tragedies of the war, and what the old manager thought he'd been looking at during Brissie's workouts was the ruins of what might have been a fine major league pitcher. When Mack said goodbye to Brissie in late summer he felt certain he was also saying goodbye to Brissie the ballplayer. "He never expected to see me on a ballfield again," Brissie said.

But Mack was wrong. Brissie went back to Greenville and after a period of convalescence resumed a personally designed regimen of workouts. He switched to a lighter, more flexible brace and continued to experiment with pitching mechanics that might relieve some of the strain on the leg while still giving him the speed and movement on his pitches he knew he'd need if he hoped ever to rise above the level of textile ball. When spring came and Mack asked Brissie if he wanted to try it again, Brissie went to Florida where the manager sent him out against minor league opposition in the spring games. And when the big club broke camp to barnstorm northward Mack offered Brissie a spot on the A's club in Savannah of the South Atlantic League. If you pitch regularly there, Mack said, you'll find out whether you can make it all the way back, adding that he'd tell the Savannah manager to keep sending Brissie out there until the pitcher himself said he'd had enough. Brissie had a pretty good spring, but Mack doubted he could in fact make it all the way back; the odds and the injuries were too great, he thought.

Mack was wrong again. Brissie rang up a 23–5 record at Savannah with a brilliant 1.91 earned-run-average, and by the end of the season he was back in Philadelphia as an active player—and as one of the great rehabilitation stories to emerge from the war. He would never have the career he might have had he been physically whole, but Brissie would become a fine major league pitcher and with mediocre Philadelphia teams would win a total of 30 games in the next two seasons.

★ ★ ★

/n August labor relations intruded once again into the national pastime, and instead of following Feller, the pennant march of the Red Sox, or the torrid National League race, baseball fans heard almost as much about pension plans and player representatives as they did about diamond heroics.

In a move they openly admitted was inspired by their fear of the American Baseball Guild, the Mexicans, and potential legal challenges to the Uniform Player's Contract, the owners announced they were ready to make some changes in the way baseball conducted its business and invited player participation in the process. Such was the general recommendation of the executive committee the owners had formed in Boston during the All-Star break. The committee included the league presidents, Frick and Will Harridge, and owners Yawkey, MacPhail, P. K. Wrigley of the Cubs, and Breadon, still very much in Chandler's doghouse but acknowledged to have learned more about player dissatisfaction than anyone else.

And there was plenty of that, as the executive committee found once the teams had elected their player representatives and given them their instructions. The chief complaint the owners heard was about the low level of salaries in this inflationary period and the absence of a minimum wage. The owners quickly conceded that $5,000 was not an unreasonable figure for the latter, and foreseeing the unfavorable publicity that would accompany the news that there were a number of major leaguers currently drawing less than this, most owners now quietly tendered "bonuses" to the most impoverished members of their clubs. What probably helped the owners to move with unaccustomed speed on this issue was the knowledge that while they were considering it a spirited debate was being waged in Congress about the future of the embattled O.P.A., the nation's chief bulwark against runaway inflation. The terms of the debate plainly revealed that America had hardly begun to resolve its postwar labor crisis and that rough seas lay ahead before any resolution appeared. Baseball, the owners now felt, probably couldn't hope to be exempt from the turmoil.

In his initial pitch to the players Robert Murphy had said that economic justice required the owners to give a player a percentage of his sale price if his club either sold him or received cash for him in a trade. He also had listened to enough players to include the ten-day severance clause as one of the grievances his Guild had been formed to redress. Now the player representatives brought these same issues to their meetings with the executive committee. But the representatives were all without legal background or training in labor relations, and they yielded fairly easily on the former issue, but they stuck on the severance clause and forced a concession from the owners that at least the clause needed modification, if not abolition.

The players got two further concessions from the owners. The owners agreed that a major leaguer under contract who was sent to the minors should play there for his big league salary. And they agreed in principle that players should receive some sort of weekly stipend during spring training which heretofore had been run as if the players really were chattel on a plantation: as long as they were at work or in their quarters, they were taken care of, but if they wanted a haircut, a shoe shine, or to take in a movie, they were on their own. And if they elected to bring their wives and children with them to camp, they bore the full expense of this. Talking figures currently ranged from $35 to $50 a week.* There were other player requests made as well, all of them respectfully put and having to do with conditions in the workplace and scheduling, but the players gave a wide berth to the one issue that most concerned management—the reserve clause.

It is likely that the owners, through their executive committee, had early on advised the player representatives that this was not a negotiating issue. Back in July MacPhail had made management's position clear when he called the clause baseball's foundation. The *Sporting News* reiterated this when it editorialized that the player representatives now meeting with ownership were rightly being reminded that the reserve clause protected them as well as the great game itself: the annual peddling of players' services in an open market situation, the paper said, would "destroy fan allegiances" and ultimately Organized Baseball. Even Mur-

---

* For years thereafter, this expense money was known among the players as "Murphy Money," a shorthand reference to Robert Murphy, and an acknowledgment of the importance of his pioneering efforts in their behalf.

phy, as he outlined what his Guild stood for, had shied away from any direct assault on the clause, though he had at one time questioned its fairness. It wasn't surprising, then, that there was no public player sentiment in favor of bringing it up for discussion: in this dawn of player-owner negotiations it simply wasn't realistic. Even years later when he'd become active as a player representative Ralph Kiner said the abolition of the clause remained unthinkable. "We never, *never* thought we had a chance of getting rid of it," he said. Despite the sacrosanct status of the clause, the owners were uneasy enough about it to continue moving quickly to incorporate the new reforms into a revised contract they could offer players before the end of the season. They wanted very much to avoid a situation in which the players would finish out their current contracts and thus remain attached to their teams only by the reserve clause. This, the magnates believed, would leave them especially vulnerable to legal challenges as well as to new incursions from south of the border.

But for the moment, at least, the owners believed Robert Murphy and his Guild were not a threat. He'd certainly scared them, but on August 20 when his Guild went down to defeat in another Pirates team vote, the American Baseball Guild seemed dead. This time when the Pirates voted only eighteen of them bothered to do so, and of these, ten who'd voted earlier to strike now voted against the Guild. Murphy got only three votes. Again Rip Sewell led the opposition, and he now had the added authority of his position as the Pirates player representative. In this capacity, he lectured his teammates, he could do a lot more for everybody than a outsider who didn't understand how baseball really operated. Subsequent to the vote Murphy announced, somewhat plaintively, that he was planning to file unfair labor practice charges against a number of clubs, though the Pirates weren't among them. But even he knew the Guild was as dead as management thought it was. The players, he said, had settled for an apple when he'd offered them the prospect of the orchard.

★   ★   ★

*F*rom Murphy's point of view the changes in the standard contract and in workplace conditions were largely cosmetic since they didn't really improve the employee's bargaining position. From the players' point of view, however, Murphy's announced agenda had seemed more like a pipe dream than a program that could actually be achieved, even in the current climate of labor unrest. For them, the concessions the owners had granted were tangible, and in general they were happy enough to have gotten them. This was especially so by late September when it began to appear that the threat of the Mexican League might prove pretty hollow after all. Mickey Owen was back in the States again, petitioning Organized Baseball for reinstatement and carrying hair-raising tales of the tempestuous and tyrannical behavior of Jorgé Pasquel. The Mexican League wasn't a major league, Owen said, and it never would be as long as Pasquel insisted on running it as his private plaything, hiring and firing managers at whim, arranging phoney player trades, even interrupting games to order pitching changes or argue with an umpire's decision. Luis Olmo too was said to be petitioning for reinstatement, and the league playoffs had been canceled when most of the imported players left the country, saying they hadn't been paid to participate in them. Max Lanier was back home in Denton, North Carolina, nursing a sore arm that had become progressively worse in Mexico. If the Mexican challenge had scared the owners into making some of the concessions, that was fine with the players, but it certainly didn't look as if Pasquel's league was going to prove an attractive, viable alternative to Organized Baseball in 1947, or any time thereafter, for that matter.

The most significant improvement in the players' lot came not out of the direct negotiations between the players and owners in August and September, though doubtless it was powerfully conditioned by those meetings. The idea of a pension plan for ballplayers developed on a separate, parallel track and emerged from long talks between Marty Marion and Doc Weaver.

All the Cardinals testified then and in later years that Weaver was a remarkable man. He'd been the team's trainer since 1927 but was far more than the glorified locker room attendant who passed for a trainer on most other teams in those days. Weaver was an ingenious inventor of items from nasal filters his players wore to help them with the coal dust on trains to foam rubber inserts they wore in their baseball shoes to cushion their feet and legs against hot, hard diamonds. He was also a farsighted observer of the baseball world who'd seen many a talented player come through his clubhouse, have his day in the sun, then go back to the farm or factory with little to show for it. He thought there ought to be some kind of cooperative effort made to provide players something for their sunset years. Many of them, he knew, were rough and untutored men, lacking in financial skills or solid advice, and even with their small salaries they were often improvident. In Marion he had an apt listener.

Mr. Shortstop was something of an anomaly among his peers in that he didn't eat, breathe, and sleep baseball. In an era when players routinely spent time before and after games talking over the opposition analyzing what they'd done well or poorly, Marion preferred to take a break from the game once the last out had been recorded and turn his mind to other things. He'd played baseball since childhood and richly deserved his distinguished nickname, but Marion never really developed that deep, visceral love of the game that Country Slaughter had, or Terry Moore, or Marion's double-play partner, Red Schoendienst. And every time he bent over to lace on a pair of spikes, his back painfully reminded him that a ballplayer's career was after all a very brief one, even if you were one of the best. Doc Weaver worked daily on Marion's back so that he could stay in the lineup, but the condition was growing worse, and he now played with a corset that Weaver had to lace him into every day. In 1946 he knew this couldn't go on much longer, and there were hot afternoons and cool, clammy nights when he wasn't so sure he wanted it to. He was a shrewd negotiator who'd been able to bargain his pay past the levels of Mize, the Coopers, Hopp, and the others who'd been sent away when their salaries had gotten too high, and he'd put some money by. But like Weaver, he'd been around long enough to know that he was the exception, that many ballplayers ended up with nothing to show for the fact that their unique skills had brought hundreds of thousands of fans into the nation's ballparks.

The plan Weaver and Marion worked out called for matching contributions from players and clubs to establish a fund that would eventually pay retired players a modest annuity—$1,200 a year for a ten-year veteran, collectible from age forty-five. In addition to those matching contributions they envisioned revenues coming from the All-Star Game, sale of the World Series radio broadcast rights, and from eight special midseason exhibitions between interleague rivals. By the time the first benefits would be paid ten years hence the two men estimated the fund would contain almost $4 million.

Like the idea of collective bargaining, the Weaver-Marion pension plan had its immediate opponents among the players when they first heard of it: the prospect of having their paycheck docked, even slightly, was opposed by some who said they were getting little enough as it was and would rather take their own risks with their money instead of entrusting it to some new and mysterious entity. What if it failed? The memory of the Depression with its bank failures was still vivid for all. In the main, however, the players saw the value of the idea, and so did a majority of the owners. The ever-generous Tom Yawkey, who had come to the aid of more than a few indigent former players, lobbied strenuously with his Red Sox for the plan and even told a few holdouts that he'd put in their shares for them if they didn't want to.

But after so many years of oligarchic rule, the owners were hardly of a mind to cede too much too easily to their employees, and in return for their participation in the pension plan and for their other concessions, they now advanced some proposals of their own. For one thing, they wanted to tighten the reins of discipline on the players, spelling out what the players could do or say publicly during the season, what kinds of endorsements they might make, and requiring them to make themselves available to the club for a variety of publicity purposes. More important, however, the owners now floated proposals to expand the regular season and to exclude the players from any future revenues accruing from the sale of television rights.

The idea of expanding the season to 168 games was probably Larry MacPhail's, and the reasoning behind it wasn't hard to figure out: if the owners were going to pay their players more and contribute to the comfort of their post-baseball years, they wanted to get more out of them. Besides, the unprecedented and astonishing attendance marks set this season amply bore out the rosy preseason predictions of those who saw baseball entering a golden era. Surely the fans would enthusiastically support a longer season with fewer open dates in it.

As for television rights, the restrictive clause was tucked away in a longish paragraph of a draft version of the new contract. This was, to be sure, the paleolithic age of TV, and no one yet knew the new medium's shape and scope. But already there was regular telecasting by the networks in the area from Boston to Philadelphia, the sale of TV sets had jumped dramatically, and a few games had even been televised from Ebbets Field and Yankee Stadium. So far, profits to the clubs from these had been negligible, but the prospects were intriguing. MacPhail had championed the idea of night baseball as a way of expanding the game's audience, and, though the war had temporarily short-circuited night ball, he'd been right. Now night ball was back in force and was being received with enormous enthusiasm: the Dodgers, for instance, had sold out all their night games before the season even began. Television looked as if it might have even greater commercial possibilities, certainly far greater than radio, which like the passenger train was beginning to look like a prewar phenomenon.

Fortunately for the players, Dixie Walker and a few other player representatives instantly spotted the restrictive clause and indicated they would urge their constituents to oppose its retention in the contract's final draft. The *Sporting News* gave the issue even greater exposure with a front-page story in its September 25 edition. The paper also came out against the proposed expanded schedule, saying the idea was ill-conceived and had a distinctly punitive smack to it, coming as it did at the end of the protracted negotiations in which owners had been forced to make some long overdue concessions.

But the paper, the owners, and most baseball writers regarded the negotiations as both the beginning and the end of the game's necessary adjustment to postwar realities. Writer Dan Daniel called the new contract baseball's "Magna Carta" and said management's timely response to employee unrest had averted more serious problems down the road. In fact, baseball's big problems hadn't been solved, only postponed for future owners and players to wrestle with.

17

*W*hen the Indians and the Red Sox took the field September 13 at old League Park in Cleveland, the two teams presented a striking contrast, the Indians loose and smiling, the Sox grim and tight. The Indians were simply playing out the string, and within a matter of days their season would be over. The Sox, however, were trying to nail down a championship that curiously continued to elude them.

When they'd started out on this road trip the Sox were hot, and they expected to get the clincher quickly. But after opening at Washington with their eighth straight win, they'd fallen into a strange and disquieting slump. They'd lost the next day to Bobo Newsom, then had moved on to Philadelphia where the awful A's had beaten them twice, Phil Marchildon picking up his thirteenth win in the second game. From there, they'd gone to Detroit where the Tigers had whipped them twice. In the series opener here in Cleveland Feller had won his twenty-fourth and struck out seven, running his season's total to 308. That made it six straight losses for the Sox, and after the game the team seemed sour and sullen. The champagne that traveling secretary Tom Dowd had been carting around for the celebration was still sitting tight in its bottles, and Yawkey, traveling with the team, was getting impatient to uncork it with his boys.

From the way they started out that day against Red Embree, Yawkey might just have to wait some more as the first two batters went meekly out. That brought Williams to the plate, and he stood outside the batter's box, waiting while the Indians went into a radical defensive alignment that put five players to the right of second base, leaving only left fielder Seerey, playing a very short left-center, to handle any ball hit to the left of second. Lou Boudreau had gone to the shift (now being called the Boudreau Shift, even when employed with variations by other teams) in desperation in the second game of a July 14 doubleheader: in the first game the playing-manager had cracked four doubles and a homer, and still his team had lost because Williams had hit three homers and a single, driving in eight runs. Between games Boudreau had sketched out a defense he wanted his team to use when Williams came up with nobody on base. Boudreau had his first baseman and right fielder play almost on the foul line. He positioned himself to the right of second and had his third baseman playing almost directly behind second. The center fielder played where the right fielder normally would, while the second baseman played essentially a wide first base and back on the outfield grass. When the Indians had first gone into the shift Williams had laughed, then asked plate umpire Bill Summers if it was legal. Summers assured him it was, and then Williams had swung at the first pitch and grounded out to Boudreau. He had no hits in that game, but for the remainder of that home stand had been better than ever, hitting at a .526 clip.

But the shift proved a smart move, both tactically and psychologically, and as the season wore on it began to bother Williams. For one thing, of course, it took away hits he might have gotten, particularly with the positionings of the second baseman, center fielder, and right fielder. Williams's power swing with its slight upward arc produced a large percentage of his hits in the air to right and right-center, and now there were defensive players stationed where some of these balls would otherwise have fallen in. For another, Williams couldn't quickly adjust his swing and stance to beat the shift by hitting to left. He'd perfected the swing and stance through the years, and they were central parts of a total philosophy of hitting. He was too conscious and scientific a hitter to start some mid-season tinkering, knowing that in trying to go to left he might well end up being unable to pull pitches with consistency. Meanwhile, sportswriters, players, and former stars showered him with criticism and advice. "Stubborn," some said; "stupid," said others, pointing out how many ordinary grounders and medium-deep fly balls would become doubles if Williams would make the adjustment and hit to left. Al Simmons, a persistent Williams critic, said the shift merely exposed Williams's deficiencies as a hitter. Ty Cobb said that if they'd tried anything like that on him, he'd have made them rue the day; he could hit into left field any time he wanted to, he said. Babe Ruth pointed out that an earlier Indians team had once tried a shift against him, and he'd hit five singles, all to left, and the fans, he recalled, "booed the shit out of me." He understood the Kid's refusal to alter his swing. That would be a "bullshit" tactic for sluggers like himself and Williams, he told writer John Lardner. You have to hit to your natural power, he said.

As July moved to August and August to September Williams continued to face the shift and his critics, and while he continued also to hit better than almost anyone else playing, he wasn't hitting with quite the consistency and authority he had before Boudreau had introduced the new alignment.* Trying too hard to smash the ball through the clustered defenders—or over all of them into the seats—Williams lost his once commanding leads in all three major offensive categories: average, homers, and runs batted in. Though baseball was obviously a team game, Williams never made any bones about his desire to win the Triple Crown this year, and at the All-Star break it looked as if he'd do it easily. Now, though, Mickey Vernon of the Senators had zoomed past him in batting average and even teammate Johnny Pesky had gone a couple of points ahead. Meanwhile, in Detroit, Hank Greenberg, sore of foot and with an aching back, had begun to come on strong in the power hitting departments and was threatening to overtake Williams. Frustrated by the shift, annoyed and then angered by what he saw as ignorant criticism, and worn down by the long season, Williams snapped at reporters, stopped speaking to some of his teammates, and sulked on the field. He was sick of coming to the ballpark, he told writer Jack Malaney, sick of looking at his teammates, sick of writers trying to make trouble. He wished he didn't have to depend on baseball to make a living. If he didn't, you wouldn't find him anywhere near a ballpark, he said.

The nadir came on September 1 at Fenway when A's right fielder Elmo Valo, who already in the series had taken two homers away from Williams with great catches, raced to the low wall in right for another Williams drive, leaped high and caught it, then slammed into the wall and fell to the warning track. The first base umpire ran out to see whether Valo had held onto the ball, and when he saw that he had, he signalled Williams out. Williams, standing at first, kicked viciously at the bag as Valo's teammates raced out to assist him from the field. The glaring contrast between Valo's heroic effort and the Kid's petulant response to it didn't sit well with the fans, but it was nothing compared to their boisterous displeasure two innings later when Williams made only a token

---

* Before the shift Williams hit .353 with 26 homers. After July 14 he hit .329 with 12 homers.

swing at a pitch, sent a weak roller to second, then ran just two steps toward first before turning aside to the Red Sox's dugout. The fans booed him lustily when he took his defensive position at the end of the inning, and when a routine fly ball came his way to end that half-inning, he caught it and flung both it and his glove high in the air. Much later he would call this a "childish stunt," but even then he couldn't help adding that he'd done it because he'd been "disgusted" by Valo's great play.

Cronin said he wasn't going to do anything with his sulking star. So close to the prize, he was hardly going to risk a potentially rancorous confrontation with him, but Rudy York wasn't intimidated and gave Williams a dressing down in which he told him that his behavior was spoiling what ought to be an exciting time for the whole team. In the last meeting of the year between the Yankees and the Sox, York was talking at first base with Tommy Henrich, and Henrich said something like, "Well, you guys have about got it nailed down now." York had looked at Henrich and replied, "You know, sometimes I think I'm the only guy on this team who realizes that." In truth, the team did seem to be waiting for Williams to snap out of it and put them over the top.

With the Indians now positioned in their shift Embree threw Williams a pitch on the outer portion of the plate, and Williams hit a line drive to left center that probably would have been center fielder Felix Mankiewicz's ball, but Mankiewicz was pulled around into right-center, and clearly Pat Seerey had no play since he was stationed just behind shortstop. The ball rolled all the way to the wall and into a drain before Mankiewicz could get to it, and even then he had some trouble fishing it out. Meanwhile, Williams with his long, loping gait had gotten into high gear and Cronin, coaching at third, gave him the sign to go home. Williams did, scoring well ahead of the throw on the first, and only, inside-the-park home run he ever hit.

Hughson took it from there. He shut out the Indians on three hits, and the Sox won, 1–0, assuring them of no worse than a tie for the championship. In the Red Sox clubhouse afterward a cameraman asked Hughson to pose with Williams and he refused, evidently still annoyed with Williams for his recent behavior. Williams, on the other hand, was bending over backwards to give Hughson the credit for the big win. At the time, Williams was allowing a ghostwritten column to appear under his name in a Boston paper, and now he wanted to make it clear to his writer that the real story here in Cleveland wasn't his homer but Hughson's gutsy pitching.

By the time the Sox had showered and left the clubhouse for the Statler Hotel they didn't yet know if they were champions outright because Detroit still had a mathematical chance to stay alive in the race if they could beat the Yankees in Detroit. The players went back to the hotel and then dispersed, some waiting around in the lobby for the news, others going up to their rooms, and others out for a snack. Johnny Pesky went out with some old navy buddies. While still in the clubhouse Williams had told someone that even if they should clinch it today, he wouldn't be coming to any victory party tonight. He had other things to do, he said. When the news came in from Detroit that the Yankees had beaten the Tigers and Newhouser on DiMaggio's twenty-fourth homer, the players in the lobby grinned broadly and shook hands. Then it was up to Tom Dowd to collect them all for the victory party.

It took him a while, but eventually he did get the players, the owner, and the champagne all together in a banquet room at the Statler for what turned out to be a brief and oddly subdued celebration. All except Williams. York clowned around a bit and some champagne was drunk, but not too much. Yawkey, who had waited so long for this moment, gave the briefest of speeches, then sat down, and it was over. The Boston writers, who had been excluded from it, were standing outside on the street when Bill Veeck came by and asked, "What the hell are you guys doing out here? Where's the party?" Clif Keane told him it was all over, and when he heard this, Veeck invited them to a lounge around the corner that he owned an interest in, and they had their own victory party there. But the official celebration, Keane said, "wasn't a very pretty sight for a team that had just won the pennant."

From the writers' point of view the only story about the event was that Williams hadn't gone to it, and Dowd tried to put the best face on this he could by telling reporters Williams had gone to a local hospital to visit a dying vet. The *Globe* ran with that the next day, though writer Hy Hurwitz investigated the story and found it wasn't so. Some team members came to Williams's defense and said they understood his reasons for skipping the celebration. Ted wasn't a drinking man, his roommate Charlie Wagner explained, and never liked parties, one of the reasons they got along so well. Ted's attitude was that winning the pennant was celebration enough, Wagner said, and that anything extra was superfluous. But Dave Egan of the Boston *Record* wasn't buying any of this, nor was he about to let so juicy an opportunity pass him by.

By all accounts, Egan was as complex and mystifying a character as Williams, his favorite target: brilliant, mercurial, by turns generous and vicious. This year he'd come out strongly for the rights of those players returning from the service and for the integration of the game. He'd also made it his business to knock Williams whenever he could. He'd graduated from Harvard in three years, then gone to law school before joining the *Globe* as a twenty-two-year-old. By the time he'd moved on to the *Record* he'd acquired a reputation as a heavy drinker who wanted to be paid off for his stories by the promoters of the horse races and boxing and wrestling matches he covered. He was also known among his peers as one of the best and quickest writers in the business, a man who could cover an event, whip off nearly flawless copy, and file it before his colleagues had so much as gotten started. Keane went with him to the first Joe Louis–Jersey Joe Walcott fight in 1947, a match in which the challenger floored Louis twice and carried the fight to him all night. Immediately afterward, "a lot of people thought Walcott had won," Keane said, "so there was a lot of milling around, people wondering what the judges had said and so forth. And there was Egan, three chairs away from me with his typewriter in his lap, pounding away. And while everybody else is still wondering what the hell has happened here, Egan's through with his story. He was just a beautiful writer. He'd never have you wondering, 'What's this guy trying to tell me.' He was clear and easy to read, like Red Smith. But an impossible guy to figure."

Just why the "Colonel," as he liked to style himself, got it in for Williams nobody knows. Keane wondered whether Egan ever actually met the slugger and thought he might not have. Pesky and Joe Dobson thought it was simply that Williams was such an obvious mark for any writer. Everybody knew Williams had no use for writers and their prying questions, they said, and so the easiest thing in the world was to go up to him in the clubhouse and ask him a provocative question. "*Boom!*" Johnny Pesky said. "There's your story." Egan's readers came to expect his special brand of vitriol applied to Williams, and Charlie Wagner recalled the experience of watching readers on street corners tearing open their copies of the *Record* to see what the Colonel had to say today about Williams. What Egan had to say about Williams's absence from the pennant celebration was the essence of what he'd been claiming all season long: "Williams is for Ted Williams and Ted Williams alone."

The situation wasn't improved any when Williams announced in Chicago that he wouldn't be accompanying the team to its next stop in St. Louis but instead was going back to Boston to rest. Lost in his announcement was the fact that Cronin himself and most of the other regulars were also returning to Boston. Cronin said he was going over to Braves Field to scout the Cardinals, and several others said they would be going over as well. Not Rudy York. He told writers he'd signed to play 154 games, and he was going on to St. Louis to do just that. When the team took the field against the Browns he was the only regular in the lineup.

While the team finished out the year as champions for the first time since 1918 (the year Williams was born) Colonel Dave Egan schemed to spoil what pleasure Williams might take from this. He'd gotten wind of a story he thought might just do that and was biding his time to break it.

★   ★   ★

*M*eanwhile, the Cardinals and Dodgers battled down to the wire and Feller and Jackie Robinson concluded their heroic individual quests.

In Detroit on August 27 Feller pitched five innings and struck out six to tie Waddell. Two days thereafter, Boudreau gave Feller the ball again in the last game of the season, and again it was against the Tigers with New-houser going for his twenty-seventh win. In Cleveland a week earlier in the exact same match-up that Veeck had billed the "pitching duel of the century," Newhouser had bested Feller, 3–0. After the game Feller had complained that the Tigers batters had almost been bunting at the ball in an effort not to strike out, all except Dick Wakefield who'd taken his full cuts. Now as he worked his way through the Detroit order for the first time he found them taking the same kind of defensive chops, and he got no strikeouts until he faced Newhouser. Feller struck him out to go past Waddell, then went on to fan four more and set what was believed to be a new record of 348. Though subsequent research credited Waddell with 349 strikeouts in 1904, there was no question that Feller had put together an astonishing season with his strikeout total, his no-hitter and two one-hitters, his ten shutouts, and his 371 innings pitched—a total that would go unsurpassed for the next twenty-five seasons. Of all the players who came back from the war and attempted to resume their careers, Feller's comeback was the most spectacular, and his 1946 season remains one of the great ones of modern times.

Montreal wasn't the big leagues, of course, but in many ways what Robinson achieved there was more remarkable than the feats of Feller or Williams or Musial, who was about to win his second batting championship. Against beanballs, high spikes, and often hostile crowds, Robinson led the Royals to the pennant by a huge nineteen and one-half games, then starred in the Junior World Series, which the Royals also won. All season long he fought a case of nerves that at one point threatened to hospitalize him, for he not only carried his own burden there at Montreal but the additional ones of the other blacks in the Dodgers system who looked to him for leadership and sometimes called him for advice. Despite all this, he led league batters in average and runs scored, stole 40 bases, and was the consensus pick as the league's best at his defensive position.

His example was tremendously heartening to the other blacks at Three Rivers and Nashua. After replacing Wright on the Montreal roster, Roy Partlow had then joined him at Three Rivers, less because he lacked ability than that he was unaccustomed to the more regimented, less improvisational ways of Organized Baseball. But he saw Robinson making the adjustment superbly, and he himself settled down at Three Rivers, as did Wright. Partlow compiled a 15–1 record there, including the playoffs, and when manager Frenchy Bordagaray played him in the outfield he batted .404.* At Nashua, Don Newcombe and Roy Campanella were clearly the outstanding newcomers in the league. Newcombe was 14–4 and like Partlow was a tough out at the plate. His batterymate Campanella was the league's best defensive catcher and in 113 games drove home 96 runs.

Whatever might befall Robinson when he went up to the majors, it was now obvious to everybody that Rickey's experiment must result in the game's integration: if not through Robinson in 1947, then the year after that or the year after that. For through his performance and iron-steady example Robinson had thrown the national spotlight on the deep talent pool so long untapped in the Negro leagues. Too late for Partlow. Too late, as well, for Josh Gibson and Buck Leonard. But not too late for Newcombe and Campanella, Larry Doby, Sam Jethroe, Monte Irvin, Junior Gilliam, and all the other black stars who would follow where Robinson had led.

---

* Partlow never really made the adjustment to white baseball. Like slugger Willard Brown who would play briefly with the Browns in 1947, Partlow had been kept too long in the Negro leagues and couldn't adapt his style of play and training to the demands of his white managers. He reported late to spring training in 1947, was casual about rules, and soon was released, despite his obvious talent.

★ ★ ★

*W*hen the Cardinals came to Ebbets Field on September 12 leading by a game and a half and then flattened Higbe and the Dodgers, 10-2, in the series opener, it looked as if Durocher had at last run out of ways to keep his club alive in the race. Higbe retired Schoendienst and Harry Walker to start the game but then gave up hits to Musial and Slaughter. When Kurowski topped a ball to the left of the mound Higbe froze and all the runners were safe. That brought up Dick Sisler, whom Dyer had been using in left lately since he'd been swinging the bat better, and he continued to do so, singling sharply to drive in Musial and Slaughter. Higbe was rattled now, but he was Durocher's ace and this early in the game his manager had to hope he could get the final out of the inning and minimize the damage. With the rookie catcher Joe Garagiola at the plate with his .224 batting average this seemed like the right strategy. Higbe threw him a high curve, and Garagiola sent a high fly toward the right field wall that was plastered with advertisements for shoe polish and razor blades. Dixie Walker drifted back, looking up and expecting to make the catch, but the wind gave it a little push, and to the dismay of everybody in Flatbush, the ball sailed out onto Bedford Avenue, giving the Cardinals a five-run lead before their ace left-hander Howie Pollet even went out to the mound.

There was nothing fancy about the slender, gentlemanly Cardinals pitcher. He threw a fastball, curve, and changeup, and while none of these was outstanding, Pollet threw them for strikes and rarely beat himself. Garagiola said the hallmarks of a winning pitcher were his ability to throw a ball when he wanted to and to throw a strike when he needed it, and this described Pollet well. Because he had no single outstanding pitch and threw with an easy motion, batters looked forward to facing him, but at the end of a game they were likely to find that they'd gone hitless. Lately, though, Pollet had begun to show disturbing signs of running out of gas and had been hit hard in his last two starts. He wasn't a robust man, and Dyer had been leaning heavily on him all season, using him occasionally in emergency relief roles as well as in his starter's slot, and the strain was beginning to show. His back was aching, and to favor it he was altering his delivery slightly, putting a strain on his shoulder, which soon enough would begin to give him additional misery. Today, however, pitching with the big early cushion, Pollet simply threw strikes and after

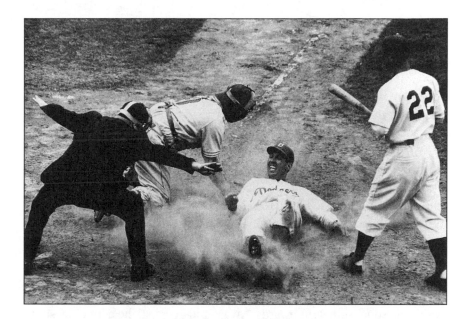

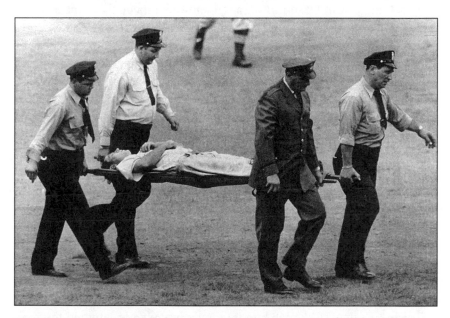

Pistol Pete's style of play—and its consequences. In Reiser's single healthy season the veteran Billy Herman said he was the greatest player he'd ever seen. (Bettmann Archive and National Baseball Library and Archive, Cooperstown, N.Y.)

some early trouble shut out the Dodgers for the last seven innings for the win.

In the second game, Dyer took another necessary chance when he started the newly activated Red Munger against Hatten. No one questioned the big Texan's ability: he probably had more stuff than any other pitcher on the staff. But since he'd rejoined the team August 21 his performances had been very uneven, clearly a consequence of the fact that he hadn't been able to work out at all after leaving Germany. In 1944 and '45 while stationed in the States Munger had pitched a good deal of service ball, but when he went to Germany he switched to the outfield. "The one game I pitched over there," he said, "I struck out fifteen in five innings." Almost all the professional ballplayers had already gone back to the States, Munger said, "and it was just awful going out there and striking all those kids out. After that I played center field." And not too much of that, either. Mainly, Munger sat around, hearing rumors that soon he'd be rotated back, then finding the rumors unfounded. By the time he caught a troop ship homeward it was mid-August, he'd put on some weight, and his arm wasn't in shape. It showed, especially in his stamina and control, but recently in a game against the Cubs he'd looked something like his old self, and Dyer decided to go with him. Besides, if Munger were to be of any use to him in what remained of the season and through the postseason, Dyer would have to send him out there and hope that he rounded into shape. There wasn't time for a more leisurely program of conditioning.

Today, it was evident from the start that Munger wasn't up to the challenge. Augie Galan began a one-out charge with a single off Schoendienst's glove, and before the inning was over Brooklyn had four runs. But with Brazle, Wilks, Burkhart, and Dickson shutting out the Dodgers the rest of the way the Cardinals made it interesting by scoring single runs in the fourth, fifth, and seventh, and Higbe had to come out of the bullpen in that inning to prevent further damage. And this day Hig was tough; he held the Cardinals hitless the rest of the way to save a game his team had to have. In winning, however, the Dodgers lost Reiser yet again when he pulled a hamstring while singling in the game's first run.

Thirty-two thousand, nine hundred and sixty people jammed the park for the last meeting of the season between the clubs, a crowd that boosted Brooklyn attendance past the 1.5 million mark, setting a new league record. And once again Durocher reached into his bag of tricks, announcing that he was starting the seldom-used Ralph Branca against Brecheen. Just why Durocher hadn't used Branca much in a season when he'd had to scratch so hard for starters was a matter of some dispute. Certainly Branca had shown enough ability in 1945 to warrant more work than Durocher had given him, and the pitcher himself claimed Durocher was under orders from Rickey to let him languish in the bullpen—punishment, Branca said, for having been a spring holdout. According to Branca, Rickey's idea was for Durocher to use him only in mop-up roles, thereby deflating his value and giving Rickey the upper hand in negotiations for 1947. But Branca had also experienced spells of arm trouble, and there had been times when Durocher couldn't have used him, even if he'd wanted to. Now, suddenly, in the most important game the Dodgers had played this year, here was Durocher calling Branca's number.

Durocher's secret plan was to announce Branca as his starter, getting Dyer to stack his lineup with left-handed batters, and then, after he'd pitched to the switch-hitting Schoendienst, bring in the left-handed Lombardi. Before the game Durocher told Lombardi to go down to the bullpen and get loose, while Charlie Dressen informed Branca of the scheme. Angry at the way he'd been treated during the season, Branca thought, "Ah, the sacrificial lamb, my ass!" Then he went out and retired Schoendienst, Harry Walker, and Musial on five pitches. Durocher had to like that and decided to go with him for another inning. "He shuts 'em out in the second inning," recalled Lombardi, "and I'm still warming up. He shuts 'em out the third inning, the fourth. In fact, he shuts 'em out the whole game, and I pitched the whole game, down in the bullpen. Then, afterwards, Leo asks me how I feel, and I say, 'Well, I'm pretty tired. After all, I pitched the whole game down there.' He just laughed. He was pretty easy to get along with as long as you won the ball game." The Dodgers had done that handily, 5–0, to move into a virtual tie with the Cardinals. They had sixteen games to play while St. Louis had thirteen. Dyer had been correct back in mid-July when he'd predicted it would go right down to the wire.

At first, it appeared the Cardinals had the greater staying power as they swept a three-game series with the Giants while the Dodgers struggled. Brooklyn dropped two of their first three against the Cubs but then came grimly back to take the finale and avert disaster. Three days later they looked like they might drop a doubleheader to the lowly Pirates who won the first game on Ralph Kiner's twenty-first homer. But Branca held the

Pirates in the second game until the hitters could get going and ended up pitching his second consecutive shutout.

With four games to go, the Dodgers blew a game to the Phillies that was debated well after the end of the season. The Dodgers led 1–0 at Ebbets Field when Phillies pitcher Oscar Judd tied the score with an inside-the-park home run. Judd struck again in the next inning when he climaxed a four-run rally with a two-run single. But in the Dodgers' fourth the Phillies showed why they were a losing team, committing three errors as Brooklyn scored three times to take a 5–4 lead. Then they began to pull steadily away, scoring three more in the fifth and another in the seventh to take a 9–5 lead into the eighth. At this point the Dodgers pitcher was Hank Behrman, the talented but erratic right-hander. "He was a cocky guy," said Phillies outfielder Del Ennis, "always talking to you out on the mound: 'Watch out!' He'd give you that out there and then pitch inside." Ennis was virtually the only long-ball threat on his team, and all season he'd seen a lot of high, inside pitches as hurlers tried to intimidate the rookie and drive him back from the plate. Now, out of the corner of his eye Ennis caught Durocher flashing Behrman the knock-down sign, and Behrman complied—only too well, throwing right at Ennis's head. Ennis went down, flinging his left hand up in a protective reaction, the ball striking him on the wrist. He had to be removed from the game, thus depriving the Phillies of their prime power hitter, but in ordering Behrman to knock Ennis down Durocher had violated an old baseball tenet: if a team is asleep, don't do anything to wake them up. The Phillies were at the end of another miserable year with nothing to look forward to but the off-season. Many of the players knew they wouldn't be asked back next spring, but today, at least, they'd played the contending Dodgers tough, as the saying went. Now Durocher's unnecessarily aggressive and even dirty strategy enraged them. They picked up Ennis's run in the eighth and then assaulted Behrman, Lombardi, and Higbe for five more in the ninth to win a game they'd been resigned to losing. When the Reds beat the Cardinals that night, it meant that Brooklyn had missed a chance to gain a full game on the Cardinals at a critical juncture.

The next day the Dodgers regrouped and beat the Cubs, but in doing so they lost Pistol Pete Reiser for the last time this year. Since his hamstring injury in the St. Louis series he'd been hobbling along, deprived now of this last of his once superlative gifts, but Durocher played him whenever Reiser said he could play. Today he told his manager he could play but he couldn't run. Yet when he walked in the first, Durocher flashed him the steal sign. Reiser took his lead, but when the Cubs pitcher made a routine throw over to first to hold him close, the crippled Reiser caught his spikes in the dirt and fell to the ground, writhing in pain. Durocher raced from the dugout, screaming to Reiser that he was all right. "Get up!" he ordered his fallen warrior. "You're all right!" "Not this time, Skip," Reiser gasped. His fibula was protruding through his skin.

★   ★   ★

*B*oth teams ended their seasons at home, the Dodgers in a two-game set with the Braves, the Cardinals with three against the Cubs. On the next to last day both won. The Dodgers had by far the tougher assignment, going up against twenty-game winner Johnny Sain whose curveball had been buckling batters' knees all season, but they lit into him with a three-run first and won easily, 7–4. Thus, when the Cardinals took the field against the Cubs that night, they knew what they had to do. Like the Dodgers, they went right to work and got two first-inning runs off Paul "Li'l Abner" Erickson, with Musial and Slaughter getting the rbi's. Harry Brecheen, victimized by poor support during the past month, was determined to make those runs do, and he pitched a four-hitter as the Cardinals won, 4–1.

On Sunday, the season's final day, the past decisively influenced the present both in Brooklyn and St. Louis. At Ebbets Field castoffs Mort Cooper and Billy Herman combined to beat the Dodgers. Cooper gave his erstwhile Cardinals teammates a big boost by shutting out the Dodgers, 4–0. By this point he was pitching on sheer guts. His arm hurt so badly he chewed aspirin all through his starts to dull the pain, and his career would effectively be over after this game. But he had an old Cardinals dislike of Durocher, and he had heart and guile, and with these he stopped Brooklyn on four scattered singles. Herman, too, had his reasons for wanting to beat Durocher and the Dodgers. In the first game of a doubleheader between the two teams the previous Sunday Durocher had elected to walk Herman in a situation that normally called for the Dodgers to pitch to him. Between games when some of the players gathered in the runway that connected the clubhouses beneath the stands, Herman asked Charlie Dressen about that move, and Dressen had said, "Billy, you know Leo's not gonna let you beat him in a ball game."

Today, Cooper began the third inning with a single off Lombardi, and one out later here was Herman again. Now, Herman said in recalling the situation, "he [Durocher] can't walk me with a runner at first, and Lombardi threw me a curveball up high, and I hit it off that right field fence where they had that Gem sign. Gave me a lot of satisfaction." Eventually Cooper scored, and that was the game's only run going into the last of the eighth. Durocher sent Joe Medwick to pinch hit for Lombardi, and he got the fourth and final Dodgers hit. But Cooper was still in charge, and the Dodgers didn't score. "Then," said Lombardi, "Durocher brought in Higbe and it was *pow! pow! pow!*: four to nothing. You go into the ninth inning against Mort Cooper down four to nothing, and it's 'Katy Bar the Door.' You just don't have a four-run rally against Mort Cooper in the ninth, even with a bad arm."

When the Cardinals took the field against the Cubs later that day, they could see from the scoreboard that Cooper and the Braves were clinging to the slimmest of leads. And here, too, the past was to intrude. A couple of weeks earlier two New York writers floated a story to the effect that Charlie Grimm's Cubs so detested Durocher and his Dodgers that in games against the Cardinals the Cubs weren't really trying to win. The source of the allegation almost certainly was Durocher himself. Despite his tough-guy persona and approach to the game, Durocher was a whiner who characteristically looked for someone to finger for his problems. (When Reiser had broken his leg, Durocher blamed the grounds crew for the condition of the dirt rather than accept responsibility for ordering Reiser to steal.) Locked in a sizzling stretch run with the Cardinals, he looked to Grimm and his Cubs and suggested to the journalists that the bad blood spilled earlier in the season in the Stanky-Merullo brawl had been influencing Grimm's decisions in subsequent games against St. Louis. Both the nature of the allegation plus the meticulous dissection of Grimm's strange blunders against the Cardinals pointed to Durocher as the likely source.

Besides, the charge was good strategy in itself. Durocher knew the schedule, knew the Cubs ended up against the Cardinals, and knew that Grimm would hardly suffer this tremendous insult silently. As indeed he didn't. When the story surfaced the wounded manager roared: everybody knew how much he loved this great game, how much he loved to win. The fact that his team hadn't done better against St. Louis, he said, was due to the fact that the Cubs batters had trouble with those tough lefties. And now that it had come down to the final day, Grimm wasn't about to let anybody say his team—and its manager—hadn't done their damnedest.

He was going to play his best players and give it his all, thus producing precisely the effect Durocher wished.

The most effective Cubs pitcher this season against the Cardinals had been tall, thin left-hander Johnny Schmitz. Schmitz had an outstanding curveball and what was more, he could throw it for strikes. But when the Cubs went down to St. Louis for the final games of the season Schmitz was in the hospital with an infection in his right foot that he'd picked up months before in the South Pacific. Since his return from the service the infection had been dormant but now had flared into a huge boil between his fourth and fifth toes, and it was clear Schmitz's season was over. Then came Grimm's call to Schmitz in the hospital: get down to St. Louis as quick as you can.

With his foot heavily bandaged Schmitz flew to St. Louis to pitch the Sunday finale against Red Munger in a game that pitted two ex-servicemen suffering in different ways from the lingering effects of the war. "They had to cut out part of my shoe so that the foot could kind of spread," Schmitz said, "but at least I could get centered on the mound with my left foot, and at first I actually felt pretty good. Then they got two in the third when Musial hit a home run. We got a run back in the fourth, and we got five in the sixth, and two in the eighth. In the sixth, I got a hit and drove in a run, and when I hit second base that infection broke wide open. I felt a little funny in the seventh, and I told 'em to get somebody warmed up, but I finished the game." His courageous effort preserved the tie between St. Louis and Brooklyn: both finished with 96–58 records, the first time in major league history that teams had tied for the pennant and the first time the championship would be decided by a post-season playoff.

★ ★ ★

*C*handler and Frick had been prepared for this possibility and had devised a three-game format. The winner of a coin-toss got to decide how he wanted to play the series: opening at home, then finishing with two on the road, or the other way around. Durocher won the toss and elected to go to St. Louis for the opener, then come back for two before the faithful at Ebbets Field.

Nobody questioned the wisdom of this decision, but when he named Branca to start in St. Louis against Pollet, Durocher raised eyebrows. True, Branca had pitched brilliantly of late, but he was untested in such an intensely pressurized situation as this, and in Pollet he faced one of the league's best; he couldn't count on his hitters giving him much support. On the other hand, Durocher had used Higbe and Lombardi in the final-game loss in Brooklyn, and the team had only one travel day before the playoffs began on October 1. If Branca could beat Pollet and the Cardinals in St. Louis, then Durocher would have Higbe, Lombardi, and Hatten ready in Brooklyn with three days' rest. And in Brooklyn before those "nutty people" Jeff Cross had spoken of, the Dodgers had run up an extraordinary season's record of 56–22 (.718).

And Pollet wasn't the Pollet of May, June, and July, so the match-up wasn't as one-sided as it might have seemed. He was an exhausted pitcher and an injured one as well. Dyer wanted Dickson to pitch the second game and Brecheen the third, if it were necessary. He couldn't use Munger to open the playoffs since he'd just pitched him against Schmitz in the finale, and he'd already told Beazley he couldn't stay with him any longer (for his part, Beazley had indicated he'd retire after the season). That left Pollet, and Dyer went to him, asking him if he thought he could win. Don't tell me you'll give it your best, Dyer said. I already know that. What I want to know is whether you think you have enough left to win for us. Pollet thought about it a moment and answered that, yes, he thought he had enough left to beat the Dodgers again.

The night before the playoffs began a Cardinals victory party was held at Ruggeri's, a famous old Italian restaurant located near Garagiola's home. "It was kind of a salute to Breadon along with being a general celebration," writer Bob Broeg said. But near the end of the festivities the mood turned sour when it was J. Roy Stockton's turn at the microphone. The writer had a well-deserved reputation for a candidness that often became acerbity, "especially after he'd had a few belts," his colleague Broeg said. Now with his glass in one hand and trademark pipe in the other, Stockton addressed Breadon in the seat of honor. "Sam," he began, "you've always like to slice the baloney thin, but this year you may have sliced it a little too thin." This, of course, was a broad reference to Breadon's legendary parsimony as well as to his selling of Walker Cooper, Hopp, Verban, and Ray Sanders. For a moment, said Garagiola, Stockton's remark "just kind of laid there." Then the reaction set in. "Breadon was pissed," Broeg said, "Dizzy Dean [by now a Cardinals broadcaster] was pissed, Harry Caray was pissed. But what Roy said was perfectly true: if Breadon had kept Cooper and Hopp, and if he'd paid

Lanier what he was worth, there wouldn't have been a playoff, and Stockton was simply pointing out that nobody knew how this thing was going to turn out."

To Caray, a twenty-two-year-old in his second season of broadcasting, Stockton's criticism of Breadon was both senseless and ill-timed. "Here was a team just going into the first playoffs ever the next day, and here comes Stockton, really blasting Breadon," Caray said. "Well, people began to yell, all over the audience, 'We want to hear Harry Caray!' " Propelled to the podium by pro-Breadon sentiment, Caray launched into a spirited defense of Breadon's character and policies that he concluded by remarking that Breadon's generosity was of the private kind and his reputation as a cheapskate undeserved. "I told them," Caray said, "that Sam Breadon was still taking care of Grover Cleveland Alexander, Old Pete, who pitched the Cardinals to the first World's Championship in the history of this town—1926—that he sent him three, three-fifty every month. He did that for a lot of people and never got the credit for it." Caray's speech was greeted with enormous enthusiasm by everyone except Stockton. "I got a hell of a hand," Caray said, "and after everything was over and I was standing there talking with someone, here comes Roy Stockton, and so I said, with a smile on my face, 'Hi Roy.' He looked at me, and, boy, if you ever saw hatred in someone's eyes—. He walked right on by."

★ ★ ★

*T*he Cardinals had pushed the Ruggeri's business from their minds when they took the field the following afternoon under a bright, hot sky. Scalpers had been at work outside the park since early morning, but the crowd was actually a bit smaller than the one that had seen the Cardinals lose to Schmitz and the Cubs on Sunday.

Pollet retired the side in order in the first, and Branca also began well, catching Schoendienst looking at a called third strike. Moore looped a single over shortstop, but Branca slipped another called third strike past Musial, and the Cardinals got on plate umpire Beans Reardon for the call. It was the beginning of what would be a very long afternoon for that official, and now he gave it right back to them. Musial himself said nothing to Reardon, only looked at him and went back to the bench. But that quiet look, Reardon said, made him feel worse than if he'd tangled with Durocher because he knew Musial didn't take many called third strikes that really were strikes. With two out and Moore still at first, Slaughter grounded a single past Stanky, sending Moore around to third. Branca pitched carefully to the clutch-hitting Kurowski and walked him, clearly preferring to take his chances with young Garagiola. Thus far, no one had really hit the ball well off Branca, and Garagiola didn't either, but he hit it in the right place, a high bouncer over the mound that Reese could glove but couldn't make a play on. Moore scored, and the Cardinals had the lead.

The Dodgers pulled even in the third when Howie Schultz timed a Pollet curve and drilled it into the left field bleachers, but in the Cardinals half of the inning they drove Branca to the showers with three solid singles and a walk and took a 3–1 lead. It stayed that way into the seventh with Pollet pitching gamely. In the fifth he gave up singles to the first two batters and then, one out later, filled the bases with a walk. But he got Stanky to hit into a double play and escaped with his two-run lead still intact. Meanwhile, the hollering from both benches had continued unabated and was clearly getting to Reardon. So was Garagiola's incessant questioning of his ball-and-strike calls. At one point after Garagiola had asked where a Pollet pitch had come in, an exasperated Reardon had snapped in his high, piercing voice, "I don't wanna hear this all afternoon! Shut up, dago! You're lucky you're not pushing a damn wheelbarrow selling bananas!" That shut up Garagiola for a time, but not the two dugouts. "They were going crazy," Garagiola said. "Where was this pitch, that pitch. It was 'fucking this,' and 'fucking that,' and Beans is really hollering back: 'Don't give me that shit! I'm not gonna listen to you assholes!'" When the teams changed sides to begin the sixth Dodgers coach Clyde Sukeforth came out of the dugout to deliver a message to the steaming, embattled umpire. "Beans," Sukeforth told him, "Frick sent me up here to tell you to cut that language out." To which Reardon responded, "It's fucking hot out here, and if he wants to umpire, you tell him to get his fucking ass out here!" Sukeforth didn't deliver that message, and the game and the cursing went on.

In the seventh the Dodgers came closer. Reese, Bruce Edwards, and Schultz singled in succession with one out, and on Schultz's hit to right-center Dressen, coaching at third, waved Edwards around to third. With the pitcher due up and with the notorious condition of the Sportsman's Park outfield, this looked to the coach like a good situation to gamble, but the bounce was true and so was Slaughter's strong throw and Edwards was out. What might have become a big inning against an obviously tiring Pollet didn't happen as he took a deep breath and retired pinch hitter Bob Ramazzotti.

Unaccountably, Durocher sent Lombardi out to face Musial in the last of the seventh, and "The Man," as Brooklyn fans had recently taken to calling him in tribute to his hitting heroics, lashed a high drive that hit the wall in right-center for a triple. Two outs later, though, and with Melton now the fourth Dodgers pitcher, Musial was still at third with a very big insurance run and Garagiola was at the plate.

"Melton had me two strikes," Garagiola remembered, "and he threw me a curveball—a hell of a curveball. I hit it on the handle. It went over Melton's head, and both Cookie Lavagetto and Reese tried to make a shoestring catch of a pop fly in the infield. Unheard of in the history of baseball. The ball hit like a bad wheel, spun around, and Musial scored. I ended up at first base, and Durocher's over there, screaming, 'What the hell did you use, a tennis racket?' But we got the run."

But the Dodgers weren't quite finished against the tottering Pollet. In their half of the eighth Stanky led off with a walk, and one out later Medwick singled to right, but this time Dressen held Stanky rather than challenge Slaughter's arm again. Durocher sent Joe Tepsic to run for Medwick, but it made no difference as Pollet jammed Dixie Walker and got him to hit into a force out at second. Carl Furillo then hit the ball hard but right at Marion, and Pollet had only three more outs to get. Reaching into his last reserves of strength, he got them and finished by striking out his tall tormentor Schultz to end the game.

★   ★   ★

*O*n the long train trip across the country to New York some Cardinals played cards while others kibitzed. Some read magazines, and as always, the players gathered to talk over the game and its implications. The reporters traveling with them sat down with individual players for interviews, and at the stops along the way they got off and filed their stories.

Much of the talk was about Durocher's use of his pitchers and what this portended for the rest of the series. Branca hadn't really pitched badly, but perhaps a veteran pitcher might have been able to wiggle out of that third inning jam, whereas Branca had clearly caved in to the pressure of the situation. More important in terms of what lay ahead was the fact that Durocher had used both Higbe and Lombardi in St. Louis. Late in the regular season Higbe had gone to Durocher and said, only partly in jest, that if the manager really wanted to win this thing, he'd give old Hig the ball every day, and lately it seemed as if Durocher had been doing just about that. Clearly, though, Durocher wouldn't start Higbe in Thursday's game; he'd start Hatten and hope to save Higbe for the third game on Friday. But whatever pitching strategy Durocher devised, Terry Moore was confident the Cardinals could solve it. Moore was a rover on these overnight trips, moving between groups, talking with individual players, encouraging, cajoling, exhorting. He loved the way the opener had turned out, of course, because now, he told his teammates, "we only have to win one out of two in Brooklyn, and I *know* we can do that." But like the rest of them, Moore thought it would be a lot better if they could finish this thing off in Thursday's game and not have it all come down to the final game in that bedlam of Ebbets Field.

When the teams got off the train in New York the headlines told them that one of the last chapters in the war had just been written with the verdicts rendered on the twenty-two high Nazis who'd been on trial all summer. Eighteen had been convicted, Goering, Ribbentrop, Keitel, Jodl, and Neurath on all counts. During the trial Goering had claimed the proceedings amounted to little more than another instance of the victors sitting in judgment on the vanquished. Yet now with the verdicts in and he himself scheduled to hang with Ribbentrop and the others, he appeared to accept it all with a calm grace and even congratulated one of the acquitted.

Dyer's choice for Thursday's game was Dickson who'd won 14 during the regular season and except for one brief spell had been very tough down the stretch. Outwardly, he appeared to have "ice water in his veins," as the cliché had it. But in truth, Dickson was always nervous before his starts and instead of resting before he was to pitch he liked to engage in some kind of time-consuming activity: if he could, he'd get his roommate Harry Brecheen to go fishing with him all day. "I'd tell him he ought to get his rest before the game," Brecheen said, "but he just wouldn't." One thing "Dick" couldn't stand, said Brecheen, was to lie around in a hotel room, waiting to go to the park and pitch. Now, of course, the playoffs schedule had forced him to do a lot of sitting around and waiting, and in the game's first inning he looked jittery as the Dodgers broke through for a run on two singles sandwiched around a walk.

But the Cardinals came right back. Dyer had Dusak in left field today against Hatten, and after Galan had thrown out Slaughter to begin the second, Dusak hit a high drive to left. Dick Whitman raced back and leaped against the wall, catching the ball, but the impact knocked it from his glove, and Dusak ended up at third with a triple. When Marion flied deep to Furillo, Dusak scored easily, and the game was tied. But not for long. Clyde Kluttz singled to center to keep the Cardinals alive, and Dickson came to the plate. Like a number of other Cardinals pitchers, he could handle the bat well, could get a bunt down, hit behind the runner, and chip in his own hits: as he faced Hatten he was hitting a very respectable .253. Now he hit a high line drive that sailed far over Furillo's head for a triple that scored Kluttz with the second run. But that was all St. Louis could get in the inning.

His own hit seemed to settle Dickson down, for after walking Edwards in the second he retired eight in a row, and as he came to the dugout for the St. Louis fifth he was pitching as if that one-run lead might be enough. As it turned out, his teammates were about to take a good deal of pressure off him, for with two outs in their half of the fifth they landed on Hatten and drove him to the showers. As usual in Ebbets Field where he hit so magnificently, the instigator was Musial, who doubled to right. Durocher ordered Hatten to walk Kurowski in order to pitch to the left-handed hitting Slaughter—orthodox strategy but risky since Slaughter had led the league in runs-batted-in. Moreover, it was the kind of challenge the combative Country relished. "For years," he recalled, "they always said the way to stop the Cardinals was to stop Musial and Slaughter with left-handers. But we saw so many of 'em that I got to where I could almost hit a left-hander better'n I could a righty. Didn't bother me a bit." It certainly didn't bother him now as he hit one of Hatten's curves between Furillo and Dixie Walker for a triple that scored Musial and Kurowski and opened some daylight between the two teams. When Dusak singled in Slaughter, the gap got wider, and Durocher lifted Hatten in favor of Behrman who got out of the inning without further scoring.

Dickson and the Cardinals cruised into the last of the ninth inning with an 8–1 lead, and it hardly seemed to matter when Augie Galan led off with a double, the first Dodgers hit since Stevens's run-scoring single in Dickson's jittery first. One out later, Stevens drove in his team's second run with a triple. When Furillo followed with a single, scoring Stevens, it became evident that Dickson had either lost his stuff or his concentration. Then he bounced a pitch into the dirt, allowing Furillo to move up a base, and walked Reese. Dyer had had Brecheen loosening up in the bullpen, but he'd also wanted to save him if he could to open the World Series. But quite suddenly things were threatening to get out of hand, and Dyer felt he needed Brecheen here and now.

The Ebbets Field crowd had been hushed by the Cardinals big fifth, and they'd watched with gathering grimness as Dickson marched through the Dodgers order in the sixth, seventh, and eighth. Now they came alive with a vengeance, screaming encouragement to their beloved Bums as Brecheen took his warm-ups. For the first time this afternoon the Dodgers bench was standing, and they stayed up when Brecheen promptly gave up a hard single to left to Bruce Edwards. Now it was 8–4, and still only one out. Durocher sent the veteran Cookie Lavagetto up to hit for the pitcher, and Brecheen walked him, filling the bases and bringing up Stanky and the top of the Dodgers order. Brecheen was well aware of Stanky's customary offensive strategy and knew he rarely offered at the first pitch. Besides, in this situation, Stanky would be especially eager to coax a walk, forcing in a run and keeping the bases full for the heart of the order. "The best way to pitch him," Brecheen said, "was to go right after him with strikes," and this is what he did. But with two strikes on him, Stanky went into his routine of spoiling one good pitch after another, fouling them off. Against a left-handed screwball pitcher the right-handed batter is deprived of his natural advantage because the screwball breaks away from him, and now Brecheen broke off a beauty that umpire Babe Pinelli said caught the outside corner for strike three. In close calls everyone in the league knew umpires weren't going to do Eddie Stanky any favors: that was both the history Stanky had made and the law of human nature. Pinelli had called him out, and Durocher and his Dodgers were down to their last out.

Durocher lifted Whitman in favor of the right-handed hitting Schultz who'd had a big day in the opener of the playoffs and who now represented the winning run if he could hit one out of the park. Schultz pulled Brecheen's first pitch hard down the left field line, but it landed outside the foul line and was only a long strike. Then, working with the greatest of care, Brecheen brought the count full. This was the situation, Ted Williams used to tell his teammates, that as a hitter you had to love because then you knew damn well what you were going to get: you were going to get the pitcher's best pitch, whatever that was. But Schultz was no Williams, and when Brecheen took some pace off his screwball, Schultz could only lunge futilely at it, striking out and ending both the game and his team's valiant battle against a more talented squad.

In the dead quiet of the Brooklyn dressing room, Durocher had little to say to his players. As Augie Galan remarked, "What the hell could you say except, 'Thanks, and we'll get 'em next year'?" Durocher then went into his office where several of his celebrity friends were waiting, among them movie actor George Raft, a heavy bettor on ball games. Over in the Cardinals clubhouse the scene was quite different, of course, and Eddie Dyer took the opportunity to remind his many well-wishers that the play-offs just concluded had really been between two organizations built by one man. Branch Rickey had signed so many of these players, Dyer said, and had gotten him started in the game. He owed the Mahatma a great deal for the success he'd just achieved. It was a handsome gesture that contrasted sharply with Dyer's refusal to make the customary bow in the direction of his defeated adversary. Clearly, he had no use for Leo Durocher.

PART 3

World Series

18

*W*hile St. Louis and Brooklyn were fighting it out for the right to meet Boston in the Series, someone in the Red Sox front office got the idea of gathering a team of American Leaguers to play some games against the Sox to keep them sharp during the week they had off. A squad that included Snuffy Stirnweiss, Joe DiMaggio, Cecil Travis, Luke Appling of the White Sox, Phil Marchildon, Dizzy Trout, Hal Newhouser, and Hank Greenberg came to Boston for games on the first three days of October. They were to be paid with the receipts of the games while the Sox would be paid a pro-rated share of their yearly salaries.

Though sound in theory, the idea proved bad in practice. Only 1,996 turned out on Tuesday, October 1, a raw, miserable day for baseball. In the fifth inning Williams batted against Mickey Haefner, the little left-hander whose offspeed stuff usually gave Williams trouble. This time Haefner served up even more trouble when his curveball hit Williams on the point of his right elbow. Cronin immediately pulled him from the game, but before it was over the elbow was twice its normal size. So, while the exhibitions went on, Williams soaked his elbow in a whirlpool bath and hoped for the best. But now, in addition to the injury, he developed one of the fall chest colds that so often plagued him, and he wasn't feeling at all well when the team departed for St. Louis on October 4. Things quickly got worse because en route the Colonel, Dave Egan, struck again, choosing this uniquely opportune moment to write that he had it on the best authority that whatever the outcome of the Series, Ted Williams wouldn't be a Red Sox in 1947. Yawkey, Egan asserted, was offering the Kid to the highest bidder: already there'd been serious talk with the Tigers about a Williams-for-Newhouser deal; and Yawkey had also talked with MacPhail about a Williams-for-DiMaggio swap.

At the Chase Hotel where the Sox put up, Egan's story created exactly the explosion he'd hoped for as Clif Keane and the other writers scrambled frantically to track down the truth of the story. Yawkey was nowhere to be found, but Keane did come across Williams talking with famed columnist Grantland Rice, and it was immediately obvious that Egan's primary objective had been achieved: Williams was both disturbed and worried. He hated New York as a town, he said, and Yankee Stadium as a park. It had a lousy hitting background, he thought, especially when there were big crowds in the center field seats and a haze of cigarette smoke hanging in the afternoon sun.

While there may have been nothing to the Newhouser rumor, and there is no doubt that the timing of Egan's story was maliciously motivated, apparently there was something to the Williams-for-DiMaggio story. The well-connected writer Roger Kahn claimed years later that Yawkey and MacPhail had had a boozy conversation in Toots Shor's in New York early in the season when DiMaggio was playing poorly and MacPhail was disenchanted with his big star. The two owners, according to Kahn, discussed the trade and even agreed on it, but sober reflection the morning after prompted Yawkey to call MacPhail to say he couldn't go through with it. Another Boston owner had let Babe Ruth go to New York, Yawkey reminded MacPhail, and if he let Ted Williams travel the same route—even for Joe DiMaggio—he wouldn't be able to show his face in the city.

The rumor (which Yawkey was oddly slow to deny) and Williams's elbow injury notwithstanding, the betting line on October 6 as the Series opened had the Sox the prohibitive favorites at 4–1. The real action here, however, was whether the Red Sox could sweep the Cardinals. They had a dynamite offensive team, the odds makers pointed out, with three .300 hitters (Pesky, DiMaggio, and Williams); three men who'd driven home well over a hundred runs each (Doerr, York, and Williams); and they had four outstanding starters. In short, they could overpower you with their bats, and their pitchers could stifle your offense. In Slaughter, Kurowski, and batting champion Musial the Cardinals had three .300 hitters of their own, and both Slaughter and Musial had driven in more than a hundred runs. But the Red Sox lineup was considered to be far more explosive, and as a team they'd scored almost a hundred runs more than the Cardinals. And while no one was scoffing at Cardinals starters Pollet, Dickson, and Brecheen, everybody knew that Pollet was coming into the Series hurt and that Munger hadn't yet shown he was capable of taking up any slack. Could this staff stop the Red Sox bats? Most doubted it, probably even the Sox. In a team meeting before the opener Mike Ryba, who'd once pitched for the Cardinals, cautioned his teammates not to pay any attention to the odds makers who'd made Boston such heavy favorites. Cardinals teams always hustled like hell, he told them, and they never gave up. There were a few guffaws from the players, and somebody said, "Aw, Mike, once a Cardinal, always a Cardinal, right?" But Ryba persisted. "All right, all right," he said, "but if we don't watch out, they're gonna beat our ass."

★   ★   ★

*T*he pitching match-up for the first game pitted Tex Hughson against Pollet. October 6 was a day of brilliant sun and deep blue shadow, and those sitting in the field-side boxes soon felt the sun's power while those in the shadows of the stands wanted to keep their jackets on. Even as the grounds crew attempted to groom the scabby infield the shadow of the first base stands and light towers extended almost to the first base line, and for much of the game batters would be standing in shadow, trying to pick up pitches speeding at them from the sunlit mound. Outside the park, scalpers were asking and getting $85 for a block of three tickets and $25 for a single grandstand seat. Inside, among the current stars of the game and dignitaries like the commissioner and the league presidents, was a scattering of former stars including Cardinals greats Rogers Hornsby and Grover Cleveland Alexander in the rumpled three-piece suit he seemed to live in. The Cooper brothers, Mort and Walker, were there as well, perhaps lamenting Sam Breadon's fiscal policies that had exiled them to Boston and New York and prevented them from participating in another Series with their old mates. Frank Crespi was also there, still in the army and still recuperating from his injured leg. Sitting in Breadon's box as his honored guest was one of the Pasquel brothers, Gerardo, a sight that was distinctly upsetting to Happy Chandler. But the Breadon-Chandler rift was now so open and deep that it was being said that Breadon was seriously thinking of selling the Cardinals rather than having to face the prospect of further dealings with the commissioner. One of the more intriguing rumors had him selling to movie mogul Louis B. Mayer who would then move the club to Los Angeles.

In batting practice Williams hoisted several balls over the screen in right, and his elbow was feeling better than he'd expected. He did not, however, feel really "swishy," as he put it, meaning loose and fluid in his swing, and he was not to feel that way throughout the Series.* The odds makers and bettors who watched him take his practice cuts could discern no impairment in his superb swing, and the heavy money stayed on the Red Sox.

After both teams had gone quietly in the first, Williams led off the second against Pollet. When he got his sign, Pollet looked into the Cardinals dugout and stepped off the rubber as his infield went into a version of the Boudreau shift. In pre-Series meetings with his infielders and pitchers Dyer had discussed employing the Boudreau shift, but his scouts who'd been following the Sox through September thought Boudreau's positioning was too extreme, especially after they saw Williams hit his inside-the-park homer in Cleveland. Dyer's modified version had Kurowski the lone infielder on the left side, playing where Marion normally would, but both players suggested that if this was the way he wanted to defense Williams, then it ought to be Marion at short with his greater range and stronger arm. And that was what now took place, Kurowski trotting over to the right of second, Schoendienst playing a wide first base, and Musial hugging the line. In the outfield, Slaughter and Moore were pulled around toward right, but Harry Walker played a normal left field.

Before the Series Dyer had given an interview to Clif Keane and Dick Young of the New York *Daily News* in which he'd said he wasn't going to use any kind of shift, and both writers thought they had a scoop. Evidently Williams had read what they wrote because now he looked a trifle nonplussed as the Cardinals shifted around, Kurowski shading his eyes for a moment with his glove now that he had to look into the sun. Then Williams shrugged his shoulders in a show of resignation and took his stance. When he grounded sharply to Schoendienst the strategy seemed vindicated: against a conventional alignment the ball would have gone through for a hit.

In the last of the eighth with the score tied, 1–1, and the cold-eyed Hughson pitching brilliantly, Kurowski lined a single to left after Hughson had easily retired Musial and Slaughter. Garagiola followed with a high drive to right-center, the ball rising up out of the deep shadow of the

---

* Williams's roommate Charlie Wagner said he asked him several times during the Series if the elbow was giving him trouble, and each time Williams said it wasn't. "He never made an excuse of the elbow," Wagner said. "Never."

Ted Williams bats against Pollet and Eddie Dyer's version of the Boudreau Shift in Game One of the World Series at St. Louis. Left fielder Harry Walker and shortstop Marty Marion are the only fielders covering the left side of the diamond. (Bettmann Archive)

infield into the bright October sun. DiMaggio gave chase, only to realize at the last moment that he'd overrun the ball and that it was going to drop behind him. Desperately, he wheeled about, took a couple of strides the other way, and caught up with the ball yet again, but his balance was off, and Garagiola's drive ticked off his glove and fell safely. Meanwhile, Kurowski, who'd been running on Garagiola's swing, was nearing third, but as he tore around the bag, Red Sox third baseman Pinky Higgins stepped into his path and gave him a hip—one of baseball's oldest illegal defensive plays. Kurowski got momentarily entangled with Higgins, then headed for home again and scored, but not before DiMaggio had alertly recovered and thrown to Pesky whose relay to Higgins caught the sliding Garagiola. Garagiola was called out and Kurowski's run didn't count.

But both third base umpire Charlie Berry and Lee Ballanfant behind the plate saw what Higgins had done, and Ballanfant ruled that Kurowski's run would count. That brought Cronin and his boys boiling out of the Boston dugout and swarming around Ballanfant. Hal Wagner kept trying to get at Ballanfant and had to be restrained by teammates, but the umpire stood his ground. "The first SOB who lays a hand on me is *through!*" he told them, and when Berry, a big, rough ex-football star, came striding into the melee to back him up, Cronin and the others went growling back to their places. The Cardinals would take a 2–1 lead into the ninth.

Things began well for them as Pollet fanned Doerr to open the inning, but then the Sportsman's Park "Rockpile" became a factor as Higgins hit a high, bouncing ball to shortstop. Marion moved a few quick steps to his right and was in a perfect position to field it when the ball took a freakish dive, skidded under his glove, and rolled into the outfield. The official scorer, taking into account the field's notorious idiosyncrasies, credited Higgins with a hit. But Marion, with his high standards, said later, "That wasn't any single. That was a plain, old error. I missed it." Now Cronin went to his bench. He sent reserve infielder Don Gutteridge to run for Higgins, and Gutteridge raced around to third when pinch-hitter Rip Russell lined a solid single to center off a plainly weary Pollet. With Hughson due to hit, Cronin sent up Roy Partee for him, but as he had so often during the season, Pollet was able to reach back to get the big out, striking Partee out on a high outside pitch. Now Pollet and the Cardinals were just one out away from victory.

The batter was right fielder Tom McBride who hadn't hit the ball out of the infield in his four previous trips and twice had rolled meekly to

Kurowski. With two strikes on him now, Garagiola flashed Pollet the sign for a fastball, but Pollet shook him off. The club's rule, Garagiola said, was that if a pitcher shook you off, you gave him the same sign. If he shook you off again, you went out to the mound to talk with him. If he shook you off after that consultation, you looked for help from the manager. "It was shadows in there," Garagiola recalled, "and I wanted fastball. Well, Dyer came out and asked, 'What the hell is going on?' Pollet said, 'He wants a fastball; I think I can get him with my curve.' Dyer asked me, 'Why do you want a fastball?' And I said, 'Because it's hard to see back there now.' Pollet said, 'I think he'll have more trouble seeing my curve,' and that was the end of the conversation." Garagiola went back behind the plate, Pollet threw the curve, and McBride hit what Garagiola called a "nineteen-hopper" that just squeezed between Kurowski and the racing Marion for a hit that tied the game. Then Pollet got the final out, and after reliever Earl Johnson had easily retired the Cardinals in their half the teams headed into extra innings.

Though he had available the lefty-righty relief duo of Brazle and Wilks, Dyer stuck with Pollet, even though it was evident on the bench that Pollet was tired and pitching in pain. Apparently the manager believed that even in such a condition Pollet was still the best he could send out there and was remembering how in the heat of the race his southpaw had completed eleven consecutive games. As he had in the ninth, Pollet began well, getting DiMaggio to ground out and Williams to pop up to Musial. That brought York to the plate. All afternoon Pollet had had the big slugger guessing wrong and lunging at the ball. Twice York had fouled out and had looked overmatched against the clever Cardinals left-hander. But York could look helpless three times in a row and hurt you badly the fourth, and late in the game he'd made another of his predictions to his teammates. "He's gonna throw me a changeup one time," York said, "and when he does, I'm gonna hit it." And that was the pitch Dyer now signalled he wanted Pollet to throw. When he did, York was waiting for it, kept his weight and his bat well back, then hit a tremendous soaring drive to left. When he connected, York hesitated a moment at the plate as if admiring his ball's trajectory, and then began his trot to first. Garagiola, on the other hand, looked down and removed his mask. In left field Harry Walker took a couple of quick strides toward the wall, then gave up as the ball carried deep into the packed bleachers and crashed against a hot dog stand. When Earl Johnson again set down

Rudy York crosses the plate after smashing a tremendous home run off Howie Pollet in the tenth inning of Game One. York, a notorious "guess" hitter was looking for a changeup, and that was the pitch manager Dyer signalled Pollet he wanted. Joe Garagiola tosses out a new ball as Bobby Doerr offers his congratulations. (*The Sporting News,* October 16, 1946)

the Cardinals in the last of the tenth, the Sox had inflicted a particularly disheartening defeat on the Cardinals. They'd beaten the best of the Cardinals, and they'd done it without any help from Williams, who was certain to be heard from soon. Betting action on a Boston sweep increased substantially.

★ ★ ★

*B*ut there would be no Boston sweep: Harry Brecheen saw to that. The wiry left-hander stopped the Red Sox in the second game on four scattered singles, one of them a scratch, as the Cardinals won, 3–0. And as he had all year, he helped himself with his bat when he drove in the game's first run with a single off Red Sox starter Mickey Harris.

Harry (the Cat) Brecheen showing how he turns his wrist over in delivering his screwball. His catcher Joe Garagiola said Brecheen not only effectively utilized the pitch but also the threat of it. (Broeg, *Redbirds*)

Brecheen was coming into the Series in the best physical shape he'd been in all season. Though he'd pitched well over 200 innings, the strain on him wasn't as evident as it was on pitchers who depended more on velocity for their effectiveness and who often lost some of it in the late season going. Brecheen's pitching was built more on finesse and out-thinking the hitter than on overpowering him, and now his arm actually felt better than it had in the earlier part of the season when it had been consistently sore and badly swollen after games: his wife, Vera, said that often after he'd pitched, his arm would be so swollen he couldn't slip it into the sleeve of a jacket. At one point, both Brecheen and Beazley had secretly been going to the same St. Louis chiropractor, but neither got relief from his treatments. But gradually, though his arm still ached after games, Brecheen found that it was gaining in strength and that he was getting better movement on his pitches with a bit less effort, and he'd pitched brilliantly in some crucial games in September.

In many ways this second game effort was typical of him: he had a definite game plan, he was able to execute it—and his teammates didn't give him much support. His relatively undistinguished season's record of 15–15 reflected that lack of support while his 2.49 earned-run-average was more indicative of his accomplishments. Most of the walks Brecheen gave up in games were purposeful, and of the three he'd doled out today, two were to York. "That park wasn't as big as that boy," was his laconic comment on York, whom he'd pitched against in the minors.

What drama there was to the game came from watching Brecheen work on Williams. In the pre-Series strategy sessions Brecheen had announced he intended to throw screwballs to Williams, thus, in a sense, negating a left-hander's purpose in developing the pitch in the first place, which was to use it almost exclusively on right-handed batters where it would break away from them. Throwing it to Williams was throwing it to break into his power zone. Yet this is what Brecheen told Garagiola and Del Rice he was planning to do.

"I never heard of a left-handed pitcher throwing a screwball to a left-handed batter," Garagiola said, and he was both perplexed and worried. In team meetings, protocol called for a rookie like Garagiola to keep his mouth shut. After matters had been discussed, Dyer might ask if there were any questions, but that remark was really addressed to the veterans. Therefore, Garagiola said nothing in public about his concerns, but he needed advice and reassurance from somewhere because he knew the critical importance of being on the same wavelength as his pitcher. A catcher thinking along a line not shared by his batterymate constantly puts down signs that contradict what his pitcher wants to throw, and the result is confusion and a loss of rhythm. Brecheen put it this way from his pitcher's perspective: "If you're thinking screwball and he's thinking curveball, then you're just kind of wishy-washy the whole game. But if you're thinking together—if he puts down curve, and you're thinking curve—that's when you pitch your best." So Garagiola sought out Pollet in private and asked him, "Can you throw a screwball to a left-handed hitter?" "Brecheen can and will," Pollet replied. And that, as far as the young catcher was concerned, was that.

Brecheen's plan had its origin in spring training when he'd noted the success some of the Cardinals pitchers had had crowding Williams. "It looked like he didn't like the ball in on him," Brecheen said. "Nobody wanted to pitch him in there, of course, because if you missed that little spot, he's liable to hit it out of the park. But if you could get it in that little spot, if he did hit it, he's likely to foul it off." Pollet had successfully jammed Williams in Game One, though Williams had twice hit the ball sharply, once leading off the second when he'd grounded to Schoendienst, and again in the sixth when he'd singled. Watching Pollet was heartening to his fellow left-hander who said to himself, "With Howard being a left-hander and pitching Williams so good, if I throw the ball where I'm looking, I can do it, too." And Brecheen had done just that. He got Williams to ground out to Musial leading off the second. He struck him out swinging in the fourth. In the sixth with one out Williams lined to Schoendienst on a ball that would have been a hit against a conventional alignment. But the measure of Williams's frustration with Brecheen's pitching pattern and the deployment of the shift came in the ninth.

DiMaggio led off with a scratch single, bringing up Williams with York and Doerr to follow. And Williams, thinking to cross up the shift by going to left, waited a fraction of a second on the pitch Brecheen threw him. It was another tight screwball that Williams hit near his fists, and he could produce only a weak pop foul that Marion took near the St. Louis dugout. Then York hit a fly to Slaughter and Doerr flied deep to Walker and the game was over. Brecheen had not only gotten his team back into the Series and stilled all that talk of a sweep, but he'd confirmed the validity of pitching Williams inside. Williams was a great hitter—all the Cardinals pitchers knew that, and Brecheen himself said that aside from Musial, the batter he most admired was the Kid. But as great as Williams was, what Pollet and Brecheen had done against him strongly suggested that before he could figure out how to adjust the Series might be over. If the Cardinals could neutralize him, a huge obstacle in their path to the championship would be removed.

★   ★   ★

*B*efore the Series began there had been some talk about the fact that Cronin was holding back his twenty-five-game winner, Dave Ferriss, until Game Three when the Series shifted to Boston. But Cronin's strategy was sound, and Ferriss himself never questioned it. Cronin hadn't wanted left-hander Harris to have to pitch in Fenway Park with its cozy left field wall, and he wanted Hughson, who pitched high in the strike zone, to have the advantage of the slightly bigger park in St. Louis. Both Hughson and Harris had pitched well enough to win, though neither had, and now it was Ferriss's turn, opposed by Dickson on a chilly, sunny day with temperatures in the high fifties and most of the fans in coats and hats.

Fenway Park's dimensions didn't bother Ferriss at all, and this season he'd gone 12–1 there. Early in his career he'd learned what he had to do to win, what he could and couldn't do as a pitcher. Like some others, he'd learned this in the service. Stationed at Randolph Field near San Antonio, Ferriss had the good fortune to come under the stern tutelage of Bibb Falk, the hard-hitting outfielder who'd replaced the disgraced Joe Jackson with the White Sox. Falk was a rough-tongued man with an old-fashioned, warrior's approach to baseball, but he knew the game thoroughly and could communicate that knowledge to those who'd listen. "He ran our army team just like he would a pro team," Ferriss said. "He wouldn't stand for any foolishness: we were there to play ball and to win." When he came to Falk, Ferriss was a straightforward power pitcher who relied primarily on his fastball. With this and his excellent control he'd enjoyed great success in amateur ball in Mississippi and then had made a solid debut in the minors in 1942 before entering the service. But Falk saw that Ferriss wouldn't be able to advance through higher levels of baseball and get batters out this way. His fastball, Falk convinced him, wasn't quite good enough to overpower hitters at the higher levels, especially when he had to come in with it when he was behind in the count. Ferriss was an intelligent man and a good listener, and he was appealing to Falk because the coach found that his pupil loved the game as much as he did. Falk taught Ferriss the art of pitching: how to set a hitter up for a certain pitch, how to spot the ball, how to make his fastball sink. When Ferriss got a medical discharge for severe asthma in February 1945, he was a far more accomplished pitcher than anyone knew, except Ferriss and Falk themselves.

Soon enough big league hitters would discover to their surprise and sorrow just how accomplished he really was as he recorded an astonishing 46 wins in his first two seasons. He wasn't overpowering, as Falk had foreseen, and he gave up an average of a hit an inning. But this was a deceiving statistic because many of those hits came when they counted for little: when he had a big lead, with two outs, or with the bases empty.

When it counted, batters found him very tough to hit, and his sinking fastball produced a great many ground outs and double-play balls—the pitcher's best friend. That made him ideally suited to pitch in Fenway Park where a fly-ball pitcher was always at some risk.

Warming up before the game, Ferriss felt good and loose and his ball was moving. "But," he admitted, "I had some butterflies. World Series, you know. You tell yourself it's just another game, but it isn't, with the flags flying and the bands playing." Indeed, as he threw his warmup pitches in front of the Boston dugout, he practically had to shorten his stride to avoid the crowd of photographers sprawled at his feet. "Dizzy Dean was there," Ferriss recalled. "He had that big, Texas-style hat on, and he was cutting up, and that helped me keep loose. 'Just be natural, man,' he said to me, 'just be loose. You've done it all year, you'll do it again.'" Down in Ferriss's hometown of Shaw, Mississippi, the president of Delta State College turned out classes and instead required the students to listen to the radio broadcast. And the students had something to cheer about in the very first inning as their hero easily retired Schoendienst and Moore on ground outs. Then he walked Musial who promptly stole second. But Musial was then guilty of an uncharacteristic mental lapse, wandering away from second, and Ferriss picked him off. "That," Ferriss said, "was probably the best way to pitch him: walk, steal, and pick off."*

Now it was the Red Sox's turn at bat, their first in the Series before their long-suffering New England fans. With one out, Pesky, held hitless in St. Louis, broke through in characteristic fashion, flaring a single into left. DiMaggio bounced slowly to Musial who had no chance to force the speedy Pesky and so tagged the batter out. Then came the Kid, who heard among the cheers some raucous boos for his failures in St. Louis, but with first base open, Dyer wasn't going to give him a chance to wreck things in the first inning and ordered an intentional walk. There was little rest in the Red Sox's lineup, however, and Dickson now had to face York with Doerr on deck. When Brecheen had walked York twice in Game Two, he'd done it in bases-empty situations where he could afford to pitch York high and away, hoping to get him to reach for one and pop it up. Dickson didn't have that luxury here. He had to come in to York, and

---

* Years afterward, when both men were retired from the game, Ferriss asked Musial what he'd been thinking about in that situation. Musial laughed and answered, "I have no idea."

when he did so on a full count, York slugged a soaring drive to left-center that was still climbing when it landed on top of the wall and bounded out into the street.

Handed a handsome three-run cushion in the first, Ferriss pitched with a masterful dispatch and shut out the Cardinals, 4–0. He got fourteen outs on ground balls, and of the six St. Louis hits he gave up, all came with the bases empty. When he struck Slaughter out on a curveball to end the game, he called for the ball, then trotted over to the boxes and presented it to his mother.

Except for York's big blow, Dickson had pitched creditably until replaced by Wilks in the eighth. After the homer he gave up only four more hits and no runs. One of the hits was a two-out bunt single down the third base line by Williams, yet another sign of the slugger's frustration. One Boston paper the next day would run as its headline, not Ferriss's shutout, but, "WILLIAMS BUNTS." It infuriated Williams.

★ ★ ★

*C*ronin came back with Hughson in Game Four while Dyer sent out Red Munger, giving the ailing Pollet another day's rest. In the first inning, anyway, it looked as if the hard-throwing Hughson was in good form as the Cardinals didn't get the ball out of the infield, but with the beginning of the second there were signs that this wasn't going to be one of his good outings when Slaughter lashed a wicked line drive into the lower right field seats. The ball was hit so hard right fielder Wally Moses hardly had time to react before it disappeared into the crowd. Next, Kurowski hammered one off the left field wall and with a hook slide beat Williams's good throw to second. Hughson got one out when Garagiola flied to DiMaggio, but Walker kept things going with a line single to right, giving the Cardinals a three-run lead.

Things got worse in the third. Schoendienst led off with a single to center, and when Moore laid down a bunt to the right of the mound the normally poised Hughson fumbled it, then, still trying for the out, threw wildly over Doerr's head at first; Schoendienst went around to third and Moore to second. Perhaps because of the way Slaughter had landed on Hughson in the first and because Musial wasn't hitting much better than Williams, Cronin let Hughson pitch to the National League batting champion with first base open. It was a mistake: Musial hit one of his patented drives into the right-center field gap to score Schoendienst and

Moore. That was all for Hughson, who was replaced by Jim Bagby, the first of a file of Boston relievers on what would come to feel like an endless afternoon for Red Sox fans. And before Bagby could get out of the inning Garagiola padded the Cardinals lead by driving in Musial with the first of the four hits he would get today.

With such a big early lead Munger's job was simplified: throw strikes and don't try anything fancy. The Sox got to him for a run in the fourth when Williams singled and the red-hot York hit a long double, and in the eighth Doerr hit a two-run homer after Marion had erred on DiMaggio's grounder. But by that time the Cardinals had eight runs of their own, Munger was throwing all fastballs, and when his teammates piled on four more runs in the top of the ninth (including an oddly superfluous sacrifice bunt by Kurowski), he coasted to a lopsided 12–3 victory that for the third time tied up the Series.

★ ★ ★

*W*hen a team opens on the road in the Series, traditional baseball wisdom has it that their best chance to win requires them to take one of the first two games in the enemy's park. Failure to do that brings them home in a deep hole, needing to win four of the remaining five games against the champions of the other league.* The same store of wisdom holds that, having achieved a split on the road, they put themselves in a strong position by taking two of the three games they play at home; if they accomplish this, they put the pressure on the other team to win the final two to close out the Series. The Red Sox had accomplished the first task when they'd snatched Game One from the Cardinals with Pollet one out from victory. And after splitting the first two in Fenway Park, they were sending Joe Dobson out in hopes of accomplishing that second task and shifting all the pressure to St. Louis.

On another team Dobson would have been a star. But this team was loaded with sluggers who got headlines for their batting feats, while for once the Sox had enough quality starters so that Dobson didn't get either the attention or the pitching opportunities he otherwise might have.† As it was, he'd won thirteen and established himself as a solid, reliable fourth

---

* Home teams that have won the first two games have gone on to win the Series twenty-four out of twenty-eight times through 1995.

† When injuries wrecked the Red Sox pitching staff in 1947 Dobson did get more opportunities, and his win totals mounted accordingly over the next four seasons.

man, capable with his curveball of an occasional outstanding performance. Dyer was sending Pollet against him, hoping to squeeze one more good effort from his crippled ace, but he knew he might not get it. Even in Game One Pollet's back and shoulder pain had him digging his nails into his palms between innings, and the club's physician Robert Hyland had come on to Boston to work on him and try to get him ready for Game Five.

But it was no go for Pollet. On another sunny, crisp afternoon he threw only ten pitches to four batters before retiring, and by the time Dyer had gotten Brazle to the rescue the Sox had a run in, runners at second and third, and only one out. Gutteridge, substituting for Doerr who was out with a migraine, had singled on Pollet's first pitch and then on a one-strike pitch Pesky had singled to right. DiMaggio forced Gutteridge with a grounder to Kurowski, the only out Pollet would get. When Williams singled hard to right for the run, Dyer had to acknowledge he wasn't going to get any more from Pollet in 1946. Brazle came in, walked York intentionally to set up force plays, and then got them with his hard sinker. "When you hit it," Brecheen said of that pitch, "it was like you had hit a rock."

The Red Sox picked up single runs in the second and in the sixth when Leon Culberson hit a Brazle pitch over the left field wall, and in the seventh they iced the game with three more. Into the ninth the only Cardinals run had come on Pesky's second-inning error, and now they got two more, thanks again to Pesky who with Musial at first and one out fumbled what would have been a game-ending double-play grounder. With two outs, Harry Walker picked up the runs with a single, making the final score 6–3.

Pollet wasn't the only Cardinals casualty in the loss. In the fourth inning Dobson hit Slaughter on the elbow with a slider. "He'd been pitching me tight," Slaughter said, "and this time when I leaned back from one, it just followed me and hit me on the crazy bone. I didn't rub it—I never rubbed where I got hit. I just took my base."

"I didn't do it on purpose," Dobson said, but when Slaughter had to come out of the game in the seventh, Dobson thought to himself, "Well, I don't suppose he's going to be able to play any more, and that will just be too bad." Slaughter hadn't missed an inning all season, but by the seventh the elbow was so swollen he couldn't flex his arm, and Dyer replaced him with Erv Dusak. After the game when the team boarded their train for the trip back to St. Louis, Doc Weaver closeted himself with Slaughter and wrapped the elbow in a towel infused with Epsom salts and then wrapped the towel in an electric sleeve. The pair stayed that way the entire way back with Weaver changing the towels, but when Robert Hyland examined the arm in St. Louis he found so severe a hematoma he told Slaughter the consequences of getting hit there again could be very serious. "He said he could even have to amputate in that case," Slaughter said, "and I said, 'Doc, that's a gamble I'll have to take. I'm playing.' " By Sunday, though the arm was still very sore and swollen, Slaughter found he had some movement in it and went to the park where he sought out Red Schoendienst. "I really couldn't throw hardly at all," Slaughter said. "They didn't know that, and I bluffed throwing, but I said to Red, 'Red, when the ball's hit out to me, come way out towards me and pick me up.' " When the Red Sox took the field for their pregame warmups, there was Number 9, playing catch near the Cardinals dugout. Dobson and his teammates were amazed. "I thought I had him out of there," Dobson admitted. He and the rest of the Red Sox were soon to wish he had.

★   ★   ★

*H*arry Brecheen woke up Tuesday morning feeling awful. His arm still ached from the gritty seven-hitter he'd pitched in Sunday's Game Six, but yesterday, an off-day, he'd felt something coming on, and here it was: the flu. So, in addition to the ache in his arm, which he'd come to live with, he now felt achy in every joint of his thin frame.

In Sunday's game he'd squared the Series with his 4–1 win over Mickey Harris, and once again he'd neutralized Ted Williams. He'd walked Williams in the first; got him to pop up to Musial in the fourth; struck him out on a screwball in the seventh; and in the ninth with one out Williams singled hard up the middle. But in both instances when Williams had reached base, Brecheen had gotten York to hit into double plays. In the first, Brecheen had walked Williams semi-intentionally after one-out singles by Pesky and DiMaggio because, even though York was the Series' hottest hitter, Brecheen felt he had a better chance against him than the great Williams. His strategy worked when York hit a screwball hard but right at Kurowski who started the double play that took Brecheen out of what might have been a disastrous inning. In the ninth, after Williams had singled, here was big Rudy again, and again Brecheen employed the same pitching strategy against him. York, Brecheen said, was "strictly power" and aimed to pull the ball. If you could keep your pitches low and not catch too much of the plate with them, he said, York would have to reach for them, in which case "he's liable to hit it to one of your middle infielders." Brecheen had been trying to do just that in York's previous at-bat as well, but he hadn't gotten the ball far enough away from him and York hit it off the center field wall for a triple. Now he threw one low and away, but York still got good wood on it, sending a hot shot up the middle. Around the National League they called Brecheen "The Cat" in tribute to his nimbleness on the mound: he was the league's best fielding pitcher, they said, a kind of fifth infielder. York's ball was hit a bit to Brecheen's left, but he was able to slow it up enough for Schoendienst to get to it and toss it to Marion to begin the double play that ended the game.

The big double play and the bigger win apparently concluded Brecheen's season, and the way he was feeling this morning, he certainly had to hope so. But there was never a thought in his mind of calling in sick, anymore than Slaughter had considered sitting out the Series' last two games. So Brecheen dragged himself to Sportsman's Park, dressed, and took a seat on the bench without so much as mentioning his condition to the manager. What would be the point? he asked himself. Here they all were on the last day of a campaign that had begun eight months ago in Florida. "Didn't make a difference how you might be feeling," as he succinctly put it. But along with his teammates' fervent hopes for starter Murry Dickson, Brecheen had private hopes that no situation would develop in which Dyer would have to look to him for help.

Over on the Boston side of the field Dave Ferriss felt pretty good as he took his warmups under a hot sun. Maybe he wasn't quite as sharp as he'd felt before Game Three, but he thought he had enough to win. His main concern was the five left-handed batters Dyer had in there against him because he was his most effective throwing with a sidearm delivery. Against left-handed batters, though, he was obliged to alter his delivery to three-quarters overhand because the lefties simply got too good a look at the ball from his preferred delivery point. Of course, those same five left-handed hitters had faced him in Game Three, and he'd pitched a shutout. But he knew also that of the six hits he'd given up the lefties had gotten four.

The Sox started fast against Dickson. The veteran Moses, a place hitter having a fine Series, singled to center and then went around to third when Marion couldn't stop Pesky's slow bouncer just to the left of the mound.

DiMaggio flied to Slaughter in medium-deep right, and Slaughter had no play on Moses who scored the game's first run. With Williams at the plate the Cardinals went into the modified shift they'd used since his third game bunt, with Kurowski playing a wide third base, but Williams got a good swing at Dickson's pitch and sent it deep into the unprotected area in straight-away center field. Terry Moore was swung well into right-center, but Williams's drive was up high and Moore, creaky legs and all, was able to catch up with it as it was dropping in for a certain second run. Dickson, saved by Moore's fine catch, got York to pop up to Schoendienst. The Sox had the lead, but as had happened with a telling frequency in the Series, they hadn't been able to capitalize fully on a big opportunity. Getting a single run after two were on, none out, and your big hitters up wasn't the way to win a ball game against a team as talented and determined as the Cardinals.

The Cardinals mounted a threat of their own in the home half of the first, but Williams threw out Schoendienst trying to stretch a single into a double, and after Musial had doubled, Ferriss got out of the inning by slipping a called third strike past Slaughter. They made good on another threat in the second, though, when Kurowski doubled, moved up a base while Doerr was tossing out Garagiola, and got the run that tied it when Walker lined out to Williams.

The Kid gave the ball another long ride in the fourth, hitting this one deep to left center. When it left his bat, he thought it would also leave the park, but as he saw Walker racing for the ball he knew it was too high and that Walker would be able to make the catch. So, his frustration mounted.

In the fifth the Cardinals played with the skill and infectious enthusiasm that mark a team that believes it will win. In the Boston half of the inning, Moore made another outstanding catch, plucking off Pinky Higgins's lead-off drive just before it hit the left-center field wall. Then Kurowski raced back of third to make a difficult over-the-shoulder catch of Wagner's foul. And Dickson closed out the inning by getting the good-hitting Ferriss to tap back weakly to the mound. It was the kind of defensive inning that can carry over into a team's next at-bat, as it did now.

Walker got another hit, this one a looping single to center. With Marion at the plate and the pitcher to follow, conventional strategy called for him to hit away, possibly with the runner going. But Marion was showing the wear of a long season, both at bat and especially in the field, and Dickson was a very good-hitting pitcher. Dyer ordered Marion to bunt

Walker into scoring position, and Dickson made the move look brilliant by doubling over Higgins. Schoendienst followed with a single to center, scoring Dickson, and when Moore singled to the same spot, Cronin came out to get Ferriss and replaced him with Dobson. With the Cardinals threatening to blow the deciding game wide open, Dobson was equal to the challenge. He got Musial to ground out to Doerr with the runners moving up, and then, with first base open, he intentionally walked Slaughter to take his chances with the right-handed Kurowski. Kurowski hit a Dobson curveball to Higgins whose throw to Doerr easily forced Slaughter at second, ending the inning. But now the Red Sox would have to catch the Cardinals in their own park, and they had only four innings left to do so.

Both Dobson and Dickson continued to pitch well through the sixth and seventh, and neither team did anything offensively until the top of the eighth when Rip Russell, pinch-hitting for Wagner, led off with a single. And now, remembering the second game of the National League playoffs when Dickson had faltered late in the game, Dyer looked along his bench, met Harry Brecheen's returning glance, and told his left-hander to get down to the bullpen to warm up. Brecheen went. "The crowd was roaring, and it hurt my head so bad," Brecheen said, "it like to kill me whenever they'd let out a yell." As he began his warmups his arm felt heavy and so did the ball. If it felt light in your hand, that was generally a good sign, he said; if it felt heavy, "then you got problems." But he quickly began putting everything he had into his pitches as a second successive pinch-hitter, Catfish Metkovich, got a hit, this time an ominous double into the left field corner. That put the tying runs in scoring position with none out and the top of the Red Sox ordering coming up: Moses (hitting .454 in the Series), Pesky, and DiMaggio. And beyond them waited the heavy guns, Williams, York, and Doerr. So now the call came down that Brecheen had hoped wouldn't be necessary, and it was no use, he said, "wishing you felt better, 'cause you don't have a choice. The manager says, 'Come here,' you come."

First base was open, but Dyer didn't want to put the potential winning run on for Pesky, DiMaggio, and Ted Williams, and Moses was a left-handed hitter. Brecheen would have to pitch to him—and to the batters who followed. There was very little room to "nibble" around the edges of the plate, either, lest in working too finely Brecheen should walk Moses. He'd have to go right after him, throwing strikes—or what looked like strikes. And this he did, surprising Moses by throwing three straight strikes, the last one catching the inside portion of the plate. Moses turned on plate umpire Al Barlick, complaining loudly about the last call, and Cronin let out a blast from the third base coach's box, but the call stood, and Moses was out without having moved his bat.

Pesky was at his best hitting to the opposite field, so Brecheen pitched him inside and got him to loft a fly ball to medium right, high enough so that Slaughter could set himself to throw. No one on the Red Sox knew precisely the condition of Slaughter's arm at this point, but the risk of having Russell thrown out at the plate to end the inning with the big hitters waiting wasn't worth it to Cronin, and he held Russell. It was well he did: Slaughter put everything he had into his throw to Musial, and it left the Cardinals relay man in perfect position to throw home. Russell would have been out. Now it was up to DiMaggio to keep the rally alive.

"Brecheen's first pitch I thought was high," DiMaggio recalled. "I told Barlick I thought so. He said, 'Well, maybe it was, but get in there and hit.' I said, 'Don't you worry about me: I'll hit.' I felt he was, in a way, questioning my desire." DiMaggio stepped back in and Brecheen threw a curve that nearly hit him in the foot. Brecheen tried another curve that missed, then a screwball that also missed, running the count to three-and-one. Now DiMaggio put one foot out of the batter's box and looked down at Cronin coaching at third. "I looked down at him for what seemed to me the longest time," DiMaggio said, "but what was probably only a few seconds. Of course, he gave me the hit sign immediately, so it wasn't so much that I was still looking for the sign. More, it was to *think* what Brecheen was going to throw me.

"By process of elimination I ruled out the fastball. He wasn't going to throw me a fastball three-and-one: it was conceivable I could hit it out of the park. I don't think he wants to walk me and pitch to Ted, so he's not going to throw me a curveball: he hasn't been able to get his curve over. He's going to throw me a screwball. I said to myself, 'He's going to throw me a screwball on the outside part of the plate, and I'm going to take it to the opposite field.' I stepped up to the plate looking for the screwball, and sure enough, there it was. I took a nice, smooth, firm swing. The ball started out over the second baseman's head, and I knew there was no way Slaughter or anybody else was going to catch it. It was in the gap." What DiMaggio didn't see was that his hit had taken off and continued to rise as it soared into the outfield. Both runners saw this, however, and scored, tying the game, and now as he rounded first base DiMaggio, too, saw how long his hit was and began to think "triple." If he could get to third, he was thinking, anything might happen: he might score on a wild pitch or a slowly-hit infield grounder, or a passed ball. But as he dug in even harder between first and second, DiMaggio felt his left hamstring pop, and instead of a triple, he barely made it to second.

He'd had thigh and hamstring problems off and on all season and had been able to play through them, though often he went out there heavily taped. Some years earlier, sportswriters had dubbed him the "Little Professor" because of his stature and spectacles. It wasn't an apt nickname, for this was an intense, determined, highly competitive man who now was finding it very difficult to accept the fact that he was going to have to leave the game. Play was suspended for almost twenty minutes while the Boston trainer taped his thigh and he tried vainly to walk some bit of suppleness back into the leg. He couldn't, and when Cronin reminded him that he represented the potential winning run at second and might not be able to make it home on a hit, DiMaggio knew he had to come out, replaced by Leon Culberson who would also fill his defensive slot. Fifty years later DiMaggio would say the injury in this situation was the greatest disappointment in his baseball career.

When play was at last resumed it had to be suspended again almost immediately when Williams swung at Brecheen's first pitch and hit a foul tip that split open Garagiola's finger. Now he, too, had to leave the game, replaced by Del Rice. The two long delays might have helped Brecheen settle down a bit while at the same time increasing the pressure on Williams who had nothing to do but stand around waiting and perhaps reflecting on his compounded failures.

The night before the final game Williams had been paid a friendly visit by Grantland Rice in his hotel room. The dean of American sports writers knew what turmoil Williams was in and just how upset he'd been by the Egan story, and he thought he'd try to cheer Williams up a bit. The slugger told Rice he wanted to win so badly in the deciding game that if this could somehow be accomplished without his contributing so much as a measly single, he'd be happy—a huge concession from a man who thought hitting day and night and practiced his swing with rolled-up newspapers in front of hotel room mirrors. Now here he was in a situation that demanded that he produce: two out, the winning run there on second for him to drive home, and the World Championship on the line.

But Brecheen got him to pop up to Schoendienst, and the Cardinals escaped the inning no worse than even.

For the Cardinals eighth Cronin sent Culberson to center field, Partee behind the plate, and right-hander Bob Klinger out to face Slaughter, Kurowski, and Walker. Down in the Boston bullpen Earl Johnson and Hughson were already beginning to throw hard. Klinger represented another of Cronin's hunches. He hadn't appeared yet in the Series and hadn't, in fact, pitched in any kind of game since September 19, not even in the three postseason exhibitions. The reason for this, or at least part of the reason, was that Klinger had been called home by the serious illness of his son. Earlier in the season he'd pitched very effectively, posting a 2.37 earned-run-average and saving nine wins for his team, more than anyone else on the staff, but a layoff of almost a month is a very long time for a pitcher, especially one like Klinger who relied on finesse and control to get batters out.

Cronin's thinking here was that with the pitcher due to hit in the Boston ninth, he would hope to get through the eighth with Klinger, pinch-hit for him, and have Tex Hughson take it from there. Johnson, who was throwing with Hughson as the last of the eighth began, had thought that with two left-handed hitters coming up he'd get the call, but he said later that Cronin felt Klinger was the better choice since he'd pitched against the Cardinals before the war when he was with the Pirates and knew their weaknesses. Indeed, Klinger himself in a joking exchange around the batting cage before Game Six had told the hot-hitting Harry Walker that he knew how to pitch him. "Damn if you'd hit me like you're hitting these other guys!" he laughed. Whatever Cronin's precise thinking was, or whether the choice of Klinger was pure hunch and devoid of real theory, Klinger now faced Slaughter to begin the inning and quickly gave up a single to him. On the Boston bench there was a nervous rustle and murmuring, and Joe Dobson claimed he and a couple of others went up to Cronin and begged him to get Klinger out of there while there was still time.

Over in the first base coach's box Dyer was going to play for Slaughter's run and hope that Brecheen could make it stand up, and he ordered Kurowski to bunt. Cardinals baseball was built on the successful execution of fundamentals like this, but here Kurowski failed, popping the ball up, and Klinger made a lunging, running catch of the ball as he neared the baseline. Now the bunt was clearly out. Barring accident, the Cardinals would have to hit Slaughter home if they wanted to get the run, and it didn't look as if they would when Rice flied out to Williams. Two outs and Walker at the plate.

Like Slaughter, Moore, Kurowski, and the others with whom he'd come up through the Cardinals system, Walker had an intense focus on winning: winning the game you were playing that day, no matter what the inning or the score; winning the pennant; winning the World Series. That, he said, was simply the way you were trained to think with the Cardinals. Never to be happy just to be in the big leagues (though they were); never to accept defeat before it became a reality; always to have your sights set on the ultimate goal, the World Championship. He'd been there as a member of the 1942 champions and the 1943 pennant winners, and he knew how it felt and what it took. This year, however, he hadn't hit well in the regular season. Dyer, he thought, played favorites, and for some reason he couldn't figure out, he wasn't one of them. The manager was constantly disparaging his ability and harping on the fact that Walker needed to pull the ball and hit for distance. That wasn't really Walker's natural style of hitting, which was rather to use more of the field and take his extra base hits as they came, and the consequence of trying to be a power hitter was a very mediocre .237 mark. At one point in the season his brother Dixie had said to him that unless he learned to take the ball to the opposite field quite a bit more than he was doing, he might not have much of a future in the big leagues. These pitchers, Dixie said, are just killing you when you try to pull everything. So Walker began the process of retooling himself as a hitter. Whenever he could, he got someone to throw to him so that he could practice taking the ball to the opposite field, and as he took his swings he kept hearing Dixie's instruction: *Wait, wait, wait. Feel like the ball is in the catcher's mitt before you swing.* Hitting in this more natural way he'd had an outstanding Series, and Dyer had stayed with him. As he stepped in to face Klinger he had six hits in sixteen at-bats (.375), and today had driven in one run, singled and scored in the fifth, and drawn a walk in the sixth. As he swished his brown and white two-toned bat over the plate, he waited to see whether Klinger was up to that boast he'd made the other day, whether he knew how to get Walker out.

On a two-ball, one-strike pitch Walker swung and hit the ball over shortstop. What happened next is one of the most celebrated—and controversial—plays in World Series history.

★ ★ ★

*O*n this much everybody agrees: Slaughter was running on the pitch and Walker's hit fell into left-center where Culberson fielded it and threw it to Pesky whose relay home was too late to catch Slaughter who scored all the way from first. After these few facts are stated, the controversy begins.

Klinger was primarily a sinkerball pitcher, one reason Cronin found him useful in Fenway Park and a reason to stay with him in this situation, in hopes he could get Walker to hit the ball on the ground for a force play on Slaughter that would end the inning. But thus far all three batters he'd faced had hit the ball in the air, indicating that Klinger's pitch wasn't dipping as it was supposed to (a common problem for sinkerball specialists who haven't worked enough lately). Nor did his ball sink on the two-and-one pitch to Walker, and Walker got a good look at it. "I was thinking 'inside-out' all the way," he said, meaning he was planning to begin his swing close to his body and extend the bat outward in its sweep, guiding the ball toward the left side. In the coach's box at first, Dyer knew Klinger's reputation and that the Sox would be hoping for the force at second, and to avoid that possibility, he gave Slaughter the steal sign. As soon as Klinger committed himself to throw to the plate Slaughter put his head down and took off for second.

Partee had an inkling Dyer might send Slaughter in this situation: the count was right, and if Slaughter made it, he'd be in position to score easily on an outfield single. Partee debated whether to call for a pitch-out but decided against it, principally because if Slaughter wasn't going, that would run the count to three-and-one and raise the risk of a walk, thereby moving Slaughter into scoring position anyway. What he decided to call for instead was a pitch on the outer portion of the plate so that if Slaughter was running, he'd have a better chance of throwing him out. Klinger in fact threw to the outside, but this played to the very strength Walker had been working to develop, and he met the pitch solidly.

In the years after the 1946 Series as the legend of Country Slaughter grew ever larger and more colorful, Harry Walker's hit got shorter and shorter until his ball fell just behind shortstop. In fact, it was a well-hit ball that landed in left-center and was certainly not a "Texas Leaguer," as the players termed short, bloop hits that just managed to fall between converging defenders. The game's official scorer credited Walker with a double, and that was probably the correct call since by the time Pesky got the ball from Culberson, Walker was within a few strides of second base and Pesky had no play on him there.* The real questions about Walker's hit cluster around Culberson's and Pesky's handling of it. The Red Sox were unanimous in believing that had DiMaggio still been in center field, Slaughter would never have dared try to score on the hit. DiMaggio was a skilled, aggressive fielder with an outstanding arm, as the Cardinals had learned: he'd thrown three of them out in the Series and just missed getting a fourth. Culberson wasn't a bad fielder, but he was no DiMaggio, and in any case was playing out of position in center. "Slaughter would *never* have scored if I'd been in center field," DiMaggio said emphatically. "In fact, I might have had a play on him at third base, because I'd have been playing that much farther over, and I'd have been charging the hell out of that ball. That's how strongly I feel." Slaughter wasn't the kind of man who could admit he'd scored because a lesser man had fielded Walker's hit, but he was too canny a player not to have known who he was taking his bold chance on.

Then there was the issue of Culberson's pickup of the ball and his throw to Pesky. Players on both teams agreed later that Culberson's throw to Pesky was curiously casual and weak, almost a lob, and that to get it Pesky had to go still farther into the outfield. It was as if Culberson never imagined the danger the racing Slaughter really represented. "It wasn't a real strong throw," said Walker, "and it didn't leave Pesky in a very good position." Yet at the time and all through the intervening years the majority of criticism for the way the play was handled landed on Pesky, not on Culberson. "Pesky held the ball," they said, allowing Slaughter to score; there was even a song written, retrospectively and repeatedly imploring him to throw it. Pesky, a friendly and self-effacing man off the field, probably encouraged this interpretation by making statements at the time suggesting that he was basically to blame for Slaughter's run.

He was certainly less to blame than Culberson, and over the years Pesky seemed to repent that willingness to be the goat. "Remember," he said, "I had to cover second with Slaughter running and a left-hand batter

---

* Bob Broeg, who saw the play from the press box, was adamant then and remains so that the hit was not a double but instead a "king-sized single." When he walked past the official scorers' table on his way to the victors' clubhouse Broeg said to them, "Gentlemen, by scoring that a double, not a single, you've taken the romance out of a great play." Slaughter himself has always maintained that Walker's hit was a single.

Two views of the finish of Enos Slaughter's famed "Mad Dash," which was actually less that than a calculated gamble that came straight out of the heart of the Cardinals tradition. Marty Marion is the on-deck batter and Roy Partee the vainly waiting Red Sox catcher. (Courtesy of Roy Partee)

up. So now I'm at the bag, and the ball's hit behind me, and I've got to go out to left-center field. For some reason, Culberson just lobs the ball to me. I get the ball, bring it down, and take a look. It's late in the afternoon, and I'm out there in the sun, looking into the shadows and the haze from the cigarette smoke. So, I see Slaughter, and he's about fifteen feet from home plate. Shit, I would have needed a gun to get him out. But, they put a pair of horns on me."

The man with the best view of the entire play was undoubtedly Roy Partee who was waiting for Pesky's relay at home plate. "I can still see Culberson coming in," he recalled, "and then I see the ball hit off the heel of his glove and trickle out, and then he grabs it with his hand, and Pesky's hollering for the ball. Why Culberson doesn't throw through [to the plate], I don't know. He had to see where Slaughter was—at third base. But instead, he soft-tosses it to Pesky. And Doerr's out there, hollering at Pesky, *'Home! Home!'* But Pesky can't hear him. Pesky caught the ball, and then he stopped. He may have taken a step in before he threw it, but it was up: he tried to reach me on the fly, and he didn't have that kind of arm. The ball is up in the air, and I can tell—I *know*—that Slaughter's got the ball beat. But if it had come to me, I'd have been up in the grandstand somewhere if I'd have tried to block the plate on him."

In the last analysis, though, neither Culberson nor Pesky was really at fault here. It was Enos Slaughter who made the play with the daring and determination that were the heart of the Cardinals tradition. Earlier in the Series Slaughter had been angry when a coaching decision had prevented him from playing the Cardinals way and scoring a run that might have won the game. With two outs in the fourth inning of Game One, Slaughter had tripled to right-center, and when DiMaggio's throw got away from Pesky Slaughter made the turn at full steam and started for home. But third base coach Mike Gonzalez was afraid Pesky could recover the ball quickly enough to throw Slaughter out, and so he'd stopped him. When Kurowski flied out to end the inning the Cardinals failed to score. "There never would have been a tenth inning for York to bat in if I'd scored that run," Slaughter said. "I was mad as hell, and I went to Dyer and told him so. 'All right,' he says, 'if another situation like that comes up where you think you can score, go ahead, and I'll take the responsibility.' When I saw where Walker's ball was as I came by second, I said to myself, 'God dang, boy! You can score on this!' The only thing I was worried about was

Roy Partee blocking the plate, and I thought to myself, 'Well, if he is, I'm just gonna take him with me.' "

★   ★   ★

*B*recheen still had to retire the Red Sox in the top of the ninth, and for a while it didn't look as if he could. York pounded a single to left and was replaced by pinch-runner Paul Campbell. Doerr followed with another single to left, but the ball got out to Walker so quickly that Campbell had to stop at second. Cronin now ordered Higgins to bunt the runners up a base, but in a crucial failure to execute a fundamental play, Higgins bunted so hard to the charging Kurowski that his throw caught Doerr at second and Marion's relay nearly got Higgins at first. When Partee fouled out to Musial the Red Sox were down to their last out.

Cronin sent McBride up to hit for Earl Johnson, but Harry Brecheen had another good screwball left in him, and McBride hit it off the end of his bat, sending a ball that twisted and caromed along the surface of the "Rockpile" toward second base. Brecheen had no chance at it, but Schoendienst quickly moved into position to handle it. "I charged the ball; I didn't lay back," he said, "and it was the toughest play I had to make in the Series, not because it was the last out, or anything like that, but because that ball was tricky. I came in on it, and it hit me in the shoulder." With Higgins bearing desperately down on him, Schoendienst grabbed for the ball as it rolled up his arm, while behind him he could hear Terry Moore hollering, *"Get him out! Throw the damn ball!"* But first Schoendienst would have to get control of it. When he did, Higgins had already launched into a barreling slide, and Schoendienst had to shovel the ball backhanded to Marion who waited with outstretched arms at the bag. The ball arrived ahead of Higgins, Marion touched the bag, then leaped out of the way as Higgins plowed into it and came to rest on his hands and knees in the dirt. Higgins looked vainly back to see what the call had been, but he knew, and so did the Cardinals who converged on Brecheen and lifted him onto their shoulders where he swayed above them, looking suddenly very frail and tired as they carried him from the field.

In the St. Louis clubhouse all was bedlam as the players tore off their uniforms and sailed caps, shirts, mitts, and towels through the air. In the crush of the wrestling, milling players, reporters, and well-wishers a par-

Scenes from the victors' clubhouse. *Top*: Country Slaughter, Harry Brecheen, manager Eddie Dyer, and Harry Walker whoop it up. (Bettmann Archive) *Bottom left*: Dyer stands between the plainly uncomfortable Happy Chandler and Sam Breadon, who hadn't been on speaking terms since the latter went to Mexico. (*The Sporting News,* October 23, 1946) *Bottom right*: Slaughter planting a kiss on a dazed-looking Brecheen. (UPI/Bettmann)

tition collapsed, bottles rolled and broke, and flashbulbs popped. "Beer!" the players hollered, "Another beer over here!" Forgotten was the B-1 vitamin drink Sam Breadon insisted on for the players' after-game refreshment during the season. A somewhat rumpled Happy Chandler was finally shoved into a small clearing and made to pose there with a stiff and unsmiling Breadon, but American League president Will Harridge was just another guy in the crowd as he tried to offer his congratulations to Breadon and Dyer. The normally taciturn Slaughter, usually the first one out of the clubhouse after a game, happily mugged for the cameramen and planted a big kiss on Brecheen's cheek. And for a few minutes Brecheen was able to forget how bad he felt even while his teammates pounded him and pulled him this way and that, snatching his cap from his sweaty brow, then slapping it back on sideways. When he found a little breathing room, Brecheen caught hold of Red Schoendienst. "Red," he said, "that was a pretty bad hop." And Schoendienst, so boyish-looking that twice this season he'd been turned away by clubhouse attendants who couldn't believe he was old enough to be a big leaguer, coolly replied, "There are no bad hops. If you play the ball right, you should never get a bad hop."

Epilogue

The next day's newspapers carried the traditional and contrasting images of victory and defeat, the Cardinals players shown mugging for the camera, pouring beer over each other, their mouths wide in happiness; and of the Red Sox there was the lone figure of Ted Williams, slumped in front of his locker, looking vulnerable and drawn, his belt unbuckled, uniform half off, as if he were reluctant to remove it and so have to confront the finality of defeat. But it really was over, and he'd driven in only one run on five paltry singles. He simply couldn't believe this had happened to him. Finally, though, he shucked his flannels, showered, and got aboard the train for Boston. Sitting there in his compartment, his deep sorrow finally broke through his stunned incredulity, and he wept. But even as his failure on the field had been public, so was his grief off it, for now as he looked up through his tears he saw dozens of curious strangers staring in at him from the station platform: he'd forgotten to pull down his window shade.

The players had to share today's front page with the news flash from Germany reporting the executions of the Nazi war criminals; and also with the unfolding story of the domestic meat crisis that had housewives standing all night in lines outside butcher shops. The Nazis had been hanged in the first hours of the new day—all except Goering. Ever since his capture Goering had insisted that he was no criminal but the second-ranking statesman of a defeated nation, and to avoid being hanged like a thief or a murderer he'd taken a cyanide capsule that was probably supplied him by one of his American guards. So, just as it had from the beginning of spring training, this last big story of the war continued to keep baseball a ghostly kind of company. When reporters asked President Truman where he stood in the public debate between Republicans Robert

Top: Ever since the start of spring training the Nuremberg trials had kept base-ball a kind of shadowy company, and at the season's end the trials ended, too, with the hangings of the convicted and the suicide of Goering. (National Archives) *Bottom*: Joe Garagiola (*left*) and Yogi Berra were not only the idols of the baseball-minded on Italian Hill but exemplars, too, of what made America great. (Broeg, *Redbirds*)

Taft and Thomas E. Dewey over the justice of the proceedings that had condemned the Nazis, Truman replied that he thought the two men could settle their differences without his help. Neither had made a secret of his presidential ambitions, and the President clearly was not unhappy to watch them bloody each other in an internecine battle. Besides, he had his hands full with the meat crisis, the continuing problems of housing shortages and wage and price demands, and the deteriorating prospects for a good settlement in China's civil war.

On this day J. G. Taylor Spink of the *Sporting News* was on the trail of another sort of story and visited Joe Garagiola and his family on Elizabeth Avenue in the Italian Hill district of St. Louis. The Hill wasn't exactly the little publisher's beat, but he knew a good story when he saw it, and the Garagiola family looked like rich territory. Baseball was the essence of what this country was all about, he thought, and nothing more beautifully illustrated the promise of American life than the saga of this second-generation immigrant kid who grew up to star in the World Series for his hometown team. Here you had everything: the hard-working immigrant parents; the assimilation of their boy into American culture; his service to his country in the war; and then his triumphant return to baseball to help his struggling team to the pennant and the World Championship. It was like an ethnic version of the immensely popular John R. Tunis baseball books for boys, a story that was a concrete example of what made America great, why it was that victorious Americans had sat in judgment at Nuremberg and now were guiding a battered world into a new era of *Pax Americana.*

In fact, Garagiola's story did illustrate some of these things. His father Giovanni had come to the States from Inveruno, Italy, in 1913 but had to wait until World War I was over to send back for his wife, Angelina. He'd found steady work in a St. Louis brickyard, and, having lived through the Depression, felt lucky to have it. Throughout his working life he stuck to his job with a fierce tenacity, and the rest of the men on the Hill were the same: they went to work every day, came home to dinner on the table, and with their wives raised their children with a strong and clearly defined set of values. Life on the Hill centered around the church, and the children were taught that as members of the community they bore a responsibility for the quality of life in it. "The Hill was a great place to grow up," Joe Garagiola said. "You learned great values there. Before he left for work, your father might tell you to go down to the widow lady's today and help out, whether it was cutting the grass or wheeling her coal around from the alley where they dumped it. Everybody helped one another."

Inevitably, as it would seem, the children became interested in a variety of American things their parents neither had time for nor understood, like baseball. Garagiola and the four Berra boys across the street were particularly taken with this American game, and Garagiola would later say that Yogi's older brother Lefty was surely the family's best hitter. But there was no professional baseball for Lefty Berra. The older boys of the immigrant families were expected to take jobs like their fathers. "You couldn't explain to the fathers that you could make money playing ball," Garagiola said. "All they knew was the work ethic: go to work, work hard, don't get fired, and bring home a paycheck. There was no way an older brother in those days could ever sign a contract. College was out of the question. High school was a luxury."

The boys loved the game and played it when they could, after school, weekends, but even the most hotly contested game always ended when the factory whistle blew. Then, Garagiola said, "we knew we had fifteen minutes at most. All the kids went home and got the pail and went to Fassi's so that Pop would have his beer on the table when he got home. And, boy, if you didn't have it there—watch out!" Gradually, the boys developed their baseball heroes and their own private aspirations to play professionally, maybe. They learned of the stars of the Cardinals and Browns, and they admired those kids from their own neighborhood who could hit, throw hard, or handle the glove: Frank Crespi, Lefty Berra, Diz Mariani, Mario Ferrato. When Yogi Berra and Garagiola signed contracts as teenagers their parents couldn't understand it, and Berra's parents at least were never to understand the magnitude of their son's baseball accomplishments.

Still, in their own ways they were proud of their boys because they could see they'd made successes of their lives, even if their line of work remained puzzling. Neither of Garagiola's parents had attended any of the Series games, and yet when Taylor Spink came calling Giovanni Garagiola had smiled on his son and told the newspaper man Joe was the finest boy on the Hill. Spink led Garagiola through a brief description of his career, which had begun in 1941 at Springfield where Garagiola was batting practice catcher and general factotum, then his service experiences and how much he'd learned playing for Kirby Higbe's Manila Dodgers, and finally the thrill of joining the Cardinals and helping them get into the Series. The pennant race had been tremendously exciting to a rookie, of course, and he'd felt a lot more pressure in the playoffs than he had in the Series. There, oddly, he'd felt more at ease, he told Spink, and he'd actually had some fun kidding around with the great Williams. But in that seventh game all the kidding had stopped, and the players had been in silent, deadly earnest. Now it was over, and he could relax for the first time in quite awhile and savor this first great success. He wore the bandage on his finger like a medal and said he would take a busted finger any day for the thrill of winning it all. The whole thing, he told Spink, had been like a dream, a diamond version of the American Dream.

"Mr. Spink," he said, "I can't believe it. Here I am on the same ball club as Stan Musial, in the same league as Blix Donnelley. In Springfield, I took care of their uniforms. I shined their shoes and handled their laundry. I get up in the middle of the night and say to myself, 'Hey, Joe, this ain't on the level. You have been dreaming.' "

Acknowledgments

*I*n reconstructing the events of the baseball season of 1946 my primary source has been the interviews I conducted over a three-year period with players, writers, and broadcasters. The great majority of these were in person, though a few were conducted by telephone. In a number of instances following the initial interview I called back to check on facts or on incidents where I felt I needed either clarification or amplification. In general, I found the men's memories of the season and its personalities sharp and vivid, especially about critical games and situations, though inevitably some of the daily details of the long season have faded through the years. (Interestingly, I found that pitchers recalled things with a greater fidelity and attention to detail than hitters did.) Throughout this lengthy process I was treated with an unfailing generosity and graciousness, even when I made repeated requests of an individual for further information. In particular, I have to thank Lou Brissie, Bob Broeg, Bob Feller, Dave Ferriss, Joe Garagiola, Donald Honig, Monte Irvin, and Ralph Kiner for their patient willingness to try to answer all my questions. None of them, of course, is responsible for whatever errors I may have made, either of fact or interpretation, nor are any of the following:

Ace Adams, Harry Brecheen, Tommy Brown, Milo Candini, Harry Caray, Sam Chapman, Gil Coan, Jeff Cross, Alvin Dark, Dominic DiMaggio, Bob Dillinger, Joe Dobson, Bobby Doerr, Del Ennis, Augie Galan, Danny Gardella, John Grodzicki, Tommy Henrich, Billy Herman, Gene Hermanski, Sam Jethroe, Earl Johnson, Clif Keane, Whitey Kurowski, Max Lanier, Marty Marion, Walt Masterson, Barney McCosky, Terry Moore, Red Munger, Stan Musial, Roy Partee, Johnny Pesky, Johnny Schmitz, Red Schoendienst, Bert Shepard, Enos Slaughter, Eddie Stevens,

Joe Tepsic, Cecil Travis, Virgil Trucks, Mickey Vernon, Bill Voiselle, Charlie Wagner, and Dick Whitman.

The following answered specific questions I had about baseball or about American life in the immediate postwar period: Red Barber, William O. Brasmer, Bill Deane, Violet Forbes, Don Gutteridge, Bill Mauldin, Tommy McBride, Jim McCarthy, Pat Mullin, William Preston, Pee Wee Reese, Howie Schultz, Woody Strode, Mrs. Bob Thurman, and Morris Wachtel.

The path to the completion of a book is often a long one that passes through dark woods, sloughs of despond, and arid wastes, and the writer is fortunate indeed that along it are friends who assist him in a variety of ways. It is always a pleasure to acknowledge even so briefly their help and the many kindnesses they so freely gave: Roger Abrahams, Marjorie Abbott, Constance Baker, Stephen Brauer, Dick Bresciani, Barbara Burn, Kay Carlson, Tristram P. Coffin, Mabel Chin, Ken Coleman, Steve Gietschier, Siegfried Halus, Robert Hilgendorf, Luke Howard, Bill McGrotha, Bryan MacMillan, Jane Hunter MacMillan, Christopher Merrill, Jay O'Callahan, Terry Ryan, Frederick Taft, Elise Turner, John Henry Williams, Robert Woods, and David Zuckerman.

Finally, I want once again to pay a public sort of tribute to my long-time, long-suffering editor, Bill Strachan, and to my agent Robin Straus, as understanding as she is professional. It is said business and friendship are an often uneasy mixture, but I am proud to count them friends as well as colleagues.

Bibliography

Alexander, Charles. *Our Game: An American Baseball History*. New York: Henry Holt and Company, 1991.

Broeg, Bob. *Redbirds: A Century of Cardinals' Baseball*. Kansas City: Walsworth Publishing Company, 1992.

———. *Stan Musial*. Garden City, New York: Doubleday & Company, 1964.

Broyard, Anatole. *Kafka Was the Rage: A Greenwich Village Memoir*. New York: Carol Southern Books, 1993.

Boudreau, Lou, with Russell Schneider. *Covering All the Bases*. Champaign, Ill.: Sagamore Publishing, 1993.

Cohen, Richard, David S. Neft, and Jordan Deutsch, eds. *The World Series*. New York: The Dial Press, 1979.

Conlon, Jocko. *Jocko*. Philadelphia: J. B. Lippincott Company, 1967.

Craft, David and Tom Owens. *Redbirds Revisited: Great Memories and Stories from the St. Louis Cardinals*. Chicago: Bonus Books, 1990.

Creamer, Robert W. *Babe: The Legend Comes to Life*. New York: Simon and Schuster, 1974.

———. *Baseball in '41*. New York: Viking Penguin, 1991.

Durocher, Leo with Ed Linn. *Nice Guys Finish Last*. New York: Simon and Schuster, 1975.

Eskenazi, Gerald. *The Lip: A Biography of Leo Durocher*. New York: William Morrow and Company, 1993.

Feller, Bob with Bill Gilbert. *Now Pitching, Bob Feller: A Baseball Memoir*. New York: Birch Lane Press, 1990.

Frommer, Myrna Katz and Harvey Frommer. *It Happened in Brooklyn: An Oral History of Growing Up in the Borough in the 1940's, 50's, and 60's*. New York: Harcourt Brace & Company, 1993.

Gilbert, Bill. *They Also Served: Baseball and the Home Front, 1941–1945*. New York: Crown Publishers Incorporated, 1992.

Gerlach, Larry. *The Men in Blue: Conversations with Umpires*. New York: Viking Press, 1980.

Golenbock, Peter. *Bums: An Oral History of the Brooklyn Dodgers*. 1984. Reprint. New York: Pocket Books, 1986.

———. *Fenway: An Unexpurgated History of the Boston Red Sox*. New York: G. P. Putnam's Sons, 1992.

Honig, Donald. *A Donald Honig Reader*. 1975. Reprint. New York: Simon and Schuster, 1988.

―――. *The St. Louis Cardinals, An Illustrated History.* New York: Prentice Hall Press, 1991.

―――. *Shadows of Summer: Classic Baseball Photographs, 1869–1947.* New York: Viking Studio, 1994.

Johnson, Lloyd and Miles Wolff, eds. *The Encyclopedia of Minor League Baseball.* Durham, N.C.: Baseball America, 1993.

Jordan, David M. *A Tiger in His Time: Hal Newhouser and the Burden of Wartime Ball.* South Bend, Ind.: Diamond Communications, Inc., 1990.

Kaese, Harold. "What's the Matter With the Red Sox?" *Saturday Evening Post,* March 23, 1946.

Kahn, Roger. *The Era, 1947–1957: When the Yankees, the Giants, and the Dodgers Ruled the World.* New York: Ticknor & Fields, 1993.

Leonard, Thomas M. *Day by Day: The Forties.* New York: Facts on File, 1977.

Levine, Peter. *Ellis Island to Ebbets Field: Sport and the American Jewish Experience.* New York: Oxford University Press, 1992.

Linn, Ed. *Hitter: The Life and Turmoils of Ted Williams.* New York: Harcourt Brace & Company, 1993.

Lowenfish, Lee. *The Imperfect Diamond: A History of Baseball's Labor Wars.* 1980. Revised edition. New York: Da Capo Press, 1991.

N.A. *Major League Baseball in Brooklyn, New York, 1901–1957.* Verplanck, N.Y.: Historical Briefs, Inc., 1993.

The *New York Times,* January–October, 1946.

Okrent, Daniel and Harry Levine, eds. *The Ultimate Baseball Book.* Boston: Houghton Mifflin Company, 1979.

O'Neal, Bill. *The International League, A Baseball History, 1884–1991.* Austin, Tex.: Eakin Press, 1992.

―――. *The Pacific Coast League, 1903–1988.* Austin, Tex.: Eakin Press, 1990.

Percoco, James A. "Baseball and World War II: A Study of the Landis–Roosevelt Correspondence." *OAH Magazine of History.* Summer, 1992.

Pyle, Ernie. *Brave Men.* New York: Henry Holt and Company, 1944.

Reynolds, Doug. "Hardball Paternalism, Hardball Politics." *Labor's Heritage.* April, 1991.

Ritter, Lawrence S. *The Glory of Their Times: The Story of the Early Days of Baseball Told by the Men Who Played It.* 1966. Revised Edition. New York: William Morrow and Company, Inc., 1984.

―――. *Lost Ballparks: A Celebration of Baseball's Legendary Fields.* New York: Viking Penguin, 1992.

Ritter, Lawrence S. and Donald Honig. *The Image of Their Greatness: An Illustrated History of Baseball from 1900 to the Present.* New York: Crown Publishers, 1979.

Rogosin, Donn. *Invisible Men: Life in Baseball's Negro Leagues.* New York: Atheneum, 1983.

The *St. Louis Post–Dispatch,* April–October, 1946.

Seidel, Michael. *Ted Williams: A Baseball Life.* Chicago: Contemporary Books, 1991.

The Sporting News, 1946.

Stone, I. F. *The Truman Era, 1945–1952.* 1953. Reprint. Boston: Little, Brown and Company, 1972.

Talley, Rick. *The Cubs of '69: Recollections of a Team That Should Have Been.* Chicago: Contemporary Books, 1989.

Taylor, Telford. *The Anatomy of the Nuremberg Trials.* New York: Alfred A. Knopf, 1992.

Tunis, John R. *The Kid Comes Back.* 1946. Reprint. New York: William R. Morrow & Co., Inc., 1990.

Tygiel, Jules. *Baseball's Great Experiment: Jackie Robinson and His Legacy.* New York: Oxford University Press, 1983.

Williams, Ted with John Underwood. *My Turn At Bat: The Story of My Life.* 1969. Reprint. New York: Fireside, Simon & Schuster, 1989.

Videos

"An Hour of Ted: Swing King; My Name Is Ted Williams." Rare Sportsfilms.

"The Best Years of Our Lives." 1946. Samuel Goldwyn Home Entertainment.

"The Home Front." 3 vols. Reader's Digest Home Entertainment Division, 1989.

"Nazi War Crime Trials." Video Yesteryear.

"1946 World Series." 1946. Reprint. Rare Sportsfilms.

"World Series Footage, 1946." Black Canyon Productions.

"When It Was a Game." 2 vols. Black Canyon Productions, 1991, 1992.

Program

THE PLAYERS AND
THEIR TEAMS, 1946

Adams, Buster. Outfielder, *St. Louis Cardinals*. Wartime star.
Anderson, Ferrell. Rookie catcher, *Brooklyn Dodgers*.
Appling, Luke. Shortstop, *Chicago White Sox*.

Bagby, Jim. Right-handed relief pitcher, *Boston Red Sox*.
Barney, Rex. Right-handed pitcher, *Brooklyn Dodgers*.
Barrett, Red. Right-handed pitcher, *St. Louis Cardinals*. Wartime star.
Beazley, Johnny. Right-handed pitcher, *St. Louis Cardinals*. Injured in service.
Behrman, Hank. Rookie right-handed pitcher, *Brooklyn Dodgers*.
Benson, Gene. Negro leagues star outfielder.
Berra, Yogi. Rookie catcher, *New York Yankees*.
Bevens, Bill. Right-handed pitcher, *New York Yankees*.
Bithorn, Hi. Right-handed pitcher, *Chicago Cubs*. Wartime star.
Blackwell, Ewell. Rookie right-handed pitcher, *Cincinnati Reds*.
Bluege, Ossie. Manager, *Washington Senators*.
Bonham, Tiny. Right-handed pitcher, *New York Yankees*.
Boudreau, Lou. Manager and shortstop, *Cleveland Indians*.
Branca, Ralph. Right-handed pitcher, *Brooklyn Dodgers*.
Brazle, Al. Left-handed relief pitcher, *St. Louis Cardinals*.
Brecheen, Harry. Left-handed pitcher, *St. Louis Cardinals*.
Brissie, Lou. Left-handed pitcher, Ware Shoals semipro team. Injured in service.
Brown, Bobby. Rookie infielder, *New York Yankees*.
Brown, Tommy. Infielder, *Brooklyn Dodgers*. Drafted into service, 1946.
Brown, Willard. Negro leagues star outfielder.
Burkhart, Ken. Right-handed pitcher, *St. Louis Cardinals*. Wartime star.

Campbell, Bruce. Former American League outfielder. Sued *Washington Senators* under
    G.I. Bill.
Campanella, Roy. Negro leagues catcher signed by *Brooklyn Dodgers* to play in minor
    leagues in 1946.

Case, George. Outfielder, *Cleveland Indians*. Stolen base king of 1940's.

Casey, Hugh. Right-handed relief pitcher, *Brooklyn Dodgers*.

Chandler, Spud. Right-handed pitcher, *New York Yankees*.

Chapman, Ben. Manager, *Philadelphia Phillies*.

Chapman, Sam. Outfielder, *Philadelphia A's*.

Christman, Mark. Infielder, *St. Louis Browns*.

Coan, Gil. Rookie outfielder, *Washington Senators*.

Cooper, Mort. Right-handed pitcher, *Boston Braves*.

Cooper, Walker. Catcher *St. Louis Cardinals*. Sold to *New York Giants* prior to start of 1946 season. Brother of Mort.

Crespi, Frank. Infielder, *St. Louis Cardinals*. Injured in service and inactive, 1946.

Cronin, Joe. Manager, *Boston Red Sox*. Former star shortstop for that club and *Washington Senators*.

Cross, Jeff. Infielder, *St. Louis Cardinals*.

Culberson, Leon. Outfielder, *Boston Red Sox*.

Dark, Alvin. Rookie shortstop, *Boston Braves*.

Deininger, Bill. Catcher in *New York Yankees* minor league system.

Dickey, Bill. Catcher, *New York Yankees*. Named manager of team, 1946.

Dickson, Murry. Right-handed pitcher, *St. Louis Cardinals*.

Dillinger, Bob. Rookie infielder, *St. Louis Browns*.

DiMaggio, Dom. Outfielder, *Boston Red Sox*. Younger brother of Joe.

DiMaggio, Joe. Outfielder, *New York Yankees*.

Dobson, Joe. Right-handed pitcher, *Boston Red Sox*.

Doerr, Bobby. Second baseman, *Boston Red Sox*.

Dressen, Charlie. Coach, *Brooklyn Dodgers*.

Dreisewerd, Clem. Left-handed relief pitcher, *Boston Red Sox*.

Durocher, Leo. Manager, *Brooklyn Dodgers*.

Dusak, Erv. Outfielder-infielder, *St. Louis Cardinals*.

Dyer, Eddie. Manager, *St. Louis Cardinals*.

Dykes, Jimmy. Manager, *Chicago White Sox*.

Early, Jake. Catcher, *Washington Senators*.

Edwards, Bruce. Rookie Catcher, *Brooklyn Dodgers*.

Elliott, Bob. Third baseman, *Pittsburgh Pirates*.

Embree, Red. Right-handed pitcher, *Cleveland Indians*.

Ennis, Del. Rookie outfielder, *Philadelphia Phillies*.

Erickson, Paul. Right-handed pitcher, *Chicago Cubs*.

Estalella, Bobby. Outfielder, *Philadelphia A's*. Played in Mexico, 1946.

Etten, Nick. First baseman, *New York Yankees*. Wartime star.

Evans, Al. Catcher, *Washington Senators*.

Feller, Bob. Right-handed pitcher, *Cleveland Indians*. Set what was believed to be all-time single season strikeout record, 1946.

Ferriss, Dave (Boo). Right-handed pitcher, *Boston Red Sox*.

Fleming, Bill. Right-handed pitcher, *Chicago Cubs*.

Fleming, Les. First baseman, *Cleveland Indians.*
Frisch, Frankie. Manager, *Pittsburgh Pirates.* Former star second baseman with *St. Louis Cardinals* and *New York Giants.*
Furillo, Carl. Rookie outfielder, *Brooklyn Dodgers.*

Galan, Augie. Infielder-outfielder, *Brooklyn Dodgers.*
Garagiola, Joe. Rookie catcher, *St. Louis Cardinals.*
Gardella, Danny. Outfielder, *New York Giants.* Played in Mexico, 1946.
Gettel, Al. Right-handed pitcher, *New York Yankees.*
Gibson, Josh. Negro leagues star catcher.
Goolsby, Ray. Rookie outfielder, *Washington Senators.*
Gordon, Joe. Second baseman, *New York Yankees.*
Gonzalez, Mike. Coach, *St. Louis Cardinals.*
Gregg, Hal. Right-handed pitcher, *Brooklyn Dodgers.*
Grodzicki, Johnny. Right-handed pitcher, *St. Louis Cardinals.* Injured in service.
Greenberg, Hank. First baseman, *Detroit Tigers.* Led American League in home runs, runs-batted-in, 1946.
Grimm, Charlie. Manager, *Chicago Cubs.*
Gumpert, Randy. Right-handed pitcher, *New York Yankees.*
Gutteridge, Don. Infielder, *Boston Red Sox.*

Hack, Stan. Third baseman, *Chicago Cubs.*
Haefner, Mickey. Left-handed pitcher, *Washington Senators.* Wartime star.
Harris, Mickey. Left-handed pitcher, *Boston Red Sox.*
Hatten, Joe. Rookie left-handed pitcher, *Brooklyn Dodgers.*
Hausmann, George. Infielder, *New York Giants.* Played in Mexico, 1946.
Hayes, Frankie. Catcher, *Cleveland Indians.* Traded to *Chicago White Sox,* 1946.
Herman, Billy. Infielder, *Brooklyn Dodgers.* Traded to Boston Braves, 1946.
Hermanski, Gene. Rookie Outfielder, *Brooklyn Dodgers.*
Higbe, Kirby. Right-handed pitcher, *Brooklyn Dodgers.*
Higgins, Mike. Third baseman, *Detroit Tigers.* Traded to *Boston Red Sox,* 1946.
Hopp, Johnny. First baseman-outfielder, *St. Louis Cardinals.* Sold to *Boston Braves,* 1946.
Hofferth, Stew. Catcher, *Boston Braves.* Traded to *Brooklyn Dodgers,* 1946.
Hughson, Tex. Right-handed pitcher, *Boston Red Sox.*

Irvin, Monte. Negro leagues star first baseman-outfielder.

Jethroe, Sam. Negro leagues star outfielder.
Johnson, Billy. Third baseman, *New York Yankees.*
John, Bob. Outfielder, *Boston Red Sox.* Released prior to 1946 season.
Johnson, Don. Second baseman, *Chicago Cubs.*
Johnson, Earl. Left-handed relief pitcher, *Boston Red Sox.*
Judd, Oscar. Right-handed pitcher, *Philadelphia Phillies.*
Jurges, Billy. Shortstop, *Chicago Cubs.*

Kell, George. Third baseman, *Philadelphia A's*. Traded to *Detroit Tigers*, 1946.
Keller, Charlie. Outfielder, *New York Yankees*.
Keltner, Ken. Third baseman, *Cleveland Indians*.
Kiner, Ralph. Rookie outfielder, *Pittsburgh Pirates*. Led National League in home runs, 1946.
Klein, Lou. Infielder, *St. Louis Cardinals*. Played in Mexico, 1946.
Klinger, Bob. Right-handed relief pitcher, *Boston Red Sox*.
Kluttz, Clyde. Catcher, New York Giants. Traded to *St. Louis Cardinals,* 1946.
Krist, Howie. Right-handed relief pitcher, *St. Louis Cardinals*. Injured in service.
Kurowski, Whitey. Third baseman, *St. Louis Cardinals*.

Lavagetto, Cookie. Third baseman, *Brooklyn Dodgers*.
Lanier, Max. Left-handed pitcher, *St. Louis Cardinals*. Played in Mexico, 1946.
Lewis, Buddy. Outfielder, *Washington Senators*.
Lewis, Duffy. Coach, *Boston Red Sox*. Formerly a star outfielder with same team.
Lemon, Bob. Outfielder-pitcher, *Cleveland Indians*.
Lindell, Johnny. Outfielder, *New York Yankees*.
Lopez, Al. Catcher, *Pittsburgh Pirates*.
Lombardi, Ernie. Catcher, *New York Giants*.
Lombardi, Vic. Left-handed pitcher, *Brooklyn Dodgers*.
Lupien, Tony. First baseman, *Philadelphia Phillies*. Released prior to 1946 season; brought suit against Phillies under G.I. Bill.

Mack, Connie. Owner-manager, *Philadelphia A's*.
Mack, Ray. Second baseman, *Cleveland Indians*.
Mackiewicz, Felix. Outfielder, *Cleveland Indians*.
Maglie, Sal. Right-handed pitcher, *New York Giants*. Played in Mexico, 1946.
Majeski, Hank. Third baseman, *New York Yankees*. Traded to *Philadelphia A's,* 1946.
Marchildon, Phil. Right-handed pitcher, *Philadelphia A's*. POW in Nazi camps during war.
Marion, Marty. Shortstop, *St. Louis Cardinals*. Most Valuable Player, National League, 1944.
Marshall, Willard. Outfielder, *New York Giants*.
Masterson, Walt. Right-handed pitcher, *Washington Senators*.
Martin, Fred. Right-handed pitcher, *St. Louis Cardinals*. Played in Mexico, 1946.
Mayo, Eddie. Second baseman, *Detroit Tigers*.
McBride, Tom. Outfielder, *Boston Red Sox*.
McCarthy, Joe. Manager, *New York Yankees*. Replaced by Bill Dickey, 1946.
McCosky, Barney. Outfielder, *Detroit Tigers*. Traded to *Philadelphia A's,* 1946.
Medwick, Joe. Outfielder, *Brooklyn Dodgers*.
Metkovich, Catfish. Outfielder, *Boston Red Sox*.
Melton, Rube. Right-handed pitcher, *Brooklyn Dodgers*.
Merullo, Len. Shortstop, *Chicago Cubs*.
Miller, Eddie. Shortstop, *Cincinnati Reds*.
Mize, Johnny. First baseman, *New York Giants*.
Moore, Terry. Outfielder, team captain, *St. Louis Cardinals*.
Moses, Wally. Outfielder, *Chicago White Sox*. Sold to *Boston Red Sox,* 1946.

Mullin, Pat. Outfielder, *Detroit Tigers.*

Munger, Red. Right-handed pitcher, *St. Louis Cardinals.*

Musial, Stan. Outfielder-first baseman, *St. Louis Cardinals.* Led league in seven offensive categories, 1946, and was named Most Valuable Player.

Newcombe, Don. Negro leagues right-handed pitcher signed by *Brooklyn Dodgers.*

Newhouser, Hal. Left-handed pitcher, *Detroit Tigers.* Wartime star; tied Feller for most wins in American League, 1946.

Newsom, Bobo. Right-handed pitcher, *Philadelphia A's.* Traded to *Washington Senators,* 1946.

Niarhos, Gus. Rookie catcher, *New York Yankees.*

Nicholson, Bill. Outfielder, *Chicago Cubs.* Wartime star.

Niemiec, Al. Infielder, *Seattle Rainiers.* Brought suit against club under G.I. Bill.

Northey, Ron. Outfielder, *Philadelphia Phillies.*

O'Dea, Ken. Catcher, *St. Louis Cardinals.* Sold to *Boston Braves,* 1946.

Olmo, Luis. Outfielder, *Brooklyn Dodgers.* Played in Mexico, 1946.

O'Neill, Steve. Manager, *Detroit Tigers.*

Ott, Mel. Manager and outfielder, *New York Giants.*

Owen, Mickey. Catcher, *Brooklyn Dodgers.* Played in Mexico, 1946.

Padgett, Don. Catcher, *Brooklyn Dodgers.* Sold to *Boston Braves,* 1946.

Page, Joe. Left-handed pitcher, *New York Yankees.*

Paige, Satchel. Negro leagues star right-handed pitcher.

Partee, Roy. Catcher, *Boston Red Sox.*

Partlow, Roy. Negro leagues star left-handed pitcher. Signed by *Brooklyn Dodgers,* 1946.

Passeau, Claude. Right-handed pitcher, *Chicago Cubs.*

Pesky, Johnny. Shortstop, *Boston Red Sox.*

Pollet, Howard. Left-handed pitcher, *St. Louis Cardinals.*

Prim, Ray. Left-handed pitcher, *Chicago Cubs.*

Ramazzotti, Bob. Rookie infielder, *Brooklyn Dodgers.*

Reese, Pee Wee. Shortstop, *Brooklyn Dodgers.*

Reiser, Pete. Outfielder-infielder, *Brooklyn Dodgers.* Led league in stolen bases, including a record seven steals of home, 1946.

Reynolds, Allie. Right-handed pitcher, *Cleveland Indians.*

Rice, Del. Rookie catcher, *St. Louis Cardinals.*

Richards, Paul. Catcher, *Detroit Tigers.*

Rickert, Marv. Rookie outfielder, *Chicago Cubs.*

Rizzuto, Phil. Shortstop, *New York Yankees.*

Roberge, Skippy. Third baseman, *Boston Braves.*

Robinson, Aaron. Catcher, *New York Yankees.*

Robinson, Jackie. Negro leagues infielder signed by *Brooklyn Dodgers,* 1946.

Roe, Preacher. Left-handed pitcher, *Pittsburgh Pirates.*

Russell, Rip. Infielder-outfielder, *Boston Red Sox.*

Ryba, Mike. Right-handed relief pitcher, *Boston Red Sox.*

Sanders, Ray. First baseman, *St. Louis Cardinals*. Wartime star; sold to *Boston Braves,* 1946.

Schmitz, Johnny. Left-handed pitcher, *Chicago Cubs.*

Schultz, Howie. First baseman, *Brooklyn Dodgers.*

Schoendienst, Red. Second baseman, *St. Louis Cardinals.*

Sewell, Luke. Manager, *Cincinnati Reds.*

Sewell, Rip. Right-handed pitcher, *Pittsburgh Pirates.*

Shepard, Bert. Coach, *Washington Senators.* Injured in service.

Sisler, Dick. Rookie first baseman-outfielder, *St. Louis Cardinals.*

Simmons, Al. Coach, *Philadelphia A's.* Former star outfielder for same team.

Slaughter, Enos "Country." Outfielder, *St. Louis Cardinals.*

Southworth, Billy. Manager, *Boston Braves.*

Spence, Stan. Outfielder, *Washington Senators.*

Stanky, Eddie. Second baseman, *Brooklyn Dodgers.*

Stephens, Vern. Shortstop, *St. Louis Browns.*

Stirnweiss, Snuffy. Infielder, *New York Yankees.* Wartime star.

Sukeforth, Clyde. Coach, *Brooklyn Dodgers.*

Tatum, Tommy. Infielder-outfielder, *Montreal Royals.* Injured in service.

Tepsic, Joe. Rookie outfielder, *Brooklyn Dodgers.*

Travis, Cecil. Shortstop, *Washington Senators.* Injured in service.

Trout, Dizzy. Right-handed pitcher, *Detroit Tigers.* Wartime star.

Trucks, Virgil. Right-handed pitcher, *Detroit Tigers.*

Valo, Elmer. Outfielder, *Philadelphia A's.*

Verban, Emil. Second baseman, *St. Louis Cardinals.* Traded to *Philadelphia Phillies,* 1946.

Vernon, Mickey. First baseman, *Washington Senators.* American League batting champion, 1946.

Voiselle, Bill. Right-handed pitcher, *New York Giants.*

Wagner, Broadway Charlie. Right-handed relief pitcher, *Boston Red Sox.* Injured in service.

Wagner, Hal. Catcher, *Boston Red Sox.*

Wagner, Honus. Coach, *Pittsburgh Pirates.* Formerly star shortstop with same team.

Waitkus, Eddie. Rookie first baseman, *Chicago Cubs.*

Wakefield, Dick. Outfielder, *Detroit Tigers.* Wartime star.

Walker, Dixie. Outfielder, *Brooklyn Dodgers.*

Walker, Harry the Hat. Outfielder, *St. Louis Cardinals.* Brother of Dixie.

Webber, Les. Right-handed pitcher, *Brooklyn Dodgers.* Sold to *Cleveland Indians,* 1946.

White, Ernie. Left-handed pitcher, *St. Louis Cardinals.* Injured in service; sold to *Boston Braves,* 1946.

Whitman, Dick. Rookie outfielder, *Brooklyn Dodgers.* Injured in service.

Wilks, Ted. Right-handed relief pitcher, *St. Louis Cardinals.*

Williams, Marvin. Negro leagues star infielder.

Williams, Ted. Outfielder, *Boston Red Sox.* American League's Most Valuable Player, 1946.

Wilson, Artie. Negro leagues star infielder.

Wolff, Roger. Right-handed pitcher, *Washington Senators*. Wartime star.

Woodall, Larry. Coach, *Boston Red Sox*.

Woodling, Gene. Rookie outfielder, *Cleveland Indians*.

Workman, Chuck. Outfielder-third baseman, *Boston Braves*. Traded to *Pittsburgh Pirates,* 1946.

Wright, John. Negro leagues right-handed pitcher. Signed by *Brooklyn Dodgers* along with Jackie Robinson, 1946.

Wright, Taffy. Outfielder, *Chicago White Sox.*

Wynn, Early. Right-handed pitcher, *Washington Senators.*

York, Rudy. First baseman, *Detroit Tigers.* Traded to *Boston Red Sox* prior to start of 1946 season.

Zabala, Adrian. Left-handed pitcher, *New York Giants.* Played in Mexico, 1946.

Zimmerman, Roy. Infielder, *New York Giants.* Played in Mexico, 1946.

Index

Adams, Buster, 131, 173
African Americans
    entrance into major leagues, 44–49
    in wartime Negro leagues, 11–12
Alexander, Grover Cleveland, 227
All-American Girls Baseball League
    (AAGBL), 11
All-Star Game (1946)
    American League pennant race at
        time of, 149–55
    National League pennant race at
        time of, 155–65
    players selected for, 149, 156
    Ted Williams's domination of, 165,
        167–68
American Baseball Guild, 137, 138–
    44, 170, 191–93
American League
    All-Star Game and, 149, 167, 169
    pennant race in, 102–12, 149–55,
        198–204
Anderson, Ferrell, 64, 116
Appling, Luke, 225
Athletics. *See* Philadelphia Athletics
Atomic bomb, 51

Bagby, Jim, 239
Ballanfant, Lee, 230
Ballplayers
    labor union for, 137–44, 191–93
    Mexican League offers to, 125–35

military service of, 4–8
postwar return of, 20–32
in racial integration of baseball,
    44–49
as replacements during World War
    II, 9–12, 14–20
reserve clause and, 56, 61–62, 64–
    65, 136–38, 170, 192–93
salaries for, 54–59, 136–38, 169–
    70, 192–93
want-ads by, 145, 146
wartime casualties among, 83–88,
    118–21
Barber, Red, 122, 162, 179
Barlick, Al, 178–79, **180**, 245
Barney, Rex, 124
Barrett, Red, 17, 18, 59, 127, 147,
    173
Baseball
    on Italian Hill, St. Louis, 72, 119,
        258, 259–61
    in Mexican League, 176–78, 194
    played by military troops, 5–8
    See also Organized Baseball
Basinski, Eddie, 15
Battle of the Bulge, xiii, 4n, 22, 38,
    68, 118
Beazley, Johnny, 9, 117, 118–19, 124,
    125, 127, **132**, 173–74, 214, 233
Behrman, Hank, 36, 37, 73, 81, 115,
    210, 219

Benson, Gene, 11
Benswanger, William, 139, 141–42, **143**, 144
Berra, Lefty, 260
Berra, Yogi, 84n, **258**, 260
Berry, Charlie, 230
Bevens, Bill, 99, 100, 102
Biederman, Les, 140
Bithorn, Hi, 71, 84
Black, Lloyd L., 170
Blacks. *See* African Americans
Black Sox scandal (1919), 61, 76, 86
Blackwell, Ewell, 35, 82, 147, 167
Bluege, Ossie, 23, 85
Boland, Eddie, 11
Bonham, Tiny, 102, 107, 109
Bordagaray, Frenchy, 15, **53**, 205
Boston Braves, 95, 211–12
Boston *Globe*, 48, 105, 202, 203
Boston *Record*, 48, 55, 202, 203
Boston Red Sox
    All-Star team and, 149
    in pennant race, 11, 104–10, 149–51, 198–204
    as Series favorites against Cardinals, 226–27
    at spring training, 67–71
    in World Series, 227–55
Boudreau, Lou, 36, 56, 95, 99–100, 186, 198–99, 204
Boudreau Shift, 199–201, 228, **229**
Bowles, Chester, 91
Bowman, Bob, 184
Branca, Ralph, 115, 209, 213–14, 215–16, 217
Brannick, Eddie, 17
Braves. *See* Boston Braves
Braves Field, 95, 96, 124, 204
Brazle, Al, xiii, 58, 117, 163, 240
Breadon, Sam, **126**, **254**
    ballplayer contracts and, 54, 57–59, 138, 169–70, 191

character evaluation of, 214–15
    hires Eddie Dyer as manager, 72, 117
    Mexican League threat and, 131, 133, 135
    sale or trade of players by, 58, 71–72, 119
    at World Series, 227, 255
Brecheen, Harry, **132**, **233**, **254**
    in post-season playoffs, 214, 218, 219–20
    reputation of, 58, 156
    season play of, 124, 173, 211
    in World Series, 232–35, 240, 241–42, 244–47, 253, 254, 255
Briggs Stadium, 112
Brissie, Lou, 86–88, **148**, 149, 189–91
Broeg, Bob, 57, 120, 214, 250n
Brooklyn Dodgers
    All-Star team and, 156
    hometown fans of, 121–23
    in pennant race, 113–16, 155–65, 171–76, 178–85, 206–21
    in post-season playoffs, 213–21
    racial integration of, 49
    rookies on, 36–38
    at spring training, 72–73
Brown, Bobby, 35, 82
Brown, Jimmy, 72, 83–84, 142
Brown, Tommy, 10–11, 36n, 182
Brown, Willard, 11, 205n
Browns. *See* St. Louis Browns
Brubaker, W. K., 88
Brucker, Earle, 31
Buker, Cy, 15
Burkhart, Ken, 17, 18, **132**, 147, 173
Burns, Ed, 45, 48

Camacho, Manuel Avila, 63, 128
Campanella, Roy, 11, 46, 205
Campbell, Bruce, 56
Campbell, Paul, 253

Camp Claiborne, 47
Caray, Harry, 214–15
Cardinals. *See* St. Louis Cardinals
Carey, Max, 97
Case, George, 98, 186
Casey, Hugh, 49, 173, 178
Chandler, Albert B. "Happy," 44, 55, 61–62, 94, 169, 213, 227, **254**, 255
Chandler, Spud, 102, 107, 110, 153, 156
Chapman, Ben, 9, 82
Chapman, Ray, 183
Chapman, Sam, 18
Chicago Cubs, 71, 209, 210, 211, 212–13
Chicago White Sox, 94–95
Christian, John, 76–77, 116
Christman, Mark, 81
Churchill, Winston, 51
Cincinnati Reds, 94
Clark, Tom, 92
Cleveland Indians, 25, 27–28, 36, 155, 186, 198, 204
Cleveland *Press*, 140
Clifford, Clark, 92
Coan, Gil, 38–40, **41**, 81, 147, 149, 187
Cobb, Ty, 97, 199
Collins, Eddie, 54–55
Comiskey Park, 94
Conlon, Jocko, 77
Contracts, ballplayer
    club owners and, 37–38, 54–55, 57, 113, 115n, 138, 159, 169–70, 181, 182n, 191
    Uniform Player's Contract, 56, 129, 136–37, 170, 191
    See also Reserve clause
Cooper, Mort, 59, **126**, 159, 211–12, 227
Cooper, Walker, 72, 74, **126**, 129, 163, 164, 171, 227

Crespi, Frank, 118, 119, 227, 260
Cronin, Joe, **69**
    contract negotiations by, 55
    on hitting against Bob Feller, 25, 27
    in pennant race, 104, 107, 109, 150
    pitcher management by, 70–71, 107, 109
    pre-World Series moves by, 204, 225
    price Red Sox paid for, 104
    as wartime player-manager, 10
    in World Series, 230, 235–36, 238, 244, 245, 247, 253
Crosley Field, 16
Cross, Jeff, 122, 124, 214
Cubs. *See* Chicago Cubs
Culberson, Leon, 15, 106, 107, 150, 240, 246, 247, 249, 250, 252
Cullenbine, Roy, 153
Cuyler, Kiki, 33

Daniel, Dan, 104, 197
Dark, Alvin, 82, 161–62, 183–84
Dean, Dizzy, 120, 155, 171, 214, 237
Deininger, Bill, 35, 82
Derringer, Paul, 71
Detroit Tigers, 18–19, 20, 22, 66, 94, 110, 112, 153–55, 198, 202, 204
Dewey, Thomas E., 95, 259
Dickey, Bill, 35, 82, 99, 102, 103, **152**, 152–53, 167
Dickshot, Johnny, 17, 147
Dickson, Murray, xiii, 173, 174–76, 214, 218–20, 236, 242–44
Dillinger, Bob, 36, 81, 147
DiMaggio, Dominic, **69**
    in All-Star Game, 149, 150
    contract negotiations with, 54–55
    returns from military service, 15, 67
    season play of, 92, 109, 150, 151

DiMaggio, Dominic (*cont'd*)
 on Ted Williams, 30
 in World Series, 230, 235, 245, 250
DiMaggio, Joe, **154**
 on All-Star team, 153
 in military service, 9, 18
 in post-season exhibition games,
  225
 returns from military service, 29–30
 salary of, 56
 season play of, 100–101, 102,
  103–4, 107, 109, 202
 at spring training, 66, 80
 trading rumors on, 225, 226
Dobson, Joe, 67, 68, **69**, 70, 71, 105,
 106, 107, 150, 203, 239–40, 241,
 244, 247
Doby, Larry, 205
Dodgers. *See* Brooklyn Dodgers
Dodger Symphony, 158
Doerr, Bobby, 15, 25, 27, 67, **69**, 105,
 107, 149, 150, 151, 186, 232,
 232, 252, 253
Domestic problems, postwar, xi, xiii,
 52–54, 91, 92, 94
Donnelley, Blix, 261
Dowd, Tom, 198, 202
Dreiseward, Clem, 106
Dressen, Charlie, 75–76, 79, 184n,
 209, 211
Durocher, Leo, **75, 180**
 managerial style of, 10, 34, 38,
  183–85, 210
 Mexican League threat and, 62, 65
 in pennant race, 113, 115–16, 155–
  63, 178–79, 181–85, 206–21
 personality sketch of, 74–79, 212
 in post-season playoffs, 213–21
 purpose pitches and, 183–85, 210
 Branch Rickey's relationship to,
  75, 76, 78, 179, 180, 209
 at spring training, 14, 37, 72
 on Eddie Stanky, 162–63

Dusak, Erv, 179–80, 218–19, 240
Dyer, Eddie, **254**
 on Cardinals' problems, 116–19
 contract negotiations and, 59
 hired as Cardinals manager, 72, 117
 Mexican League challenge and,
  125, 127
 in pennant race, 123, 163, 170–71,
  173–76, 178–81, 206–21
 in post-season playoffs, 214–21
 purpose pitches and, 185
 at spring training, 58, 81
 in World Series, 228, 229, 231,
  232, 238, 240, 243, 244, 247–49,
  252, 254, 255
Dykes, Jimmy, 14, 20, 83

Early, Jake, 40
Ebbets Field, 10, 121–22, 172, 183,
 184–85, 196, 210, 211, 218,
 219–20
Edwards, Bruce, 64–65, 116, 173,
 216, 220
Eephus ball, 167
Egan, Dave, 48, 55, 202–3, 204,
 225–26
Eisenhower, Dwight D., xi
Elliott, Bob, 142
Embree, Red, 198, 201
Ennis, Del, 35, 82, 147, 210
Erickson, Paul "Li'l Abner," 211
Etten, Nick, 17, 18, 109
Evans, Al, 92
Exhibition games
 played by military troops, 5–8
 post-season against Red Sox, 225
 in postwar spring training, 14

Falk, Bibb, 236
Federal League, 61
Feller, Bill, 25, 26
Feller, Bob, **26, 154, 188**
 childhood of, 25

fastball velocity of, 187–88
Mexican League offer to, 61
in military service, 5, 8, 27, 28
returns from military service, 20,
    25, 27–29
salary of, 56
season play of, 94–95, 98–101,
    155, 186–89, 198, 204
at spring training, 27–28
strikeout record and, 186, 187,
    188–89, 198, 204
Fenway Park, 30, 71, 104–5, 149,
    165, 236, 237, 249
Ferrato, Mario, 260
Ferrell, Rick, 104
Ferrell, Wes, 104, 185
Ferriss, Dave, 32, 68, **69**, 71, 106, 147,
    149, 150, 153, 185–86, 235–38,
    242–44
Fitzsimmons, Fat Freddie, 9
Fleming, Bill, 20
Fleming, Les, 99
Forbes Field, 141
Ford, John, 47n
Fort Riley, Kansas, xiii, 6, 34, 48,
    119
Fox, Pete, 15, 16
Foxx, Jimmie, 9, 70, 104
Fraternity of Professional Baseball
    Players, 138, 140
Frick, Ford, 91, 179, 180, 184, 191,
    213, 216
Frick, Henry, 139
Frisch, Frankie, 42–43, 81, 142,
    147
Fultz, David, 138, 140
Furillo, Carl, 36, 38, 73, 116, 123,
    158, 182, 217, 219

Galan, Augie, 49, 72, 75–76, 77–78,
    115, 159, 161, 208, 219, 221
Galloway, Chick, 87
Gambling, 75–76

Garagiola, Giovanni, 260
Garagiola, Joe, **258**
    on Brecheen's screwball, 233, 234
    Manila Dodgers and, 115, 163
    in post-season playoffs, 216, 217
    on purpose pitches, 183
    reputation of, 72, 163
    as rookie, 163–64, 206
    Sporting News story on, 259–61
    in World Series, 228, 230, 231,
        232, 234, 239, 246
Gardella, Danny, 16–17, 60, 63, 64,
    126
Garrison, Ford, 86
Gedeon, Elmer, 83
Gehringer, Charlie, 110
Gettel, Al, 102
Giants. *See* New York Giants
GI Bill of Rights, 55–56
Gibson, Josh, 12, 205
Gilbert, Bill, 4n
Giles, Warren, 94
Gilliam, Junior, 205
Goering, Herman, 51, 257, 258
Goetz, Larry, 167, 168
Goldstein, Louis, 116
Gonzalez, Mike, 35, 252
Goolsby, Ray, 81
Gordon, Joe "Flash," 66, 103
Gordon, Sid, 17
Gray, Pete, 11, 15
Greenberg, Hank
    Mexican League offer to, 61
    in military service, 8, 20, 22
    in post-season exhibition games,
        225
    returns from military service, 22,
        29, 66, 83, 84
    salary of, 56
    season play of, 94, 153, 189, 200
    at spring training, 66, 85
Gregg, Hal, 115, 124
Greybeards, 9–10

Griffith, Clark, 4, 40, 52, 84, 91–92, 94, 138, 140, 187
Griffith Stadium, 92, 93, 188
Grimm, Charlie, 36, 81, 156, 163, 212
Grodzicki, Johnny, 119–21, 170, 171
Grove, Lefty, 104, 155
Groves, Leslie, 51
Gumpert, Randy, 102
Gutteridge, Don, 36, 230

Hack, Stan, 71
Haefner, Mickey, 18, 147, 187, 225
Harnett, Gabby, 33
Harridge, Will, 191, 255
Harris, Mickey, 68, **69**, 70, 106, 107, 149, 150, 232, 236, 241
Hasbrouck, Robert, 4n
Hatten, Joe, 36–37, 73, 81, 115, 173, 179–80, 208, 218
Hausmann, George, 61, 62
Hayes, Frankie, 98, 100, 101, 186
Henrich, Tommy, 42, 66, 99, 100, 102, 105, 109, 151, 153, 201
Herman, Babe, 10
Herman, Billy, 33, 72, 77–78, 83, 84–85, 115, 156, 159, 162, 207, 211–12
Hermanski, Gene, 36, 37–38, 49n, 73, 81, 95, 116, 158
Hershey, Lewis, 4n
Higbe, Kirby, **114**
    gambling habits of, 76
    as manager of Manila Dodgers, 115, 163, 260
    in post-season playoffs, 217–18
    returns from military service, 73
    season play of, 119, 156, 167, 173–74, 206, 208, 212
Higgins, Pinky, **69**, 150, 230, 243, 253
Hitler, Adolf, 8, 22
Hofferth, Stew, 159

Honig, Donald, 33, 48, 52n, 122
Hopp, Johnny, 72, 159, 170
Hornsby, Rogers, 30, 227
Housing shortage, xiii, 52, 92, 94, 259
Hughson, Tex, **69**
    returns from military service, 68, 70
    season play of, 92, 106, 107, 109, 149, 150, 201
    in World Series, 227, 228–29, 236, 238–39, 247
Hurwitz, Hy, 202
Hyland, Robert, 33, 118, 240, 241

Indians. *See* Cleveland Indians
Inflation, postwar, 51–54, 91
Irvin, Monte, 46, 48, 78, 205
Italian Hill, St. Louis, 72, 119, 258, 259–61

Jackson, Shoeless Joe, 86, 236
Jakucki, Sig, 11, 15
Janowitz, Vic, 182n
Jethroe, Sam, 11, 46, 48, 205
Jim Crow rules, 46
Johnson, Billy, 102
Johnson, Bob, 15, 16
Johnson, Don, 71
Johnson, Earl, 68, 109, 150, 231, 247, 253
Johnson, Walter, 155
Joost, Eddie, 72
Jorgensen, Spider, 156
Judd, Oscar, 210
Jurges, Billy, 71

Kaese, Harold, 70
Kahn, Roger, 226
Kansas City Monarchs, 46
Keane, Clif, 48, 105, 202, 203, 226, 228
Kell, George, 24, 110, 112, 150

Keller, Charlie, 18, 42, 66, 101, 102, 153
Keltner, Ken, 99–100
Kid Comes Back, The (Tunis), 34n
Kiner, Ralph, 38, 40–43, 58, 81, 139, 147, 193, 209
  photograph of, 41
Klein, Chuck, 33
Klein, Lou, 62, 72, 119, 125, **126**, 127, 129, 131, 163
Klinger, Bob, 150, 247–49
Kluttz, Clyde, 163, 179, 219
Krist, Howard, **9**, 117, 118, 170
Kuhn, Bowie, 76n
Kurowski, Whitey, **132**
  on All-Star team, 163
  contract negotiations with, 57–58, 119, 127
  Mexican League offer to, 131–32, 133, 135
  in World Series, 228, 230, 243, 247, 252, 253

Labor union. *See* Union, ballplayers
Ladies' Day, 107, 108
Landis, Kenesaw Mountain, 4, 13, 33, 44, 61, 137
Lanier, Max, **126, 130**
  contract negotiations with, 58–59
  on Mexican League baseball, 176–78, 194
  season play of, 123, 124
  signs with Mexican League, 125, 126, 127, 129, 131, 135, 163
Lauche, Frank J., 94
Lavagetto, Cookie, 182, 217, 220
League Park, 198
Leahy, William D., 92, 93
Lemon, Bob, 94–95
Leonard, Buck, 205
Lewis, Buddy, 40
Lewis, Duffy, 48
Lewis, Franklin, 140

Lewis, John L., 52, 91
Lie, Trygve, 95
Lindell, Johnny, 42, 153
Lisenbee, Hod, 10
Lombardi, Ernie, 96
Lombardi, Vic, 33, 49n, 115, 173, 175–76, 209, 211–12, 214, 217
Lopez, Al, 58, 139
Louis, Joe, 203
Lupien, Tony, 55–56

Mack, Connie, 15, 23–24, 52, 70, 87, 112, 138, 149, 189–90
Mack, Ray, 99, 101
MacPhail, Larry, 34, 80, 100, 103, 140, 151–53, 170, 191, 192, 196, 226
Maestri, Amado, 177
Maglie, Sal, 61, 62, 63
Majeski, Hank, 109
Malaney, Jack, 109, 200
Manila Dodgers, 114, 115, 163, 260
Mankiewicz, Felix, 201
Marchildon, Phil, 23–24, 85–86, 198, 225
Marching Blacks (Powell), 47
Mariani, Diz, 260
Marion, Marty, **251**
  fielding skill of, 57, 172, 228, 230
  as Joe Garagiola's roommate, 163–64
  pension plan for ballplayers of, 194–95
  season play of, 123, 179
  Ted Williams and, 167, 168
  in World Series, 228, 229, 230, 253
Marshall, Willard, 17
Martin, Freddie, 62, 125, 126, **126**, 127, 129, **130**, 131, 163
Martin, Pepper, 10, 97, 171
Mass transit problems, xi, xiii, 94
Masterson, Walt, 24–25

Mayer, Louis B., 227
Mayo, Eddie, 140
McBride, Tom, 15, 150, 230–31, 253
McCarthy, Joe, 30, 66, 102–3, 104, 110, 151–53
McCarthy, Mac, 165
McCormick, Frank, 55
McCosky, Barney, 19, 66, 67, 110, 112
McGraw, John, 16, 42, 171
McKechnie, Bill, 82
Meat crisis, 257, 259
Medwick, Joe, 57, 179, 184, 212, 217
Melton, Rube, 174, 217
Merullo, Len, 163
Metkovich, Catfish, 16, 107, 110, 150, 244
Mexican League
    labor issues raised by, 136–37, 169–70
    playing conditions in, 176–78, 194
    signing of major league players to, 125–35
    as threat to Organized Baseball, 60–65, 94, 95
Miller, Eddie, 15
Miller, Julius, 136
Milwaukee Brewers, 155
Minor leagues
    postwar resurgence of, 145–47
    rookie stars in, 39
    season openers in, 96–98
    wartime replacement players from, 10–11
Mize, Johnny, 9, 17, 29, 32, 78, 129, 183
Montreal Royals, 47, 97, 148–49, 181, 205
Moore, Joe, 76–77, 116
Moore, Terry, 5
    on Brooklyn Dodger fans, 122
    on fielding at Sportsman's Park, 172–73

leadership influence of, 164–65
in post-season playoffs, 215–16, 218
returns from military service, 3, 5–6, 72, 83, 84–85, 117, 163
in World Series, 243, 253
Moses, Wally, **69**, 150, 238, 242–43, 244–45
Mullin, Pat, 66, 153
Mullin, Willard, 21, 111, 157
Munger, Red, 118, 173, 208, 213, 214, 238–39
Municipal Stadium, Cleveland, 186
Murphy, Johnny, 102
Murphy, Robert Francis, 137, 138–44, **143**, 169, 170, 192–93
Musial, Stan, **xii**, **5**, **132**, **134**
    on All-Star team, 163
    hitting ability of, 167n, 176
    Mexican League offer to, 132–33
    in post-season playoffs, 215, 217, 219
    returns from military service, 3, 4, 5, 29, 72
    season play of, 117, 123–24, 206
    wartime service of, xiii–xiv
    in World Series, 237, 238

Nájera, Castillo, 95–96
National Labor Relations Board, 51, 137, 139–40, 144
National League
    All-Star Game and, 156, 167, 169
    first post-season playoffs in, 213–21
    pennant race in, 113–24, 155–65, 206–21
Nazi war crimes trials, 218, 257, 258, 259
Negro leagues
    integration of major league baseball and, 46, 48, 205
    wartime baseball and, 11–12

Newcombe, Don, 46, 205
Newhouser, Hal, 18–19, 29, 32, 66,
   94, 147, 154–55, 202, 204, 225
Newnan Brownies, 145
Newsom, Bobo, 187–88, 198
New York *Daily News*, 228
New York Giants, 16–17, 96, 209
New York Times, 20
New York *World Telegram*, 104, 108
New York Yankees, 35, 42, 66, 102–4,
   107–10, 111, 151–55, 202
Niarhos, Gus, 103
Nicholson, Bill, 36, 81
Niemiec, Al, 56, 169, 170
Night baseball, 196
Nimitz, Chester, 92, 93
Northey, Ron, 79
Nowak, Hank, 119
Nuremberg trials, 218, 257, 258, 259
Nuxhall, Joe, 10

O'Brien, Eddie, 182n
O'Brien, Johnny, 182n
O'Connor, Leslie, 137
O'Dea, Ken, 72, 163
O'Dell, Billy, 184
O'Neill, Harry, 83
O'Neill, Steve, 22, 107
Olmo, Luis, 61, 194
Opening day (1946), 91–96
Organized Baseball
   American Dream and, 259–61
   domestic problems and, 52–54, 91,
      92, 94
   labor union for, 137–44, 191–93
   Mexican League challenge to,
      60–65, 94, 95, 125–37, 169–70,
      176–78, 194
   postwar enthusiasm for, 145–47
   racial integration of, 44–49, 205
   replacement players in, 9–12, 14–20
   reserve clause in, 56, 61–62, 64,
      136–38, 192–93

return of military veterans to, xiv,
   20–32, 83–88
wartime continuation of, 4, 8–14
See also Baseball
Ott, Mel, 16, 42, 63, 96, 124, 162
Owen, Mickey, 62, 63, 64–65, 116,
   126, 132–33, 134, 159, 177, 194
Owners
   ballplayer salaries and, 37–38, 54–
      55, 57–59, 113, 115n, 119, 127,
      159, 181, 182n, 191–92
   pension plan and, 196
   players union and, 140–44, 191–93
   reserve clause and, 136–38, 192–93

Pacific Coast League, 146
Padgett, Don, 116
Page, Joe, 102, 109, 152
Paige, Satchel, 11
Parker, Dan, 45, 47
Parrott, Harold, 159
Partee, Roy, 67, 150, 154, 166, 230,
   247, 249, **251**, 252, 253
Partlow, Roy, 11, 46, 149, 205
Pasquel, Alfonso, 132–33, 134
Pasquel, Bernardo, 129
Pasquel, Gerardo, 227
Pasquel, Jorgé, 60–64, 113, 125, **126**,
   127, **128**, 131, 133, 169, **177**,
   194
Passeau, Claude, 71, 167
Patterson, Robert, 84
Pennant race (1946)
   in American League, 102–12, 149–
      55, 198–204
   in National League, 113–24, 155–
      65, 206–21
   opening day of, 91–96
Pension plan, 194–96
Pesky, Johnny, 67, **69**, 109, 149, 150,
   151, 200, 202, 203, 237, 240,
   245, 249, 250, 252
Pettit, Paul, 182n

Philadelphia Athletics, 198
Philadelphia Phillies, 12, 210
Pinelli, Babe, 220
Pittsburgh Pirates, 42, 81, 139–44, 193, 209–10
Players. *See* Ballplayers
Playoffs
    post-season, 213–21
    See also World Series
Pollet, Howie, 58, 123, 163, 171, 173, 179, 206, 208, 213–14, 215–17, 227–32, 234, 240
Polo Grounds, 16, 95
Powell, Adam Clayton, Jr., 47
Pravda, 51
Prim, Ray, 71
Profanity, 184–85
Purpose pitches, 183–85, 210
Pyle, Ernie, 87

Racial integration
    of major league baseball, 44–49
    military service and, 46–47, 48
Raft, George, 221
Railroad strike, 91, 131
Ramazzotti, Bob, 179, 217
Rayburn, Sam, 92
Reardon, Beans, 215, 216
Reconversion, 15, 52, 60, 91, 137
Reds. *See* Cincinnati Reds
Red Sox. *See* Boston Red Sox
Reese, Pee Wee, 33, 73, 74, 121, 217
Reiser, Pete, **207**
    injuries of, 33–34, 113, 157–58, 182, 183, 207, 208, 210–11
    meets Jackie Robinson in army, 48
    returns from military service, 29, 32–34, 61, 72, 74
    season play of, 113, 116, 157–58, 178–79, 182–83, 208, 210–11
    wartime service of, xiii, 6, 9
Replacement players, wartime, 9–12, 14–20

Reserve clause
    challenges to, 136–38, 192–93
    player salaries and, 56, 136–38, 170
    violations of, 61–62, 64–65
    See also Contracts, ballplayer
Restrictive clause, 196–97
Reyes, Nap, 16
Reynolds, Allie, 186
Rice, Bob, 142, 144
Rice, Del, 72, 163, 234, 246, 247
Rice, Grantland, 226, 246
Richards, Paul, 19
Rickert, Marv, 36, 71, 81
Rickey, Branch, **75**
    contract negotiations and, 37–38, 54, 57, 113, 115n, 159, 181, 182n
    Leo Durocher's relationship to, 75, 76, 78, 179, 180, 209
    influence of, 221
    "Mahatma" nickname for, 34
    postwar baseball season and, 34, 96
    reserve clause violations and, 61, 64–65
    signs Jackie Robinson, 44–46, 47, 48
Rizzuto, Phil, 99, 107, 110
Roberge, Skippy, 118
Robinson, Aaron, 103
Robinson, Jackie, **45**, **93**
    integration of Organized Baseball and, 44–49, 179, 204, 205
    Mexican League offer to, 62
    as minor league player, 84, 97–98, 148–49, 205
Rockwell, Norman, 25
Roe, Preacher, 58
Rookies
    minor league stars as, 39
    at spring training, 34–43
Roosevelt, Franklin Delano, 4, 13, 91

Ross, Chet, 181
Roy, Jean Pierre, 60
Royals. *See* Montreal Royals
Ruffing, Red, 102, 107
Ruggeri's restaurant, 214–15
Russell, Rip, 150, 230, 244
Ruth, Babe, 67, 68, 72, 74, 98, 104, **128**, 199–200, 226
Ryba, Mike, 227

Sain, Johnny, 162n, 211
Salaries, ballplayer
    club owners and, 37–38, 54–55, 57–59, 113, 115n, 119, 127, 159, 181, 182n, 191–92
    Mexican League threat and, 169–70
    reserve clause and, 56, 136–38, 192–93
    for returning military veterans, 54–59
Sanders, Ray, 36
San Francisco Giants, 184
Saturday Evening Post, 25, 70
Schmitz, Johnny, 71, 213, 214
Schoendienst, Red
    on All-Star team, 161, 163
    on Lanier's departure for Mexican League, 125, 135
    season play of, 58, 119, 178, 206, 209
    in World Series, 228, 238, 241, 253, 255
Schultz, Eddie, 115–16
Schultz, Howie, 156, 216, 220
Seals Stadium, 146
Season, baseball
    increase in games played in, 196–97
    opening day of, 91–96
Seats, Tom, 15
Seerey, Pat, 186, 201
Senators. *See* Washington Senators

Sewell, Luke, 62, 81, 147
Sewell, Rip, 142, **143**, 167, 188, 193
Shadows of Summer: Classic Baseball Photographs, 1869–1947 (Honig), 52n
Shepard, Bert, 84
Shibe Park, 24
Shore, Ernie, 68
Shotton, Burt, 120
Simmons, Al, 9, 24, 199
Sisler, Dick, 35, 62, 72, 81, 170, 206
Sisler, George, 35
Slaughter, Enos "Country," **5**, **251**, **254**
    on All-Star team, 163
    in military service, 4, 6, 9
    returns from military service, 54, 72, 117
    season play of, 123, 173–74, 206
    on Sportsman's Park, 172
    in World Series, 238, 240–41, 244, 245, 247, 249–53, 254, 255
Smith, Hilton, 12
Smith, Red, 203
Southworth, Billy, 14, 174
Spahn, Warren, 35, 82
Speer, Albert, 8
Spence, Stan, 40
Spink, J. G. Taylor, 31, 259–61
Sporting News, The
    on Gil Coan, 39
    on Joe Garagiola, 259–61
    on integration of baseball, 45, 47–48
    on labor issues for ballplayers, 56, 140, 192, 197
    on pennant race of 1946, 111
    want-ads by ballplayers in, 145, 146
    on wartime baseball, 14, 21
    on Ted Williams, 31
Sportsman's Park, 170, 171–72, 216, 230

Spring training
  ballplayer stipends for, 192
  barnstorming tours following, 80–81
  for returning servicemen, 14, 82
  for rookies, 34–43
  wartime engagement of, 13–14
Stanky, Eddie, 159–63, **160**, 173–74, 217, 220
Stephens, Vern, 62–64, 176
Stevens, Eddie, 73, 78–79, 115, 158, 219
Stewart, James Garfield, 94
Stirnweiss, Snuffy, 99, 100, 107, 110, 225
St. Louis Browns, 204
St. Louis Cardinals
  loss of players from, 71–72, 119–21, 125–35
  in pennant race, 116–24, 163–65, 170–76, 178–85, 206–21
  player contracts and, 57–58
  in post-season playoffs, 213–21
  as Series underdogs against Red Sox, 226–27
  at spring training, 71–72
  wartime baseball and, 5–6, 35–36
  in World Series, 227–55, **229**
St. Louis *Post-Dispatch*, 57, 170
Stockton, J. Roy, 140, 214–15
Strikes
  baseball, 141–42, 144
  mass transit, 94
  railroad, 91, 131
Strode, Woody, 47
Sukeforth, Clyde, 216
Summers, Bill, 199

Taft, Robert, 257, 259
Tatum, Tommy, 84, 97
Television rights, 196
Tepsic, Joe, 181–82, 217
They Also Served (Gilbert), 4n

Thurston, Hollis "Sloppy," 42
Tigers. *See* Detroit Tigers
Transportation crisis, xi, xiii, 91, 94, 131
Travis, Cecil, 8, 18, 22–23, 40, 83, 85, 92, 225
Triple Crown, 200
Trout, Dizzy, 18, 66, 147, 153, 186, 225
Trucks, Virgil, 19, 22, 39, 66, 67, 153, 166–67
Truman, Harry S., 50, 91–92, **93**, 257, 259
Tunis, John R., 34n, 259

Uniform Player's Contract, 56, 129, 136–37, 170, 191
  See also Reserve clause
Union, ballplayers, 137–44, 191–93
United Nations, 50
USS Alabama, 27, 28

Valo, Elmo, 200
Vance, Dizzy, 155
Vaughan, Arky, 77
Veeck, Bill, 12, 155, 186, 202, 204
Verban, Emil, 72
Vernon, Mickey, 40, 92, 200
Voiselle, Bill, 63, 138

Waddell, Rube, 155, 186, 188, 204
Wagner, Charlie, 70, 85, 86, 151, 202, 203, 228n
Wagner, Hal, **69**, 107, 149, 150, 230
Wagner, Honus, 142
Waitkus, Eddie, 71
Wakefield, Dick, 18, 20, 56, 66, 153, 204
Walcott, Jersey Joe, 203
Walker, Dixie, 61, 72, 77, 116, 157–58, 165, 179, 181, 197, 206, 217, 248

Walker, Harry, **9, 254**
  in military service, xiii, 5, 6, 8
  on Terry Moore, 164
  in World Series, 229, 231, 240, 247, 248–50, 254
Want-ads, ballplayer, 145, 146
Ward, Leo, 131
Ware Shoals Riegels, 148
War nerves, 24–25
Washington, Kenny, 47
Washington Senators, 24–25, 91–94
Waterfront Park, 3
Weart, Douglas L., 95
Weaver, Harrison "Doc," 121, 163, 194–95, 240–41
Webber, Les, 123
"What's the Matter With the Red Sox" (Kaese), 70
White, Ernie, 58, 117, 118, 129
White, Hal, 19
White Sox. *See* Chicago White Sox
Whitman, Dick, 36, 38, 73, 79, 81, 116, 158, 181, 219
Wilks, Ted, **132**, 171, 173, 174
Williams, Marvin, 48
Williams, Ted, **69**
  in All-Star Game, 165, 167–68
  defensive shift against, 199–201, 228, 229, 235
  as fielder, 30, 109
  hitting ability of, 19, 30, 165–66, 183, 199–201, 220
  Mexican League offer to, 61
  military service of, 8, 31
  newspaper stories on, 199, 203–4, 225–26, 257
  post-season injury of, 225, 226, 227–28
  returns from military service, 15, 18, 29, 30–32, 67, 68
  salary of, 56
  season play of, 20, 86, 92, 106, 109, 110, 150, 199–202

  trading rumors on, 225–26
  in World Series, 228, 234–35, 238, 241, 243, 246–47
Wilson, Artie, 11
Wolff, Roger, 18, 32, 92, 147
Wood, Smoky Joe, 68
Woodall, Larry, 48
Woodling, Gene, 36
Workman, Chuck, 17, 18, 147
World Series (1946)
  game one, 227–32
  game two, 232–35
  game three, 235–38
  game four, 238–39
  game five, 239–41
  game six, 241–42
  game seven, 242–53
  news stories following, 257–61
  odds makers' predictions on, 226–27
  winning hit controversy of, 248, 249–53
World War II
  ballplayer casualties from, 83–88, 118–21, 189–91
  continuation of baseball during, 4, 8–14
  domestic problems after, xi, xiii, 51–54, 91, 92, 94, 259
  international climate following, 50–51
  military service of ballplayers in, 4–6
Wright, John, 45, 46, 47, 49, 77, 149
Wright, Taffy, 95, 106
Wrigley, P. K., 11, 14, 191
Wyatt, Whitlow, 33
Wynn, Early, 40, 115

Yankees. *See* New York Yankees
Yankee Stadium, 107, 109, **154**, 196, 226
Yawkey, Tom, 48, 86, 104–6, 191, 196, 198, 202, 225–26

York, Rudy, **69, 232**
   hitting prowess of, 67–68
   season play of, 109, 201, 204
   traded to Red Sox, 22
   in World Series, 231, 234, 237–38,
    241–42, 253

Yost, Eddie, 10
Young, Dick, 228

Zabala, Adrian, 61
Zimmerman, Roy, 61, 62